Nuclear South Asia Impact on Conventional Arm Race

NUCLEAR SOUTH ASIA

IMPACT ON CONVENTIONAL ARM RACE

Col. S.C.Dhiman (Retd.)

NEHA PUBLISHERS & DISTRIBUTORS

DELHI

Publisher
NEHA PUBLISHERS & DISTRIBUTORS
4832/24,Prahlad Lane,S-207 Ansari
Road, Daryaganj, Delhi-110002
Ph.: 43570976, 23278261
Email: nehapubdistributors@gmail.com

Edition: 2015

ISBN: 978-93-80318-76-9

Laser Typesetting
JEE-VEE Graphics, Delhi

Price: 1195/-

Printed
Vikas Computers, Delhi

Preface

In South Asia a nuclear arms race continues, led by India and followed by Pakistan. India has acquired a ballistic missile defense system, heavily in satellites, launched a nuclear submarine (the INS Arihant), unveiled ambitious limited war fighting strategies – for instance, its Cold Start military doctrine – and moved away from a concept of deterrence to compellence. Pakistan has responded with, for instance, the fielding of Nasr (a low-yield nuclear weapon), supplemented by full spectrum deterrence. These moves have the potential to erode the prevailing deterrence stability of South Asia, and cause the region to drift toward conflict.

Although the primary purpose of Pakistan's nuclear arms build-up is to counter India, suspicions also exist that Islamabad wants to pressure Washington not to ignore it, move too close to India, or take other actions that Islamabad opposes. Another objective is to continue to receive US and other assistance despite their bilateral disputes over Afghanistan or terrorism.

A nuclear conflict can have no victor. In South Asia, nuclear deterrence may, however, usher in an era of durable peace between Pakistan and India, providing the requisite incentives for resolving all outstanding issues, especially Jammu and Kashmir.

The international community should encourage a process of peace and rapprochement, help promote the peaceful resolution of disputes, and support nuclear stabilization and restraint in South Asia. The world must also pay attention to the root causes of insecurity and instability in South Asia. Resolution of the Jammu and Kashmir dispute is indispensable for the region's peace and prosperity. The principles for settling this dispute justly have been enunciated in Security Council resolutions, which must be implemented.

It is further hoped that the book will prove to be of immense value to teachers, students and researchers.

—Editor

Contents

Preface (*v*)

1. Nuclear Arms Race 1
2. Arms Race Developing in the Asia-Pacific Region 30
3. Nuclear Deterrence Thinking Promote an Arms Race 50
4. Arms Races among New Nuclear States 78
5. Conventional Operations under Nuclear Overhang in South Asia 106
6. India and Weapons of Mass Destruction 141
7. Foundation of China's Nuclear Doctrine 197
8. South Asia Security Challenges: Terror Campaign and Nuclear Proliferation 235

Bibliography 293

Index 295

1

Nuclear Arms Race

India's defeat in war in 1962 was quickly followed by another uncomfortable military development for India, China's explosion of a nuclear device in 1964. This may have been carried out by Beijing primarily with the US and perhaps the Soviet Union in mind. However, one side effect was that India was now faced not only with a territorial foe, but also a nuclear foe, an uncomfortable power imbalance from India's point of view.

There may have been some limited moves toward reducing Sino-Indian hostilities following Rajiv Gandhi's trip to China in 1988, but relations still remained quite cool in the 1990s. Underlying perceptions of mistrust were very clear on India's side, as well as a sense of having been overtaken in the global pecking order and estimation.

China was firmly in Indian sights in the late 1990s, as someone to be strategically matched, something of an ongoing quest. At the time, 1997, Mohan felt that given "the national determination in India to liberate itself from the current second class status in world affairs ... New Delhi will find it impossible to give up its search for global status similar to that of China"; in which "New Delhi is most unlikely give up its determination to acquire a functional nuclear deterrent against Beijing ... India will remain committed to building a small but functional deterrent against China." China's installation of CSS-5s medium range missiles in Tibet, with a range of about 1,333 miles, was highlighted in the Indian media during 1997 as targeting India.

Raja Mohan's 1997 predictions were quickly met, as India moved in 1998 toward transforming its implicit 1974 nuclear capability into an explicit realized capacity. The Prime Minister Atal Bihari Vajpayee was blunt concerning China factors behind the Pokhran-II tests by India:

We have an overt nuclear weapons state [China] on our borders, a state that committed armed aggression against India in 1962. Although our relations with that country have improved in the last decade or so, an atmosphere of distrust persists, mainly due to the unresolved border problem. To add to the distrust, that country has materially helped another neighbour of ours [Pakistan] to become a covert nuclear weapons state.

Vajpayee may not have intended this letter to the US president to be publicized; but the sentiments were clear enough, objectively and subjectively. Indian commentators like General Amarjit Kalkat, who had commanded the Indian peace keeping forces in Sri Lanka in 1987, were also clear at the time where the message of India's nuclear explosions was aimed. It was not a local regional demonstration against Pakistan. Instead, Kalkat argued that:

What strikes me as being particularly significant is their effect on India-China relations.

These will be put on an even footing ... The tests are really an attempt to correct the current military and technological imbalance vis--vis China, which is already in the threshold of being a world super power ... Countries tend to respect equals and nuclear parity does help provide the level playing field needed to build such an equalitarian relationship. China has been a nuclear power for long, but India was not till it showed its capability this week.

Similar logic was apparent with India's successful testing of an Agni-II medium range (2,500-3,000 kilometers/1,550-1,860 miles) missile in 1999. Dinkar Shukla at the Government of India's Press Information Bureau asserted that "Pokhran-II and Agni-II are a symbol of a resurgent India," in which "the Pakistani threat is only a marginal factor in New Delhi's security calculus. Agni is at the heart of deterrence in the larger context of the Sino-Indian equation." Such considerations were why Chellaney argued in 2000 that "a major motivation for India's 1998 nuclear tests was the growing military asymmetry with China."

IR theory enters the picture with regard to China's differing responses in 1962 and 1998. Whereas China took military action against India in 1962, it initially responded fairly mildly to India's nuclear explosion in 1998. Lei Guang argues that different perceptions were in play. In 1962, China could feel that its identity was at stake through India refusing to negotiate over what China considered was an unequal treaty imposed on it in earlier times of weakness. Guang argues that "given the centrality of territory to the Chinese national identity, what constituted the border between China and its neighbour was no longer simply a matter of administrative marking." Instead, there was a threefold challenge to China, to its perceived territory, sovereignty and legitimacy. Consequently, this "triple assault on China's fundamental identity as a nation-state contributed to its final decision to resort to violence in 1962." Such consideration are rightly seen by Guang as an example of IR constructivism.

Conversely, China took a more subdued and restrained approach to India's nuclear testing in 1998. Guang explains this difference by arguing that China's core identity was not particularly threatened by this event; India's nuclear explosion "did not constitute a frontal attack on the PRC's identity in 1998. On the contrary, it testified to China's nuclear power and affirmed its position as a major power in the region." This did not mean that China was not concerned about India's nuclear explosion. What it did mean was that China responded in different ways and at a different pitch than in 1962. As Guang argues, "a main thrust of the Chinese reaction to India's nuclear tests in 1998 was geopolitical in nature. Unlike in 1962, what was at stake for China in 1998 was its national security, not its fundamental identity as a modern nation-state." Its power advantages enabled a cooler calculated restraint in 1998.

Nuclear rivalry continues to affect Sino-Indian relations. A nuclear arms race, and its "nuclear security dilemma" dynamics, adds a competitive spiral element to their relationship. Even as the dust from India's Pokhran-II tests was settling, further deployment of Chinese missiles was causing alarm in India, Chellaney pointing out in 2000 that "India's largest neighbor [China] is conducting the biggest expansion of missile capabilities anywhere in the world. The first of these new missiles, the Dongfeng (DF) 31, last tested in July 1999, can reach every corner of India but little of U.S. territory."

Chellaney's own sense of the political context of China's nuclear program was stark, "India's existing modest deterrent capabilities will be gravely undermined as China builds up its nuclear and missile armories. The Sino-Indian asymmetry will increase ... India will have every incentive to acquire similar assets that play a primary role in power-projection strategies." An offensive weapons spiral was in the offing from both sides. Whilst welcoming US attempts to develop a AMD (Anti-Missile Defence) system, Chellaney acknowledged and concluded that "nevertheless, the likely response of those states whose security will be directly affected, particularly China, will significantly affect India's interests. This is what India has to worry about"; even though "in due course, the action-reaction cycle triggered by missile defences could drive India closer to the United States." Strategic alignment between India and the US is Beijing's nightmare.

In terms of power projection, China's control of Tibet has seen its installation of various medium and intermediate range missile systems. These missile systems are irrelevant to curbing domestic discontent inside Tibet, but do literally and strategically point outside Tibet toward India, its capital Delhi and other major Indian cities. Indian analysts are acutely aware of these implications. For Mahapatra, this military buildup in Tibet is "not only aimed at overwhelming India militarily, but to enable Chinese coercive diplomacy in respect of the border dispute." Asymmetrics is in play. Installation of intermediate and medium range ballistic missiles enables China to immediately and easily threaten India; whereas the main centers of China, Beijing, Shanghai, Guangzhou remained far away from India. Back in 1999, Kanwal was lamenting that "realistic deterrence against China can only be achieved by developing a demonstrated capability to target major Chinese cities such as Beijing and Shanghai with nuclear weapons."

However, India's successful testing of the Agni-III intermediate range ballistic missile in 2007 and 2008, with a range of 3,500 kilometres (2,170 miles), for the first time brings many of China's main cities within range of India's nuclear strike capability. The Agni-I short range ballistic missile is clearly oriented towards Pakistan, Agni-III is equally clearly oriented towards China, "China-specific" in Pandit's eyes. India's nuclear mobility is strengthened by the submarine based Sagarika ballistic missile launches carried out in 2008. India is set to test its augmented Agni-III+/IV missile system, with a range of 5,000 kilometres (3,110 miles) in early 2009, enabling India to target all of China for the first time. From China's point of view, this increases its nuclear encirclement, in part from India, in part from India in conjunction with the United States.

Of course, India's and China's modernization and expansion of their nuclear and missile capability is not necessarily just aimed at each other. India has its ongoing concerns with Pakistan, China has its own set of concerns with the United States. Nevertheless, India and China also feed off each other's nuclear programs. The final twist in the nuclear relationship is India's drive to establish an effective anti-ballistic MDS (Missile Defence System), in part through collaboration with the United States, but in part under its own efforts. Following successful interceptor missile tests in 2006 and 2007, India claims to have developed an ABM (Anti-Ballistic Missile) capacity, with operational deployment scheduled by 2011. Classic security dilemma dynamics operate here. As admitted by Mohanty, "China would watch India's growing missile defence capability very carefully ... there is hardly any doubt that both China and Pakistan would most likely try to strengthen their missile strike capabilities to maintain the strategic deterrence." From India's point of view, China's close nuclear links with Pakistan remains a further exacerbating and exasperating factor in Sino-Indian relations, and is part of their respective encirclement and alignment scenarios to which we now turn.

GLOBAL THREATS AND NATIONAL DEFENCE POLICIES

The fight against terrorism has reshaped Japan's defence policy. The attitudes of South Korea, Japan and China with respect to non-proliferation have been widely different. The three countries are modernizing their armed forces to address new threats in more specific and suitable ways.

The Fight Against Terrorism and Defence Policies

For Japan, the significance of participating in the 'war on terror' went beyond the alliance with the United States and economic considerations, though such factors also weighed in. Japan engaged in the 'war on terror' immediately after 9/11. The policy set up included diplomatic efforts against terrorism and inter-national co-operation to combat terrorism via the freezing of assets, as well as the passing of an Anti-Terrorism Special Measures Law on 19 October 2001, which provided for the dispatch to the Indian Ocean of ships and aircraft. In comparison with the period of the Gulf War, when the Japanese government had found itself unable to obtain the swift passage of a law on co-operation with the United Nations, or the precautions inserted in the 1992 Peacekeeping Operations Law, the 2001 law is remarkable in two ways. It was adopted within a few weeks of the 9/11 attacks; it undertook to take Japanese troops as close to a country at war as they had been since the Second World War. It provided rear support to US (and allied troops) on the distant fringes of the geographical boundaries of the US–Japan alliance (the 'Far East' in the 1960 Security Treaty; 'areas surrounding Japan' in the 1997 Guidelines on Security), establishing a new legal framework that superseded previous security arrangements.

In parallel with this military response, Japan kept up the non-military and traditional aspects of its security policy. It contributed to the international effort for the reconstruction of Afghanistan, through refugee and general assis-tance to Afghanistan and neighbouring countries: in the conference held on 21–22 January 2002 in Tokyo, Japan pledged $500 million over 2.5 years for the reconstruction of Afghanistan.

Japan also supported the US endeavour to free Iraq, though initially on the grounds that there might be WMD in Iraq. At the Madrid conference on the reconstruction of Iraq, on 24 October 2003, Japan committed itself to a $5 billion assistance package of

$1.5 billion in grants and $3.5 billion in loans. It also sent 600 men to Iraq on a reconstruction and humanitarian mission in 'non-combat zones', sheltered by Dutch and later Australian troops. The Japanese government was extremely cautious in deploying troops, and effectively did so only after re-involvement of the UN in Iraq and the end of the war had been pro-claimed. The deployment of the Self-Defence Forces (SDF) took place after the end of the war, which was launched on 20 March 2003 and ended on 1 May the same year. Resolution 1483 of the UN Security Council, approving the establishment of a US-led administration, was passed on 22 May 2003; Japan's law for the dispatch of the SDF to Iraq was adopted on 26 July 2003. On 16 October 2003, resolution 1511, mentioning the vital role of the UN in the reconstruction of Iraq, was passed. The plan organizing the dispatch was adopted on 9 December and the first deployment took place on 26 December. This was Japan's first intervention in a country, which though no longer technically at war, remained highly unstable. However cautious and moderate in scale, the dispatch represented a considerable effort, caused tremendous uproar in the Diet and was highly unpopular. Nonetheless, after the adoption of the bill authorizing the dispatch, and before the plan organizing it, M. Koizumi was re-elected in September 2003 as head of the Liberal–Democratic Party and as Prime Minister in September 2005: however unpopular, his Iraqi policy bore no electoral consequence.

Furthermore, new threats – and specifically terrorism – became important parameters of the National Defence Programme Outline upon its renewal in November 2004. The previous one dated from 1995 and was now considered outdated in view of the emergence of the 'new threats' in question. The aim of the new outline was to turn the SDF into an agile, flexible force, deployed so as to be able to counter unpredictable threats, such as commando raids, for instance. Furthermore, a 'Plan for the Prevention of International Terrorism' involving the police, not the SDF, was adopted in December 2004.

Domestically, Japan was first made aware of a terrorist threat by the sarin gas attack of March 1995, perpetrated by the religious group Aum Shinrikyô. This chemical attack appeared as a stepping-stone in the era of nuclear, chemical and biological (NCB) terrorism. However, it was only after 9/11 that Japan adopted a wide range of measures for the prevention of terrorism.

In 2003–4, the Diet also adopted a set of laws on emergency situations. Though plans for emergency legislation were made in 1963 as well as 1976, the government was never able to push them through the Diet. In spite of fierce opposition in June 2003 and 2004, the majority were convinced that Japan needed a decision-making process suitable for emergencies and determining the prerogatives of local councils, what the treatment of prospective prisoners should be (intended for Japan to be able to ratify the Additional Protocols to the 1949 Geneva Conventions on the Treatment of Prisoners of War), and to provide for co-operation with US armed forces based in Japan. Terrorism has thus achieved what the Communist threat never could: it increased threat perception in the Diet to the level needed for it to pass the 2001 and 2003 dispatch laws, which have expanded the SDF's scope for intervention, as well as pass a set of laws on emergency situations, which had been regarded as anti-democratic and militaristic in nature until then. The adoption of emergency legislation has marked an important step in Japan's entry into the post-Cold War era.

The 'war on terror' has not, however, had an impact of similar magnitude on South Korea's defence policy. According to a poll held in 2002 by the Pew Research Center, 72 per cent of South Koreans opposed the US-led war against terrorism and 24 per cent supported it; in Japan, the figures were almost reversed. Nonetheless, South Korea was the third contributor in manpower to the war in Iraq, after the US and Britain: it sent 3,600 troops there, as well 660 engineers and medical personnel. It also allocated $60 million in Official Development Assistance (ODA) to Iraq. As in Japan, the National Assembly decision to dispatch troops on 21 March 2003 was very unpopular. The rationale for the dispatch of troops was to strengthen the alliance; to contribute to world peace and security; economic factors, such as energy resource security and participation in post-war reconstruction, were also brought up. Still, another global challenge that East Asia faces is the proliferation of Weapons of Mass Destruction (WMD) epitomized by the North Korean nuclear crisis, and it is to that issue which we now turn.

Nuclear Threats and Defence Policies

China was responsible for much of the nuclear proliferation that occurred in Asia and the Middle East from the late 1970s. It sold nuclear technology to Pakistan and Iran; missile technology to Pakistan, Iran, North Korea and Libya; intermediate range missiles to Saudi Arabia; materials used to make chemical weapons to Iran; and advanced communications equipment to Iran, North Korea and the Taliban when they ruled Afghanistan. Such transfers to Pakistan, Libya and Iran occurred in the late 1980s and early 1990s, even while China was acceding to the Non-Proliferation Treaty (NPT)(1992), signing and ratifying the Chemical Weapons Convention (CWC) (1993, 1997 respectively), signing the Comprehensive Test Ban Treaty (CTBT) (1996), and joining the Zangger Committee (1997). Since 1997, however, China has grown increasingly cautious in the area of arms exports. On 25 August 2002, it issued expanded missile export control regulations and revised the 1997 list (Regulations on Export Control of Military Items). In 2004, it joined the Nuclear Suppliers Group.

It is engaged in consultations with the other multilateral regimes regarding the control of arms exports, including the Missile Technology Control Regime, the Australia Group and the Wassenaar Agreement. That China has become aware of the necessity to abide by such regimes is one of the positive effects which globalization has had on its defence policy.

Today, the primary nuclear threat to East Asia's stability is North Korea and proliferation resulting from the past connections between North Korea and Pakistan, as evidenced by revelations about Pakistani scientist A.Q. Khan's activities. South Korea and Japan's positions with respect to North Korea differ substantially. To Japan, the North Korean threat dates back to the early 1990s and is therefore fairly recent. To South Korea, on the other hand, perception of North Korea as a threat dates back to the end of the

Korean War, even if this has tended to recede over the past three years.

The North Korean threat has existed as the focus of South Korean defence policy throughout the post-war period as well as the basis for the South Korea–US alliance. When US–China relations improved from the beginning of the 1970s and the Carter administration began to withdraw some of America's Korean troops in 1978, South Korea feared abandonment and started a nuclear enrichment programme in 1978, which it officially stopped only under US pressure in 1981. It had completed the ratification of its accession to the NPT in 1975, but pursued some components of its programme until 2000.

The White Paper on Defence published in December 2000 continued to designate North Korea as South Korea's 'main enemy' regardless of the change brought to the two Koreas' relationship following the historic summit between Kim Dae-Jung and Kim Jong-Il in June 2000. Only since January 2003 has President Roh Moohyun been elected on a mandate to secure peace and prosperity for Korea, on the basis of the peaceful resolution of the North Korean nuclear issue and the establishment of an inter-Korean economic community. The President has been successful in downplaying the North Korean threat and easing dialogue with the North. The 2005 White Paper on Defence no longer refers to the Communist regime's conventional weapons and WMD, and forward-deployed troops have been downgraded from a 'military threat' to a 'direct threat'. Today, South Koreans resent the North less than the Japanese.

Japan's position with respect to nuclear weapons and non-proliferation has been as anti-nuclear as the US–Japan alliance allowed. Japan is deeply aware that it has been the only country to suffer from the use of nuclear weapons, and its pacifist constitution has led it to contribute to the strengthening and widening of disarmament and non-proliferation regimes throughout the world. Japan has submitted nuclear disarmament resolutions every year to the UN General Assembly. It promoted the establishment of the International Atomic Energy Agency's Additional Protocol (1997), which provides for reinforced safeguards and verification measures, and contributed to the universalization of the non-proliferation regimes (the NPT, the CTBT) by assisting developing countries in their implementation. It also contributed to the launch of the Hague Code of Conduct against Ballistic Missile Proliferation (2002).

This non-nuclear stance has been a pillar of Japan's defence policy since 1968, when Prime Minister Satô articulated the 'three non-nuclear principles': Japan rejects the possession, the acquisition, and the introduction of nuclear weapons onto its territory. In practice, the third branch of the principle has been violated by the requirements of the alliance with the US, and the introduction of nuclear weapons into Japanese waters by US military vessels. For Japan to benefit from the protection of the US nuclear umbrella implied in itself some degree of tampering with the non-nuclear principles.

In spite of the protection thereby afforded, the Japanese have felt threatened by North Korean missiles ever since what the Japanese government considered to be a test launch in August 1998. Ronald Reagan, and George Bush after him, had sought Japan's involvement in a joint missile defence project. Four months after the test launch, in December 1998, Japan finally agreed to joint research with the US on a Missile Defence System (MDS). Between fiscal years 1999 and 2004, Japan allocated some ¥29.3 billion ($236 million) to the MDS.

The missile launch also accelerated the adoption of the 'Law Concerning Measures to Ensure the Peace of Japan and Security of Japan in Situations in Areas Surrounding Japan', in May 1999. Debates on this law started in April 1998, prior to the North Korean missile launch, and this law was required to ensure the entering into force of the new Japan–US Guidelines on Security of 1997. The missile launch did not influence substantially the pace of adoption or the content of the law. However it gave the Japanese people and their representatives a sense of increased urgency for an effective framework of co-operation with the US. The law allows Japan to provide rear support to the US in the event of an attack against Japan or in Japan's surrounding areas – a 'situational' rather than geographical concept – even though the Japanese government argued at the time that the wording referred to Asia.

New Threats and Military Modernization

Globalization has also had an impact in terms of shaping the means deployed to fight new threats, and in this regard, the South Korean and Japanese governments are modernizing their armed forces. The South Korean armed forces' modernization is being carried out with a view to enabling South Korea to play a greater role in regional defence.

At present, it lacks the ability to do so effectively without US military backing, which is why the US has recently reaffirmed its commitment to South Korea's defence. Although the US would assume command during a conflict in the peninsula, South Korea has already exercised peacetime control of its troops since 1994, and the South Korean Minister for Defence and the US Secretary of Defence have now reached further agreement, in a joint statement issued in October 2005, to 'appropriately accelerate talks about granting South Korea wartime operational control'. In the same statement, the two countries agreed to bring down the number of US forces deployed in South Korea from 33,000 to 29,500 (compared with a previous level of 37,000). This move represents a further compromise; in 2004, President Bush had announced the unilateral withdrawal of 12,500 troops, creating some uneasiness in Seoul.

South Korea's military modernization involves cutting 170,000 troops from the current 675,000 and adding more sophisticated weapons and missiles to its arsenal, including F15 jets and precision-guided tactical missiles. It is also in the process of converting its 'whole defence structure into one centring around knowledge and information, taking advantage of computers and information technology' so as to gain efficiency in war or peacetime; and this it aims to do by 2015.Consequently, South Korean defence expenditure has been increasing steadily: spending was $20.7 billion in 2005, almost double from $11.9 billion in 2001.

In Japan, the modernization of the defence forces is also taking place alongside a strengthening of the Japan–US Alliance. In October 2005, the Japanese Ministers for Defence and Foreign

Affairs, together with the US Secretary of State and Secretary of Defence, published an intermediate report on changes to be brought to the alliance in order to ensure the gradual inter-operability of the two armies. Even more than South Korea, Japan is eager to appear as a trustworthy ally: its defence policy constraints imply greater dependency than South Korea's, and it hopes to gain greater autonomy within and through the alliance by playing along.

The majority of Japanese citizens support the alliance though they do not wish to see their troops sent around the world to act alongside the US. Japan's defence policy was born in the context of the Korean War and on America's strong advice. As such, it has been limited historically to the exercise of self-defence, the three conditions of which are: an imminent and illegitimate act of aggression against Japan; the absence of alternative means to deal with the aggression; a use of arms confined to the necessary minimum. In seeking to become a 'symmetrical (economic, political, military) great power', Japan encounters many restrictions derived from Article 9 of its constitution, which renounces belligerence as a right pertaining to nationhood. Japan is keen to alleviate the inconveniences of the US presence, and it hopes to gain weight within the alliance in order to become more influential in its operation, less subject to US pressure, and better able to express dissenting views.

The modernization of Japan's defence forces, undertaken at the end of 2004, has been both qualitative and operational in character. The missile defence system is an important aspect of its new defence posture, as is the improvement of inter-operability with the US armed forces. Yet, at $44.7 billion in 2005, Japan's defence budget has been increasing only marginally (up from $40.4 billion in 2001), and is comparable in scale to France's $41.6 billion budget and the UK's $51.1 billion budget in 2005. With the new Mid-Term Defence Programme (2005–9), Japan has now entered a five-year period of decline in its defence spending.

The 'war on terror', the North Korean nuclear threat, and the modernization of defence forces as a prerequisite for responding to such 'new threats', altogether illustrate the extent to which global challenges have directly influenced national defence policies.

In other instances, globalization's impact on defence policies may be indirect.

NUCLEAR ARMS CONTROL AND DISARMAMENT

While one could give credit to China for its efforts in recent years with regard to its nonproliferation policy and practices, less can be said about its nuclear arms control and disarmament policy. On disarmament, Beijing could claim that it has held a principled position on complete nuclear prohibition since 1964, when it conducted its first nuclear test. At the same time, over the past four decades, China has maintained that the two largest nuclear weapon states should take the lead in drastically reducing their nuclear arsenals before the second-tier nuclear weapon states participate in multilateral nuclear disarmament. China's 2008 Defence White Paper argues that further U.S. and Russian reductions in "a verifiable and irreversible manner" could "create the necessary conditions for the participation of other nuclear-weapon states in the process of nuclear disarmament." In addition, the paper argues that nuclear arms control and disarmament measures cannot succeed unless the root causes of global/regional conflicts are addressed.

In recent years, Beijing has put more emphasis on how nuclear arms control and disarmament should contribute to global strategic stability and the national security of participating states, rather than undermine them. Strategic stability and national security considerations may become both a benchmark for and an excuse against China's participation in multilateral nuclear disarmament processes. Chinese analysts are not encouraged by recent developments in both nuclear and conventional armament of a number of states and are concerned that they could invite reactions that ultimately result in an arms race. Some have suggested that certain nuclear weapon states spend more on conventional systems than nuclear arsenals because the latter cannot be used; others argue that fear of being coerced and intimidated continues to be the logic for non-nuclear states to pursue nuclear weapons options. In addition, the RMA, missile defences, and the potential for space weaponization are red flags that caution, if not deeply concern, Chinese strategists. Beijing is keenly aware that

Some major powers are realigning their security and military strategies, increasing their defence investment, speeding up the transformation of armed forces, and developing advanced military technology, weapons and equipment. Strategic nuclear forces, military astronautics, missile defence systems, and global and battlefield reconnaissance and surveillance have become top priorities in their efforts to strengthen armed forces.

Beijing continues to have strong reservations about U.S. missile defences. A November 6, 2008 statement by the Foreign Ministry spokesman pointed out that "China always believes that setting up global missile defence system, including deploying such system in some regions of the world or conducting cooperation in this field, is detrimental to global strategic balance and stability, undermines mutual trust among countries and affects regional stability. The recent development of situation makes it evident that relevant countries should take other countries' concerns seriously." Indeed, Chinese analysts remain keenly attentive to this issue against the larger context of the international strategic environment at any given time. One of the key criteria for Chinese analysts is to assess how a specific offence-defence configuration could affect international strategic stability, major power relations, and global arms control processes and direction. This being the point of departure, missile defence itself would not be treated merely as a military development. Instead, one needs to look at the broader implications, since this particular military posture both reflects the threat perceptions and strategic intentions of the state adopting it and inevitably will affect the existing international strategic environment and the perceptions and interests of other major powers.

During the early 1980s, China followed the U.S. Strategic Defence Initiative closely. Beijing feared that the Reagan administration's missile defence plan could trigger certain Soviet reactions, including the development and deployment of Moscow's own ballistic missile defence, resulting in possible neutralization of China's limited nuclear deterrent force. This would exert strong pressure on China to spend more on nuclear modernization, thus taking away much needed resources from economic development priorities. At the same time, the superpower arms race raised the specter of space weaponization and hence serious implications for international security and stability.

Over a quarter-century later, the issues remain the same for China: the credibility and effectiveness of its nuclear deterrence; the danger of weaponization of outer space; and the need to determine priorities and allocate resources.

Chinese positions on nuclear arms control and disarmament could be influenced by three specific developments in U.S. defence policy. The first revolves around the overall strategic orientation of U.S. nuclear forces. Chinese analysts argue that the end of the Cold War has resulted in a unique environment in which the United States is gradually achieving unchallenged nuclear dominance, as the result of declining Russian nuclear arsenals and still-limited Chinese nuclear capabilities. Chinese analysts are concerned that Washington may be emboldened by this newfound advantage to pursue policies of unilateralism and preemptive attack more aggressively than in the past.

In addition, Chinese analysts have expressed considerable concern about perceived U.S. efforts to develop new types of nuclear weapons. The United States has already achieved unchallenged conventional and nuclear weapons dominance but is still pursuing research and development programs that will eventually make nuclear weapons more readily usable and capable of penetrating hardened underground facilities. For instance, the George W. Bush administration's Reliable Replacement Warhead (RRW) Program planned, when fully operational, for the production of 125 new nuclear warheads annually up to the year 2022, in order to maintain a sizable U.S. nuclear arsenal that is reliable, safe, and available for use. These new nuclear warheads would also be easier to maintain and have a longer service lifetime than existing systems. Despite the fact that the RRW program has been suspended due to congressional "zeroing out" of funding for its research and feasibility studies, Chinese analysts argue that the U.S. attempt to change the nuclear balance of power in this way could lead to renewed nuclear arms races between nuclear weapon states, induce threshold states to openly pursue nuclear weapon capabilities, and fundamentally undermine global nuclear nonproliferation efforts. This may give the Chinese some pause as to if and how they should proceed with regard to nuclear disarmament, given the high degree of asymmetry between the U.S. and Chinese nuclear arsenals. While China possesses about two dozen missiles capable of reaching continental United States, the United States has 830 missiles capable of striking targets in China.

Finally, U.S. missile defence deployments in East Asia pose a serious threat to China's second-strike nuclear capabilities. Given the size and sophistication of China's small nuclear arsenal, the ability to survive a first strike is critical to maintaining the credibility and reliability of its deterrence. Despite Washington's assurance that it seeks only a limited missile defence not directed at China, Beijing continues to seek—and this may well explain its current nuclear modernization efforts—to reverse the growing imbalance as a result of U.S. missile defence plans, not to mention the new nuclear security environment that China has to face, namely, the emergence of India and Pakistan as nuclear weapon states and North Korea's nuclear weapons development.

The U.S. dependence on space assets for military operations—along with the fact that Beijing sees U.S. missile defence systems as a precursor to weaponization of outer space—may also explain China's efforts to develop a limited antisatellite capability. Chinese concerns extend beyond missile defences; U.S. capabilities in long-range precision conventional strike weapons, combined with C^4ISR (command, control, communications, computers, intelligence, surveillance, and reconnaissance), further deepen China's sense of vulnerability.

If these trends continue, it could lead China to take action to redress an emerging nuclear imbalance. Given its relatively smaller and less sophisticated arsenal, there is good reason Beijing would be reluctant to endorse measures that could impose significant constraints on its ability for self-defence. China's nuclear modernization efforts in recent years—with an emphasis on qualitative rather than quantitative improvements, especially in areas such as enhanced mobility, survivability, and, hence, credibility of its deterrence—are indicative of Beijing's serious concerns.

This preoccupation with maintaining or restoring what Beijing considers to be strategic stability may be a major factor affecting its decision on CTBT ratification. Indeed, it was with great reluctance that the PLA and the nuclear weapons community endorsed China's decision to sign the treaty. While China signed the CTBT in 1996, Beijing has not yet ratified it, mainly because of the U.S. Senate's rejection of it in 1999. Since then, a fierce internal debate about CTBT ratification has been raging in China. Some support ratification because China has already stopped testing, giving China the moral high ground on this global arms control issue. Others in China argue that ratification would prevent China from resuming testing in response to a new round of U.S. testing. Some Chinese analysts believe China was duped into signing the treaty before the United States initiated its missile defence programs. A few of them have even suggested that it is probable the United States could start testing again to develop a new generation of small nuclear warheads. China's signature of the CTBT means that China continues to accept the constraints imposed on its ability to test, a critical step in the development of new nuclear weapons, especially the miniaturization of warheads for new ballistic missiles currently under development. If this is the case, then Beijing's acute concern about the shifts in U.S. nuclear thinking could precipitate shifts in Chinese policies on nuclear testing.

Related to the testing issue is the issue of fissile material production and China's position on an FMCT. Clearly, if there are serious concerns among Chinese strategic analysts about the need to maintain a sufficiently sized nuclear arsenal that could survive a first strike and still be able, in both quantitative and qualitative terms, to retaliate against the striking country by penetrating and defeating missile defences, then China would have to consider the question of how much is enough as a hedge against future contingencies. China is believed to have stopped producing weapons-grade highly enriched uranium and military plutonium, although it retains a fissile material stockpile for future expansion of its nuclear arsenal, should the need arise. In this context, the "how much" question is informed by three factors: changes in nuclear doctrine, the international security environment, and military technology.

It is widely acknowledged that there is no evidence to suggest that China's NFU policy has changed; the country's security environment remains favourable. However, changes in military technology may pose the most serious challenge to China. Chinese analysts refer specifically to: U.S. discussions about developing new types of nuclear warheads, U.S. missile defences, and advanced U.S. conventional weapons. These issues could have a major impact on Chinese decision makers as they determine the size of China's nuclear arsenal and on the question as to whether to retain the ability to produce fissile material for nuclear warheads or sign onto an international treaty that could deprive it of that option.

WEAPONS DEVELOPMENT AND THE NATIONAL DEFENCE ECONOMY

It is common knowledge that modern warfare is not only the competition of weapons on the battlefield but is also, at the same time, an all-out competition of the total strength of the opposing side's politics, economics, military, and science and technology. During the development of weaponry, the four aspects of politics, economics, military and science and technology are completely brought into play. In today's climate of rapid development of national defence science and technology and the daily emergence of new weapons, the material base of the actual national defence economy should be not only strong but also exceptional.

- With the upgrade in the tactical and technical performances of weapons, manufacturing costs would correspondingly be also more expensive. Since the end of WWII, science and technology development has flourished. There has been a multitude of achievements in science and technology that have continuously increased weapon precision, its powers to cause casualties, and its military effectiveness. The explosive power of a small atomic bomb has the same effectiveness as 100 bombers from WWII. The fire power of today's tank is tenfold greater than that of WWII. A mission to destroy 60 percent of the equipment of a tank division would today require only 1 percent of the aircraft used 40 years ago. During the Falklands War between England and Argentina, the EXOCET missile, which cost only $200,000, fired by the Argentinean Air Force was able to sink a British SHEPHARD missile destroyer that costs $200 million. The ratio of the two costs effectiveness is 1:1,000. The precision of precision-guided bombs and artillery shells is 2 to 3 times better than that of non-guided bombs and artillery shells. However, the upgrading of weapons performance has also brought with it the consequence of more expensive manufacturing costs. The cost of scientific research and technical components compared to the cost of a system with microcomputer technology, new materials, and new techniques imported in great quantities would appear to be prominently greater. Each of the U.S.'s HELLFIRE antitank missile costs about $28,100 to buy, but the scientific research to produce it costs $310 million. Each of the LEOPARD-II tanks of the Federal Republic of Germany costs $3.58 million to buy, yet the scientific research cost was $360 million. The research cost of Japan's MODEL 61 tanks cost 500 million to research and develop in the 1950s, its MODEL 74 tanks cost 2.5 billion to develop in the 1960s, and the MODEL 88 tanks that currently are under research and development have a budgeted cost that could reach 25 billion. The research and development expenditures of three generations of tanks seem to have increased geometrically. According to statistics, the costs of fighters and tanks increase about tenfold every 20 years and the costs of aircraft carriers increase by tenfold every 30 years. Weapons development has come to rely more and more on the national defence economy, causing great burdens for many countries.

- The increase in weapon power has also created battlefield situations where the consumption of battlefield material and economic losses are immense. It requires a huge quantity of material reserves. The 4th Middle East War lasted only 18 days and both sides, Egypt and Israel, suffered economic losses of over $5 billion. The loss of aircraft by both sides was comparable to the combined loss in aircraft in a year by all of the participant countries during WWII. In the first 3 days after the war started, the total number of tactical missiles launched by both sides was equivalent to the combined total of all the reserves of the countries in NATO. The loss of tanks was equal to one-third the number of those in the possession of NATO countries at that time. Both sides strategic reserves and materials were exhausted a week into the war. We can infer the amount of economic loss that could be created by modern warfare from this. In the Falklands War, the English spent a total of $2.16 billion, about $1.2 million every hour. This kind of consumption, to fight one mid-size modern war, is difficult for even an economically great power to support.

The production of weapons, ammunition, technical facilities and engineering equipment all consume large amounts of metal and various kinds of nonferrous metals. They also need the support of the chemical industry and energy resources, as well as military industrial products. According to the statistics from affiliated departments at the United Nations, 15 to 16 percent of the world's copper output and 10 percent of it tin, nickel, lead, and zinc outputs are used for weapons production and toward the building of other national defence installations. The consumption of energy resources is even greater. During WWI, the consumption of fuel by each soldier for each day averaged about 6 kg. During WWII, it was increased to 20 kg for each person each day. In the several local area wars fought in recent years, the fuel consumption of each man each day increased to 90 kg. The consumption level is shocking! This not only raises problems for logistics support, it also increases the economic and energy resources burden.

- The rapid increase and shorter intervals in the updating and replacement of weaponry have sharply increased military expenditures and expenses. The advancements of science and technology have caused new weapons to emerge in an endless stream and greatly accelerated replacement and updating of weaponry. Before and after WWI, the time period for a weapons system to go from research and design, through trial tests and production to its deployment within the service required about 20 to 30 years. At present, this procedure requires only 10 to 15 years or an even shorter period. According to the analysis of a Soviet economist, Maj. Gen. Guluofu, a new weapons system for the Soviet military from research to its deployment in the services requires 10-15 years. Since the 1960s, Soviet missiles have already been updated three generations. The majority of its aircraft, submarines, and surface ships underwent updating long ago. Its anti-air defence missiles, radar, command equipment, communications equipment, and other equipment have also been through several generations of updating. The research of new weapons and the updating of existing weapons have greatly increased the military expenditures and expenses of every country. According to an analysis by western observers, "The world economy is already shouldering a burden of massive destructive weapons, poverty, and debt. Militarization will further sap its strength." Since the 1960s, the global expenditure for weapons has been about $14 trillion. In 1985 it was about $800 billion, in 1986 about $900 billion. Every second of every year about $1.7 million are spent. Immense military expenditures have become serious economic problems for each of the world's countries.

- The research and production of modern weapons have made even greater demands on the national defence economy and national defence industries. Since WWII, especially during the 1960s and 1970s, the unceasing discovery of new technology has led to a great revolution in weapons and military-use equipment.

In 1945, the atomic bomb appeared. The research of computers for weapons use came in 1946. In 1952, the first transistorized computer was developed. In 1953, the world's first hydrogen bomb was exploded. In 1955, the first nuclear-powered submarine was launched. In August 1957, the first intercontinental ballistic missile was fired, and in October of that same year, the first manmade satellite was orbited. In 1960, mankind recovered its first satellite. In 1961, the world's first manned satellite did an orbit around the earth and returned to the surface. In 1967, the first integrated circuit was successfully developed. In 1969, man had his first landing on the moon. In 1977, the neutron bomb was researched and developed. In April 1981, the world's first spacecraft flew. The research and production of all these new weapons and equipment and a large portion of the new technology that entered into the sphere of the national defence economy not only greatly changed the production and industrial structure of the national defence economy, it also added a series of new production and industrial sectors. These changes helped to restructure the traditional national defence industries, moving them in the direction of technological improvement, and development of a technological reserve. The diffusion of a large quantity of high technology made it possible to turn a consuming national defence economy into a propagating field of national defence economy.

Weapons development is reliant on the development of the national economy. It also encourages the growth of national defence science and technology. Military high-technology also gave impetus to the development of the economy. Looking at this from two-dimensional space, this big "O" cycle could possibly expand further. Analysing it from a three-dimensional space, this kind of spiraling trend is perfectly suited to the objective laws of material development.

Weapons and Equipment Development and Military Scientific Theory

"Technology determines the tactics." The appearance of large quantities of technical equipment inevitably brings about great transformations in military theory and tactics; this in turn leads to great changes in strategic thinking, patterns of combat, combat style, and military structures:

- Weapons development enhances man's strategic consciousness, deepens his strategic reflections, and increases the emphasis on strategic projections. In today's world, strategic research is extremely dynamic. With the development of strategic rockets and various spacecrafts, as well as the gradual development of energy beam weapons, kinetic energy weapons, and other space weapons systems, war has extended from the surface, air, and sea toward outer space. The areas of man's activities have already extended beyond the earth and moved into space. This has opened up man's field of vision and expanded his modes of thinking. In the wideness of space, the earth is no longer "boundless and limitless," but has become one of the "global villages" in the universe. In the eyes of the strategist, the earth has become small and man's strategic reflection is becoming more profound and his strategic consciousness has been greatly enhanced. Man's heart embraces the whole of the universe. The development of strategic research is even more important than at any time in history and has become an especially important issue for all countries globally. What is coming will be conflicts in space. One of the conflicts will be the military struggle for "control of the high ground in space." The other will be exploitation and use of space, the struggle for the resources of space. For this reason, every country in the world is busily formulating and developing strategic plans. In March 1983, the United States became the first to formulate a "Star Wars Plan." This caused global commotion in strategy research. The Soviet Union responded with "defensive measures" to the "Star Wars Plan." Western Europe came up with the "Eureka Plan." Each of the COMECON countries announced a "Plan for the integrated advancement of science and technology by the year 2000." Japan had its "Policy outline for science and technology;" China had a "Policy for a new technological revolution;" India came out with "Policy statements for new technology;" South Korea had its "Conceptions for long range national growth;" and Yugoslavia had its "National science and technology development strategy." To rank within the world's family of nations, to live and survive in the "global village" in this universe, each nation must come up with ideas for a "grand strategy." "To stand shoulder to shoulder with the giants" one must intensely fix one's eye on the growth of national defence construction and weapons in the next century.

- Modern weapons are not only direct combat strengths between opposing combat opponents, they are also strategic deterrents and tools for international political struggles. The appearance of offensive strategic weapons like missiles, atomic bombs, nuclear-powered submarines, and long-range bombers has caused great changes in military strategy. The research, production, and large stockpiles of strategic weapons are already more than needed to seek out and kill an enemy. It has turned into a tool for political and diplomatic struggle. The large-scale arms race have caused the United States to stockpile over 9,400 nuclear warheads with a total nuclear weight equivalent of over 4 billion tons. The Soviet Union's stockpile of over 8,000 nuclear warheads has a total nuclear weight equivalent of over 5 billion tons. The quantity of nuclear warheads possessed by these two nuclear powers comprises above 97 percent of the global total. Both have the capacity to destroy the other several times over. Living under these conditions, the military strategy of both sides has gone through many changes; strategic ideologies have been revised about every 10 years. However, pressure from the threat that "destroying the enemy doesn't necessarily mean one's own survival" has kept them from crossing the "nuclear threshold" and taking the next step of pressing the button to launch those nuclear missiles. England, France, and China have independently and on their own developed into national nuclear powers. The limited power of these countries is not enough to compete with the capabilities of the United States and the Soviet Union, but they do play a role in the even development of political, economical, and military affairs within the world. This power is entirely a symbol of a country's independence and its existence within the world of politics, economics, military affairs, and science and technology.

In addition to nuclear weapons, the emergence of strategic weapons has definitely caused reforms within the military, changing past combat theories that we must go through war and campaigns to achieve strategic objectives to the possibility that strategic weapons could directly attack the opponent's strategic targets and achieve the strategic objectives. The development of various space weapons has not only intensified military struggles in space, it has also increased ways in which strategic objectives could be directly achieved.

- Today's weapons systems are very mobile. They also have long range, high accuracy, and great power, causing the time and spatial aspects as well as the intensity of war to change greatly. The development of these weapons and the great number of these weapons being deployed within the services have caused the arenas of war to be extended into deep sea and space, the length of war to shorten, and the suddenness, destructiveness, savageness, and mutation to increase unprecedentedly. In the "blitzkrieg" of the German armoured troops during WWII, they could advance only about 30 km daily. Today, under normal circumstances, the Soviets could do 50 km and under nuclear conditions it could reach above 100 km. When the Soviet Union invaded Afghanistan, its push towards Kabul, a distance of 900 km took only 6 days. The time it takes for an intercontinental ballistic missile to travel its whole distance is only slightly more than 30 minutes and there is no more than 20 minutes of early warning for its defence.

During the Falklands War, England's SHEFFIELD class missile destroyer did not even have the opportunity to react before it was hit by Argentina's EXOCET missile. With this short span of time, it is very difficult to react. This has made even greater demands on command and control. The largeness of the battlefield and the number of troops involved have given rise to immense increases in technical weaponry and specialized technology and have caused even greater problems in the coordination of operations and commands. According to reports, there were only 20 different military specialties during Word War I. It grew to 160 during World War II, and at present, the number of military technologies and specializations exceed 2,000. During combat, the army, navy, air force, and the other different service branches are all involved at the same time. The types of weapons used are never less than a dozen and usually are in the hundreds. This alone would demand that the commander prepare detailed plans and coordinate his commands well. There must be no mistakes in differentiating missions, allotting time, and coordinating activities. Any small error could lead to major mistakes and even greater disasters.

First strike has always been the combat phase that militarists attach greatest importance to. The success or failure of the first strike impacts the whole battle. In modern combat, because of the short time needed for combat, the phases of combat are no longer clearly delineated. The long range surprise attack or the counterattack during the preliminary period of the combat has become the main combat model for first strike. Thus, every nation has given special attention to studying the first strike phase of a war. The United States emphasizes that "every preparation must be made to win with the first strike." The Soviet Union also believes that "surprise attacks are the most effective combat opening moves to implement in future wars.... Victory can basically be determined in the first phase of a war." This will demand that commanders make complete preparations for first strikes. Intelligence, reconnaissance, personal observations with automatic and rapid analysis, processing and judgment, decisionmaking, formulating careful plans, and even reactions must be quick and accurate because only then could the "first strike win" objective be achieved.

- The extensive use of modern weapons has caused great changes in military structures. Before WWI, the military was basically composed of land forces that included the infantry, artillery, calvary, and navy. Before WWII, there was a great deal of aircraft and tanks in the military, thus the air force, armoured troops and motorized troops came into existence. The air force itself was divided into bomber, fighter, and attack aircraft forces. There were surface vessels, submarines, naval aviation forces and marines in the navy. After WWII, strategic rocket forces, army airborne forces and other service branches were formed. With the development of space technology and the successful development of various spaceflight vehicles as well as the development of various space weapons, the militarization of space will possibly strengthen the military deployment of a new independent military service branch "Space Forces." In 1982, the United States established the Air Force Spaceflight Command (a command comparable to the Strategic Air Force and Tactical Air Force Commands combined), and in 1983, the United States established the Naval Spaceflight Command. In 1985, the two commands and affiliated army commands were combined to form the U.S. Spaceflight Command. Not long after the United States had established the Air Force Spaceflight Command (1982), the Soviet Union appointed Lt. Gen. Sadaluofu as the "Aeronavigation Forces Commander." Some reports have said that "it is possible that the Soviet Union had already established a military spaceflight command like the U.S. Air Force Spaceflight Command and that the aeronavigation force was nothing but a subforce of that command." Various evidence has shown that the growth of the militarization of space has brought about the birth of the "Space Forces." With the advancements made in microelectronics, computers, and artificial intelligence technology, multipurpose robots could soon be used more and more in military applications and in those work areas where the labour is heavy and environmentally dangerous; thus a "robot force" would have to be deployed. The influence of weapons development on military administrative systems and deployment and on the overall structure can be easily seen. At present, the strategic course for overall military development is: a reduction in the overall personnel strength, a rise in the proportion of technical military personnel in the overall structure, a decrease in the proportion of personnel directly involved in combat, and a different scale for the increase in the proportion of logistic personnel (including technical support personnel).

The impact of modern weapons on military theory has been profound and extensive. The various sophisticated tools, means and methods of modern policy decision studies, projection studies, and futures studies have scientifically given impetus to and provided directions for military theories and strategic growth. It has allowed the military to grow scientifically so that it can completely anticipate conflicts and play a better leadership role.

2

Arms Race Developing in the Asia-Pacific Region

Many analysts believe that growing friction between the United States and China will define the coming decades. Certainly, China is in the midst of an ambitious bid to modernize its military by the middle of this century. A key part of this effort is to downsize its army—the world's largest—while beefing up its air force and navy. This will enable China to project military force farther beyond its borders. China's total spending is second only to that of the United States, but it is low as measured by per capita spending. However, China has expanded its military spending at a double-digit pace in the past decade, and it became the world's second-largest military power, surpassing France, in 2009. In March 2011, the Chinese government announced that it would be raising its official military budget by 12.7%, to US$91.5 billion. This marks a surge forward in military spending and reverses the government's 2010 position, when it reined in military spending to a mere 7.5% increase. The 2010 military budget was the first to fall below 10% since 1989. Military experts in the United States and elsewhere have said Beijing's real military spending is at least double the announced figure. A 2009 Pentagon report estimated China's total military spending to be between US$105 billion and US$150 billion. While growing rapidly, China's military spending is still dwarfed by that of the United States.

China clearly now intends to develop a military capability to match its new-found economic status, and is spending more on its navy and air force, and cutting back on its land forces. The idea is to put the country in a better position to project force outside its own borders. China's insatiable appetite for raw materials and energy has also widened the military's mission to protect China's strategic economic interests overseas. The country's naval and air forces certainly appear determined to impose their dominance in the South China Sea—through which vital oil supplies pass, and where several islands are in dispute—and in the East China Sea, where China and Japan are in dispute over mineral rights, and a number of contested islands. The government says that most of the increased military expenditure is focused on improving the historically poor living conditions of soldiers in the People's Liberation Army.

In addition, the authorities intend to increase spending on "informatization," in an attempt to close the gap on the United States's use of "smart" technology. Defence companies in the West could benefit from China's attempts to upgrade its military technology, although it is extremely doubtful whether Washington would allow American companies to supply technology to China.

Some analysts contend that if China's economic growth remains robust, and the country is thus able to continue to expand its defence spending significantly each year, it will pose a threat to the United States' military dominance of the globe by the mid-21st century, or earlier. In early 2009, Beijing confirmed plans to build aircraft carriers, with the apparent intent of projecting "blue water" naval power eastwards into the Pacific, bringing it into potential conflict with the United States. For its part, Beijing fears that the United States is trying to "encircle" China, by using India, and allies such as Japan and Australia, as proxies to contain China's increasing military strength. China's concerns have some validity—military ties between Washington and New Delhi, for example, are growing in a number of areas. India is also growing into a major purchaser of US military equipment, an about-turn for a country that relied on Soviet weapons during the Cold War. In a groundbreaking deal, India agreed to buy six Lockheed C130J transport planes for around US$1 billion in January 2008—New Delhi had previously procured transport aircraft from the USSR or Russia. India is expected to spend US$100 billion in the next decade on its military. India's defence minister, Arackaparambil Kurien Antony, has made it clear that he expects military spending, currently 2.5% of GDP, to increase substantially as the nation's robust economy continues to grow.

NUCLEAR ARMS RACE

The nuclear arms race was a competition for supremacy in nuclear warfare between the United States, the Soviet Union, and their respective allies during the Cold War. During the Cold War, in addition to the American and Soviet nuclear stockpiles, other countries also developed nuclear weapons, though none engaged in warhead production on nearly the same scale as the two superpowers.

World War II

The first nuclear weapon was created by the American Manhattan Project during the Second World War and was developed to be used against the Axis powers. Scientists of the Soviet Union, then an ally of the United States, were aware of the potential of nuclear weapons and had also been conducting research in the field. The Soviet Union was not officially informed of the American experiments until Stalin was briefed at the Potsdam Conference on July 24, 1945.

The Americans did not trust the Soviets enough to keep the information safe from German spies but also distrusted the Soviets and their intentions generally, despite their wartime military alliance. Even during the war several government and military figures in the USA saw the USSR as a potential enemy in the future.

Despite their official ignorance, the Soviets were well aware of the program due to a ring of spies operating within the American nuclear program. The atomic spies (including Klaus Fuchs and Theodore Hall) kept Stalin well informed of American progress. When U.S. President Harry S. Truman informed Stalin of the weapons, he was surprised at how calmly Stalin reacted to the news and thought that Stalin had not understood what he had been told. In fact Stalin had long been aware of the program. The program was top classified meaning even Truman did not know about it or the weapons until he became president.

In August 1945, atomic bombs were dropped on Truman's orders on designated Japanese cities. The first bomb was dropped on Hiroshima, and later another bomb was dropped on Nagasaki by the B-29 bombers *Enola Gay* and *Bock's Car* respectively.

Early Cold War

In the years immediately after the Second World War, the United States had monopoly on specific knowledge of and raw materials for nuclear weaponry. Initially, it was thought that uranium was rare in the world, but this turned out to be wrong. American leaders hoped that their exclusivity would be enough to draw concessions from the Soviet Union, this proved ineffective. Behind the scenes, the Soviet regime was working on building their own atomic weapons. During the war Soviet efforts had been limited due to a lack of uranium, but new supplies in Eastern Europe were found and provided a steady supply while the Soviets developed a domestic source. While American experts had predicted that the USSR would not have nuclear weapons until the mid-1950s, the first Soviet bomb was detonated on August 29 of 1949, shocking the entire world. The bomb, named "Joe One" by the West, was more or less a copy of the bomb the United States had dropped on Japan, "Fat Man".

Governments spent massive amounts to increase the quality and quantity of their nuclear arsenal. Both nations quickly began working on the hydrogen bombs and the United States detonated their first of these on November 1, 1952. Again, the Soviets surprised the Americans by exploding a deployable thermonuclear device next August, though it was not a real multi-stage hydrogen bomb, which followed in 1955.

The most important development in terms of delivery in the 1950s was the introduction of intercontinental ballistic missiles, ICBMs. Missiles had long been regarded the ideal platform for nuclear weapons, and were potentially a more effective delivery system than strategic bombers, which was the primary delivery method at the beginning of the Cold War. On October 4, 1957, the Soviet Union showed the world that they had missiles able to reach any part of the world when they launched the Sputnik. The United States launched their own satellite on the 31 October 1959. The Space Race showcased technology critical to the delivery of nuclear weapons, the ICBM boosters, while maintaining the appearance of being for science and exploration.

This period also saw some of the first attempts to defend against nuclear weapons. Both superpowers built large radar arrays to detect incoming bombers and missiles. Fighters to use against bombers and anti-ballistic missiles to use against ICBMs were also developed. Large underground bunkers were constructed to save the leaders, and citizens were told to build fallout shelters and taught how to react to a nuclear attack. These measurements were called civil defense.

Mutual Assured Destruction (MAD)

None of these defensive measures were secure, and in the 1950s both the United States and Soviet Union had nuclear power to obliterate the other side. Both sides developed a capability to launch a devastating attack even after sustaining a full assault from the other side (especially by means of submarines), called a second strike. This policy was part of what became known as Mutual Assured Destruction: both sides knew that any attack upon the other would be devastating to themselves, thus in theory refraining them from attacking the other.

Both Soviet and American experts hoped to use nuclear weapons for extracting concessions from the other, or from other powers such as China, but the risk connected with using these weapons was so grave that they refrained from what John Foster Dulles referred to as brinkmanship. While some, like General Douglas MacArthur, argued nuclear weapons should be used during the Korean War, both Truman and Eisenhower opposed.

Both sides were unaware of the capacity of the enemy's arsenal of nuclear weapons. The Americans suffered from a lack of confidence, and in the 1950s they believed in a non-existing bomber gap. Aerial photography later revealed that the Soviets had been playing a sort of Potemkin village game with their bombers in their military parades, flying them in large circles, making it appear they had far more than they truly did. The 1960 American presidential election saw accusations of a wholly spurious missile gap between the Soviets and the Americans. On the contrary, the Soviet government exaggerated the power of Soviet weapons to the leadership and Nikita Khrushchev.

An additional controversy formed in the United States during the early 1960s concerned whether or not it was certain if their weapons would work if the need should occur. All of the individual components of nuclear missiles had been tested separately (warheads, navigation systems, rockets), but it had been infeasible to test them all combined. Critics charged that it was not really known how a warhead would react to the gravity forces and temperature differences encountered in the upper atmosphere and outer space, and Kennedy was unwilling to run a test of an ICBM with a live warhead. The closest thing to an actual test was 1962's Operation Frigate Bird, in which the submarine USS *Ethan Allen* launched a Polaris A1 missile over 1,000 miles to the nuclear test site at Christmas Island. It was challenged by, among others, Curtis LeMay, who put missile accuracy into doubt to encourage the development of new bombers. Other critics pointed out that it was a single test which could be an anomaly; that it was a lower-altitude SLBM and therefore was subject to different conditions than an ICBM; and that significant modifications had been made to its warhead before testing.

INITIAL NUCLEAR PROLIFERATION

In addition to the United States and the Soviet Union, three other nations, the United Kingdom, People's Republic of China, and France also developed far smaller nuclear stockpiles. In 1952, the United Kingdom became the third nation to possess nuclear weapons when it detonated an atomic bomb in Operation Hurricane in Australia on October 3, 1952. During the Cold War, British nuclear deterrence came from submarines and nuclear-armed aircraft. The Resolution class ballistic missile submarines armed with the American-built Polaris missile provided the sea deterrent, while aircraft such as the Avro Vulcan, SEPECAT Jaguar, Panavia

Tornado and several other Royal Air Force strike aircraft carrying WE.177 gravity bomb provided the air deterrent.

France became the fourth nation to possess nuclear weapons on February 13, 1960, when the atomic bomb Gerboise Bleue was detonated in Algeria, then still a French colony [Formally a part of the Metropolitan France.] During the Cold War, the French nuclear deterrent was centered around the Force de frappe, a nuclear triad consisting of Dassault Mirage IV bombers carrying such nuclear weapons as the AN-22 gravity bomb and the ASMP stand-off attack missile, Pluton and Hades ballistic missiles, and the Redoutable class submarine armed with strategic nuclear missiles.

The People's Republic of China became the fifth nuclear power on October 16, 1964, when it detonated a uranium-235 bomb in a test codenamed 596.

Due to Soviet/Chinese tensions, the Chinese might have used nuclear weapons against either the United States or the Soviet Union in the event of a nuclear war between the United States and the Soviet Union. During the Cold War, the Chinese nuclear deterrent consisted of gravity bombs carried aboard H-6 bomber aircraft, missile systems such as the DF-2, DF-3, and DF-4, and in the later stages of the Cold War, the Type 092 ballistic missile submarine.

Richard Nixon's Program of Détente

Economic problems caused by the arms race in both powers, combined with China's new role and the ability to verify disarmament led to a number of arms control agreements beginning in the 1970s. This period known as détente allowed both states to reduce their spending on weapons systems. SALT I and SALT II limited the size of the states arsenals.

Bans on nuclear testing, anti-ballistic missile systems, and weapons in space all attempted to limit the expansion of the arms race through the Partial Test Ban Treaty. These treaties were only partially successful. Both states continued building massive numbers of nuclear weapons, and new technologies such as *multiple independently targetable reentry vehicles* (also known as MIRVs) limited the effectiveness of the treaties. Both superpowers retained the ability to destroy each other many times over.

Reagan and the Strategic Defense Initiative

Towards the end of Jimmy Carter's presidency, and continued strongly through the subsequent presidency of Ronald Reagan, the United States rejected disarmament and tried to restart the arms race through the production of new weapons and anti-weapons systems. The central part of this strategy was the Strategic Defense Initiative, a space based anti-ballistic missile system derided as "Star Wars" by its critics. During the second part of 1980s, the Soviet economy was teetering towards collapse and was unable to match American arms spending. Numerous negotiations by Mikhail Gorbachev attempted to come to agreements on reducing nuclear stockpiles, but the most radical were rejected by Reagan as they would also prohibit his SDI program.

Post–Cold War

With the end of the Cold War the United States, and especially Russia, cut down on nuclear weapons spending. Fewer new systems were developed and both arsenals have shrunk. But both countries still maintain stocks of nuclear missiles numbering in the thousands. In the USA, stockpile stewardship programs have taken over the role of maintaining the aging arsenal. After the Cold War ended, a large amount of resources and money which was once spent on developing nuclear weapons in USSR was then spent on repairing the environmental damage produced by the nuclear arms race, and almost all former production sites are now major cleanup sites. In the USA, the plutonium production facility at Hanford, Washington and the plutonium pit fabrication facility at Rocky Flats, Colorado are among the most polluted sites.

United States policy and strategy regarding nuclear proliferation was outlined in 1995 in the document "Essentials of Post–Cold War Deterrence". Despite efforts made in cleaning up uranium sites, significant problems stemming from the legacy of uranium development still exist today on the Navajo Nation in the states of Utah, Colorado, New Mexico, and Arizona. Hundreds of abandoned mines have not been cleaned up and present environmental and health risks in many Navajo communities.

India and Pakistan

The South-Asian states of India and Pakistan have also engaged in a nuclear arms race. India detonated what it called a "peaceful nuclear device" in 1974 ("Smiling Buddha") much to the surprise and alarm of the world who had been giving India nuclear technology for civilian, energy producing and peaceful purposes. The test generated great concern in Pakistan, which feared that it would be at the mercy of its long-time arch rival and quickly responded by pursuing its own nuclear weapons program.

In the last few decades of the 20th century, Pakistan and India began to develop nuclear-capable rockets, and Pakistan had its own covert bomb program with Chinese proliferation which extended over many years since the first Indian weapon was detonated. In 1998 India, under Atal Bihari Vajpayee government, test detonated 5 more nuclear weapons. While the international response to the detonation was muted, domestic pressure within Pakistan began to build steam and Prime Minister Mian Muhammad Nawaz Sharif ordered the test, detonated 6 nuclear war weapons in a tit-for-tat fashion and to act as a deterrent.

OTHER MAJOR TRENDS

The Environment

It might appear surprising, but the US military is arguably doing more to save the planet than any other organization on earth. The US Defence Department is investing huge sums in the search to develop renewable sources of energy, as well as improving energy efficiency. The key drivers behind this trend include: national security—the United States does not want to be dependent upon energy imported from politically unstable regions; cost reasons—even a 5% cut in the fuel bill would save the Department of Defence US$635 million (based on the 2007 figure); and, finally, because it makes sound military sense—many lives are lost transporting fuel to the frontline in vulnerable convoys.

The US military is already one of the largest consumers of renewable energy in the world, and it has set a goal that 25% of its energy should come from renewable sources by 2025. The US Air Force's goal is that 50% of all the fuels used in domestic training flights will come from synthetic, or non-petroleum, sources by 2016. The US military is also investing heavily in solar and wind power.

Technological Advances

The military is one of the key drivers of technological advances. There are certainly some remarkable developments taking place. The F-35 Joint Strike Fighter, being developed by Lockheed Martin, Northrop Grumman, and BAE Systems, for example, features some extraordinary features. These include technology that allows the pilot to look through the structure of the aircraft. The aircraft also features voice commands that significantly reduce the pilot's workload.

The military is also investing heavily in information technology on land. Military units constantly transmit huge amounts of data back and forth to report their position, generate situational awareness, and share information on enemy tactics. Soldiers with access to laptops, for example, can provide vital information to military commanders. Real-time management of information enables rapid decision-making, meaning that military operations can proceed quickly, possibly providing a decisive advantage during a battle.

Cyberspace: The New Battlefield

Unsurprisingly, given the new emphasis on information technology, governments around the world are investing heavily in measures to protect their computer networks from attacks, and to launch their own cyber attacks. In 2010, the *Guardian* reported (January 13, 2010) that the Chinese military has been developing capabilities to spy on, infiltrate, and compromise adversaries' computer networks for years. "Informatized war" is an integral component of its "three warfares" (*san zhong zhanfa*) strategic concept, and the achievement of information superiority is viewed as a requirement for battlefield supremacy. Many large defence companies have already branched out into cyber-security and information-technology services.

CHINESE NUCLEAR WEAPONS

After its first test of a nuclear weapon in 1964, China advanced fairly rapidly in nuclear weapons technology. In January 1969, Secretary of Defence Clark Clifford informed the Congress that:

From October 1964 through December 1967 they [the PRC] detonated seven nuclear devices, including three thermonuclear and one low yield device delivered by a missile. (On December 27, 1968, the Chinese communists detonated their eighth nuclear device.) This test was similar to the sixth, conducted in June 1967. Both were apparently thermonuclear devices with yields of about 3 MT which were air dropped.

According to China expert Brad Roberts, through 1982 there was "a steady accretion of deployed weapons systems such that China was able to threaten to attack by nuclear weapons all of its potential adversaries – and, in addition, to threaten U.S. military bases in the Western Pacific and the allies that hosted them." China's nuclear weapons complex has reflected this buildup.

Warhead Development and Deployment

The principal nuclear weapons organization, the Chinese Academy of Engineering's Institute of Physics, employs 8,500 professional technical staff members. Yu Min, described by *Xinhua* as the "architect of the country's first H-bomb" claims that China's key nuclear capabilities are "on a par with the United States and the former Soviet Union." Xue Bencheng, one of the most important scientists involved in the development of China's neutron bomb, stated that the July 1996 Chinese nuclear test was "a great spanning leap" because it solved the problem of nuclear weapons miniaturization. According to a report in the Hong Kong press, China's Central Military Commission Vice Chairman Zhan Wannian told the Commission that there will be "further upgrading, and further development [of Chinese nuclear weapons] from 2001 to 2009."

China is today heavily invested in the process of modernizing its strategic forces. Viktor Mikhaylov, while he was Russia's first Deputy Minister for Atomic Energy, stated that, "China is very closed in its weapons work and the scope of its nuclear efforts can be judged from a number of indirect signs. But one needs have no doubt that such efforts are significant and dynamic." Retired Russian Major General Valdimir Belous in July 2006 wrote that, "China is transforming itself into one of the 21st Century's most influence centres of power, something that is to a considerable degree facilitated by the reequipping of its Armed Forces and the buildup of its nuclear missile potential, which in terms of total quantity of warheads has surpassed the equivalent indicators of France and Great Britain." According to Vyacheslav Baskakov and Aleksandr Gorshkov, Russian military journalists: Specifically, it [China] will succeed in making the shift from its current megaton-class nuclear ordinance to a level of hundreds and tens of kilotons, thereby increasing the effectiveness of available forces and weapons, flexibility of use in various circumstances and combat situations on both a strategic and tactical level.

For example, it is believed that the yield of the strategic nuclear warheads with which Chinese ICBM's are now equipped will decrease from 1-4 megatons to 250-650 kilotons each. The yield of tactical and operational-tactical nuclear warheads, according to expert assessments, will total from 90-100 kilotons each.

There are convincing reports that this recent progress has not been entirely indigenous. For example, the House Select Committee on U.S. National Security and Military Commercial Concerns with the People's Republic of China, generally known as the Cox Committee, concluded that: The People's Republic of China (PRC) has stolen classified information on all of the United States' most advanced thermonuclear warheads, and several of the associated reentry vehicles. These thefts are the result of an intelligence collection program spanning two decades, and continuing to the present. The PRC intelligence collection program included espionage, review of unclassified publications, and extensive interactions with scientists from the Department of Energy's national weapons laboratories.

The stolen U.S. secrets have helped the PRC fabricate and successfully test modern strategic thermonuclear weapons. The stolen information includes classified information on seven U.S. thermonuclear warheads, including every currently deployed thermonuclear warhead in the U.S. intercontinental ballistic missile arsenal. Together, these include the W-88 Trident D-5 thermonuclear warhead, and the W-56 Minuteman II, the W-62 Minuteman III, the W-70 Lance, the W-76 Trident C-4, the W-78 Minuteman III Mark 12A, and the W-87 Peacekeeper thermonuclear warheads. The stolen information also includes classified design information for an enhanced radiation weapon (commonly known as the 'neutron bomb')....

The Cox report continued that there was additional PRC espionage in the mid-1990s that included information about "the W-70 warhead [that] contains elements that may be used either as a strategic thermonuclear weapon, or as an enhanced radiation weapon ('neutron bomb'). The PRC subsequently tested the neutron bomb...."

The Central Intelligence Agency released the following assessment of Chinese nuclear espionage: China obtained by espionage classified US nuclear weapons information that probably accelerated its program to develop future nuclear weapons. This collection program allowed China to focus successfully down critical paths and avoid less promising approaches to nuclear weapon designs.

China obtained at least basic design information on several modern US nuclear reentry vehicles, including the Trident II (W88). China also obtained information on a variety of US weapon design concepts and weaponization features, including those of the neutron bomb. We cannot determine the full extent of weapon information obtained. For example, we do not know whether any weapon design documentation or blueprints were acquired.

We believe it is more likely that the Chinese used US design information to inform their own program than to replicate US weapon designs. China reacted very strongly to the Cox report, claiming, inaccurately, that the nuclear weapons design information had been declassified by the United States and also stating that the PRC had tested an enhanced radiation weapon in the 1980s. In an interview in June 2001, Xue Bencheng, chief engineer of the PRC neutron bomb, also claimed that the July 1996 Chinese nuclear test resulted in "a great spanning leap," a significant breakthrough in nuclear weapons technology which solved the problem of miniaturization and reached the same level of technology as the advanced nuclear nations.

Whatever the source, miniaturization has enabled China to develop a number of warhead options. China is reported to have "tactical nuclear warheads, theater nuclear warheads, and nuclear mines." Hong Kong military commentator Ma Ting-sheng has even suggested on Hong Kong television that China would transport nuclear bombs into the United States "before a war breaks out."

A number of heavily-redacted CIA intelligence reports on China's nuclear weapons testing have been declassified. They include details which suggest a broad interest in developing nuclear weapons for tactical platforms, modernizing and replacing older warhead technologies, and building up a body of test data to continue the process in the context of a Comprehensive Test Ban Treaty (CTBT). What Chinese testing has occurred since the announced end of China's nuclear testing in 1996 is not certain. The Cox reported concluded that "nuclear tests related to development of the PRC's next generation of thermonuclear warheads may be continuing at the PRC test site at Lop Non Nor." In May 2006 *Chinese Defence Today* also reported possible "low yield nuclear tests" after the declared end of testing.

The Stockpile Size

The precise number of Chinese nuclear weapons is a closely guarded state secret. The assertion that China has 200 warheads is actually an invention of the Western press and academia based on inference from a 2004 claim by the PRC that it had conduct the fewest nuclear tests and had the smallest arsenal among the nuclear powers.

Other estimates of China's nuclear stockpile dramatically differ. According to Lieutenant General Michael Maples, Director of the

Defence Intelligence Agency, "China currently has more than 100 nuclear warheads." Maple's statement was in 2006, however, a declassified 1984 DIA estimate of the Chinese nuclear weapons stockpile put it, "Between 150 and 160 warheads."

Many estimates are much higher. A November 1997 Congressional Research Service report by Jonathan Medalia, citing a report by the National Resources Defence Council, concluded that "....China has perhaps 300 deployed nuclear weapons and 150 tactical nuclear weapons that are available but not deployed, and that the stockpile could actually be two or three times larger." A study by the Carnegie Institute estimated that China had 450 nuclear weapons. Other estimates span the range from 200 to 2000.

In evaluating the wide range of estimates of the number of Chinese nuclear weapons Dr. You Ji observed in 1999: "The lower end of the estimates, 200, is certainly too low.... A *Rand* report also claims that by 2003 China will possess between 600 and 1500 nuclear warheads.

This higher end of the estimates may be as unrealistic as the lower end, especially if one thinks in terms of warheads deliverable after a first strike." DIA estimated that China had 150-160 nuclear weapons as far back as 1984 and "the number of warheads is not restricted by Chinese materials production, but on what the Chinese perceive their needs to be."

THE HUMAN COST OF UNREGULATED ARMS TRANSFERS

Violations of international humanitarian law are widespread in contemporary armed conflicts, with civilians often bearing the brunt of the violence. Civilians are not only caught in the cross-fire between the warring parties, but they are often deliberately targeted. Women are subjected to sexual violence, children are forcibly recruited into the armed forces or armed groups and used to participate in the fighting, and whole communities are forced to flee their homes under threat of attack. In a number of contexts, the security situation is deteriorating for both local and international actors providing humanitarian assistance. This leaves the many civilians that depend on humanitarian aid to survive in an even more precarious situation.

The increasingly easy access to highly lethal weaponry in conflict zones both facilitates such violations and aggravates their consequences. While a single shot from a standard rifle fired into a crowded market would be a criminal incident, unloading dozens of bullets a minute from an automatic weapon or firing a mortar into the same market can transform it into the scene of a massacre. These types of incidents have unfortunately become so familiar that they seem almost inevitable to both the public and to decision-makers.

Nevertheless, such incidents can be prevented and States have both the responsibility and the opportunity to do so. It is obvious that no single measure can effectively prevent weapons from being used in violation of international humanitarian law. Yet, the establishment of strict controls on weapons transfers to prevent further proliferation is an indispensable part of the solution. Without effective measures in this area, it is unlikely that much progress will be made in reducing the misuse of weapons on the ground. And the price of inaction is high, in terms of human suffering, social and economic disruption and the burdens of intervention when the international community decides to act.

The Need for an International Arms Trade Treaty

In recent decades, State have adopted wide-ranging prohibitions and limitations on the transfer of chemical, biological and nuclear weapons, missile systems and certain components of these technologies. Yet it is conventional weapons— assault rifles, grenades, mines, bombs, rockets and missiles—that are causing most of the death and injury in today's conflicts. Until recently, however, the transfer of conventional weapons had received little attention at the global level.

The ICRC has urged States to develop strict controls on conventional arms transfers at the national, regional and global level. It has also promoted specific criteria for arms transfers aimed at preventing weapons from falling into the hands of those likely to use them to violate international humanitarian law. In recent years, the ICRC has been pleased to note the significant progress that has been made in this regard at the regional level.

A number of regional instruments now include a list of criteria to be considered before authorizing certain arms transfers—mainly of small arms and light weapons.

Still, existing regional arms transfer criteria vary and not all regions have adopted such commitments. At the national level, criteria for arms transfer decisions are even more disparate, and only rarely do they fully reflect all of States' obligations under international law.

This highlights the need for common global standards in this field to achieve consistent approaches to arms transfer decision-making among States. The ICRC therefore strongly supports the development of a treaty that would define common standards for arms transfers based on States' responsibilities under international law, including international humanitarian law. We warmly welcome the adoption of UN General Assembly resolution 61/89, which takes this initiative forward.

The parameters of an arms trade treaty: International humanitarian law obligations relevant to conventional arms transfers

In our view, an Arms Trade Treaty should, as a minimum, reflect States existing legal obligations relevant to arms transfers. The ICRC would in particular urge all States to ensure that their responsibilities under international humanitarian law are adequately reflected. International humanitarian law, which governs the use of weapons in armed conflict and protects victims of war, is a particularly relevant consideration in decisions to transfer military arms and ammunition, and other military equipment. States also have a number of obligations under international humanitarian law that are directly applicable to arms transfers.

Firstly, there are certain explicit prohibitions or limitations on conventional arms transfers contained in international humanitarian law, which arise from specific treaty obligations. States Parties to these treaties are prohibited from transferring—or have to exercise restraint when transferring—particular categories of conventional weapons. These include for example a prohibition on the transfer of:

- Certain types of landmines under Amended Protocol II to the 1980 Convention on Certain Conventional Weapons;
- Blinding laser weapons under Protocol IV to the 1980 Convention on Certain Conventional Weapons;
- Anti-personnel mines under the 1997 Convention on the prohibition of anti-personnel mines.

Second, among the fundamental rules of international humanitarian law is the prohibition on the use of weapons that are of a nature to cause superfluous injury or unnecessary suffering and weapons that are by nature indiscriminate. These are universally accepted norms, which bind all States. The use of specific weapons has been prohibited on the basis of these principles (e.g. expanding and exploding bullets). Even when these treaties do not specifically prohibit the transfer of such weapons, allowing the transfer of prohibited weapons would be difficult to reconcile with States' duty to ensure respect for humanitarian law. The same argument would apply to the transfer of weapons that—even if they are not regulated by a specific convention—would be considered prohibited based on these fundamental rules.

Ultimately, however, the majority of arms transfers concern weapons that are not specifically restricted or prohibited under international humanitarian law. In these cases, States must nevertheless consider how the weapons they transfer are likely to be used.

Although international law allows States to acquire arms for their security, under Article 1 common to the 1949 Geneva Conventions and their Additional Protocol I, all States also have a solemn obligation to "respect and ensure respect" for humanitarian law. Not only do States have to respect the law, but they also have a responsibility to "ensure respect" by others. This is generally interpreted as conferring a responsibility on third-party States not involved in an armed conflict to refrain from encouraging a party to an armed conflict to violate international humanitarian law, to not take action that would assist in such violations, and to take appropriate steps to cause such violations to cease. Because military weapons are transferred with the purpose of enabling the recipient to engage in an armed conflict, such transfers should therefore be considered in light of States obligation to ensure respect for humanitarian law. States that produce and export arms can be considered particularly influential in "ensuring respect" for international humanitarian law owing to their ability to provide or withhold the means by which violations may be committed. They should therefore exercise particular caution to ensure that the weapons transferred are not used to commit serious violations of international humanitarian law.

States party to the Geneva Conventions affirmed this responsibility at the 28th International Conference of the Red Cross and Red Crescent in December 2003. In the Agenda for Humanitarian Action adopted by the Conference, States party to the Geneva Conventions undertook to "make respect for international humanitarian law one of the fundamental criteria on which arms transfer decisions are assessed" and were encouraged to incorporate such criteria in national laws and policies, as well as regional and global norms.

The ICRC considers that to fully reflect States' obligations under international humanitarian law, any future global standards on arms transfers should include a requirement to assess the recipient's likely respect for humanitarian law, and not transfer weapons if they are likely to be used for serious violations of this law.

An increasing number of regional arms transfer instruments, as well as national laws and regulations, already contain such international humanitarian law criteria. These include documents adopted by the OSCE, ECOWAS, the OAS and the Central American Integration System. A similar provision should be an essential element in any future Arms Trade Treaty.

Conclusion

A comprehensive global agreement that would strengthen controls over international arms transfers is urgently needed. The continued unregulated supply of weapons to areas where they are likely to be used to violate international humanitarian law demonstrates that existing controls are far from adequate. In the absence of stricter controls, the human costs of unregulated arms transfers are likely to continue to grow as more weapons find their way into the hands of those who will use them to commit atrocities, to violate international humanitarian law and human rights, to spread terror and to commit other crimes.

Any international standards adopted should be comprehensive and establish concrete requirements for arms transfer decision-making. These must take full account of States' existing obligations under international law, including international humanitarian law.

Specifically, such a treaty should include:

- A requirement not to transfer arms or ammunition likely to be used to commit serious violations of international humanitarian law;
- A requirement not to transfer weapons or ammunition whose use has been prohibited;
- A requirement not to transfer weapons or ammunition that are of a nature to cause superfluous injury or unnecessary suffering or that are by nature indiscriminate;
- A reference to existing prohibitions on the transfer of specific weapons.

Governments have a responsibility not to transfer weapons if they believe they might be used for violations of international humanitarian law. For the ICRC, this is however not only a legal question. Equally compelling is the moral responsibility that rests on arms-transferring States—precisely because their actions can make a difference— to withhold the means by which violations are carried out and to contribute to the protection of civilians. By agreeing to strict arms transfer controls that would be common to all States, governments can prevent weapons from ending up in the hands of those who will use them to violate the very rules that States themselves have created. In so doing, they can also strengthen the basis for post-conflict reconstruction, the rule of law and lasting peace in many areas of the world.

3

Nuclear Deterrence Thinking Promote an Arms Race

Nuclear weapons are quintessentially offensive weapons; they cannot be used 'defensively' to bring about security. If your opponent uses them first to attack you, he has a great advantage. (This, of course, is assuming he doesn't create a nuclear winter worlwide through destroying the atmosphere - the critical point of explosion after which this would happen is not yet properly known:) your use in retaliation to such an attack can only be an act of revenge, not of security, and it may only instigate a further attack by the initiator. because there is such an advantage to the country which strikes first, deterrence thinking requires that a co7country set up what is called a "credible second-strike capacity". This means tht your opponent should have strong reasons to believe tht if he strikes first you will still have enough weapons, delivery vehicles (planes and missiles) and enough of a functioning command, control, communications and intelligence system to carry out a second-strike which will so seriously damage the attacking country tht their rulers will decide not to strike first, i.e.be deterred.

It is clear that it is not enough to simply have a nuclear stick to counter an opponent's nuclear stick. You have to have quite a few nuclear clubs. Moreover, if your opponent's nuclear clubs get more and more sophisticated then so must yours, even if not equally so. If their ability to devastate your deterring capacities increases you also have to continue to make or try to make more sophisticated nuclear clubs of different sizes, shapes, materials, purposes, etc.

Technology doesn't stand still. Nor does politics. To deter an opponent systematically and regularly means that your 'credibility' as a nuclear opponent must always be maintained. That is to say, both your will and your capability to use nuclear weapons as a last resort or in retaliation must not be doubted by your 'enemy' or 'enemies'. So this 'will' must be regularly upgraded. A pattern of instiutionalised belligerence i.e. a hostility-induced and hostility-generating arms race is established.

To cut a long story short, there is no such thing as a "stable minimum deterrence". Minimum deterrence is not a fixed position but a moving and unstable one, depending on the nuclear preparations and improvements your presumed opponent is making or can make.

Indian pro-nuclearists can never agree even among themselves on what constitutes an "adequate deterrence" against, say, Pakistan and China. So those at the extreme end of the spectrum who make the highest demands for a `viable' weapons system invariably get preferred because if you have satisfied them you have more than covered what the `moderate' nuclearists are clamouring for.

Nuclear Weapons After 1945

We cannot be confident that nuclear war will never happen. Nor can we afford to be wrong or make a mistake even once. We can also say with greater confidence and accuracy than our pro-deterrence opponents who dismiss fears of a nuclear outbreak, that as long as nuclear weapons are around they are almost certain to be used at some time or the other even if we don't know exactly when. Furthermore, if you look at the actual history of nuclear conflict, especially between the East and the West, then there were clearly occasions when, either by accident, miscalculation or design, nuclear weapons came close to being used or detonated.

Perhaps the closest we came to it as a matter's of design, was in the 1962 Cuban missile crisis when very senior defence officials and civilian bureaucrats advised John Kennedy to attack first. This has now been revealed in recently released U.S. government papers.

A number of former top officials who used to be pro-bomb during the Cold War have now said that deterrence thinking should not be relied upon.

General Lee Butler, former head of the USA's Strategic Air Command said the world "survived the Cuban missile crisis no thanks to deterrence, but only by the grace of the God". He also said that during the Cold War the honest truth was that the USA never felt nuclearly secure but constantly insecure. They were never assured by the so called state of deterrence apparently established by the respective capacities/arsenals of the superpowers.

There have also been over 224 accidents of various types concerning nuclear weapons systems. These have been classified in four ways:

Group 1 is accidental, unauthorised or possible detonation of a weapon;

group 2 covers accidental detonation without war risk but radioctive contamination;

group 3 refers to accidents to vehicles carrying nuclear weapons;

group 4 refers to other significant accidents.

In group 1 there were a least 10 such accidents. This record does not include an accident we now know about - in 1954 in North Carolina, a nuclear bomb accidentally fell off from a plane and five of its six safety mechanisms against detonation failed!

INDIAN AND PAKISTAN WILL REPEAT THE FOLLY OF THE NUCLEAR ARMS RACE BETWEEN USA AND USSR?

India and Pakistan are more likely to have a nuclear conflict than any other pair of nuclearly equipped rivals because a nuclear dimension has now been added to an already hostile relationship between the two governments. South Asia is now the only part of the world where a continuous hot-cold war has existed between the same two combatants for over 50 years. In short, the conditions for a spiralling nuclear arms race and constant tension (repeating the East-West experience) are very much in place.

The circumstances in which nuclear weapons are most likely to be used are, of course, in the framework of a war like situation or atmosphere where their use is most likely to be perceived as 'unavoidable' or in pre-emptive 'self-defence'. The hatreds and hostilities associated with the existence of such an atmosphere are not far from the surface in the case of India and Pakistan. One can easily envisage circumstances in which they could erupt.

The conflict between East and West, for all their strategic posture, was essentially an ideological one. The conflict between India and Pakistan is a concrete one centred on disputed territory, historical enmities since the birth of the two countries, and geographical proximity. Another 'hot' war is a very real possibility.

Missile flight time between USA and USSR was 25 minutes. Here it is less than three minutes. There is not even time to reverse any fateful decision to launch a conventional or nuclear exchange via missiles.

Nuclear Blackmail, Say From China?

Here, there is a question of logic and a question of historical fact. The question of logic is that to have any hope of deterring (in nuclear terms) a nuclearly equipped rival you have to have a second-strike capacity against it. The country which has most often attempted nuclear blackmail in an explicit or implicit manner is the USA. Estimates vary from 26 to 37 American attempts.

But to nuclearly deter the USA you have a 'credible minimum deterrent'against it and the only country that has had this and still has it is russia. Even China does not have this. India can never hope to have this in the next twenty years or more unless the USA rapidly reduces its current nuclear arsenal. The only country to have carried out an action that some Indians called attempted nuclear blackmail was when the USA in 1971, if it was attempted blackmail, fail but there is no plausible evidence tht any act of attempted nuclear blackmail by any nuclear weapons state has ever succeeded. it is also a matter of historical fact that in the 34 years that China has had the bomb, it has never attempted blackmail against any country including India. Nor has possession of such bombs prevented nuclear weapons states from being militarily and politically defeated by non-nuclear countries and forces - China being bloodied in a military conflict with non-nuclear Vietnam in 1979, France losing in Algeria, Britain in Suez, the USA in Vietnam and Russia in Afghanistan.

One of the most important reasons why every attempt at nuclear blackmail has failed is precisely because nuclear weapons are remarkably astrategic weapons. Apart from the most dire circumstances concerning the self-defense of one's country it is extremely difficult to justify their use by a possessor country even to its home population. Precisely because the use of nuclear weapons or even the threat of their use is so utterly disproportionate to whatever political ends governments may desire, their potential for blackmail can be safely disregarded. it is effectively nil.

The regime which the USA today wants to destroy more than any other is Cuba's. It is using every political, military, economic and other means to strangle the country. But nuclear weapons are utterly irrelevant to this effort.

Nuclear Indian and Pakistan Promote Global Nuclear Disarmament

This kind of thinking is typical of pro nuclearist but it is again an example of inverted logic as well as being contradicted by the historical evidence. Does anyone believe that the usa, for example, can be frightened, awed or worried into disarming because India has developed nuclear weapons? Well, that is what the claim amounts to saying! In reality, hawkish behaviour by one nuclear weapons states. Hawks in different countries fed off each other's importance and power.

The Indian nuclear elite has talked a great deal about how it had to have the bomb because of the potential threat posed by China and the fact that it is a potential nuclear rival. The truth is that China has never seen India as a nuclear threat so far and has not behaved as if India was such a threat. There has been no reason for it to do so. For China, the border dispute is a distant and minor matter though for the Indian elite it is something of a running sore which it constantly reminds itself of. However, after the Indian justifications that the bomb was partly directed at China, the latter country must begin to consider India as just such a nuclear rival; and if not now, then certainly in the future. And China will have to make its nuclear preparations (including targeting) accordingly. In short, India by its actions has moved a long way to making sure that China is no longer simply a potential nuclear rival but becomes an actual one. This increases Indian and Chinese nuclear insecurities.

As for the idea that President Reagan's nuclear belligerence so worried the Gorbachev leadership of the USSR that they wanted to reduce mutual nuclear tensions. It is absurd to think that you should increase nuclear tensions by nuclearly arming in order to reduce political tensions! for over fifteen years now the political relationship between India and China was improving slowly but steadily. Now this decisive set-back will ensure that things will not be as they once were.

After a gap of 34 years, India and Pakistan have become the first new additions to the group of countries openly possessing and justifying their possession of nuclear weapons. t his will encourage other countries which have the capability but have not yet decided to go openly nuclear to do the same. They will cite the same kind of national security considerations and the same kind of nuclear deterrence arguments to justify their actions.

The prospects for making the world permanently free of nuclear weapons will be worsened, not improved, by more and more countries going openly nucelar. In truth, the mindset of nuclear elites eveywhere, dominated as it is by the concept of nuclear deterrence and its illusory virtues or strengths, is exactly the same. Only the nationalities of such nuclear elites are different and therefore the 'national interests' they claim to represent and fight for.

It is this mind-set, which believes so strongly in the value of nuclear deterrence, that constitutes the greatest single barrier to bringing about universal nuclear disarmament.

The single most important reason why it has been easier to move towards universal elimination of other kinds of weapons of mass destruction like agents of biological and chemical warfare is because those weapons have not carried the same baggage of deterrence arguments which have justified their possession, deployment and use for 'national security' or other political purposes.

THE FURTHER SPREAD OF NUCLEAR WEAPONS

Contemplating the nuclear past gives grounds for hoping that the world will survive if further nuclear powers join today's six or seven. This tentative conclusion is called into question by the widespread belief that the infirmities of some nuclear states and the delicacy of their nuclear forces will work against the preser-vation of peace and for the fighting of nuclear wars. The likelihood of avoiding destruction as more states become members of the nuclear club is often coupled with the question *who* those states will be. What are the likely differ-ences in situation and behaviour of new as compared to old nuclear powers?

NUCLEAR WEAPONS AND DOMESTIC STABILITY

What are the principal worries? Because of the importance of controlling nuclear weapons—of keeping them firmly in the hands of reliable officials—rulers of nuclear states may become more authoritarian and ever more given to secrecy. Moreover, some potential nuclear states are not politically strong and stable enough to ensure control of the weapons and of the decision to use them. If neighhouring, hos-tile, unstable states are armed with nuclear weapons, each will fear attack by the other. Feelings of insecurity may lead to arms races that subordinate civil needs to military neces-sities. Fears are compounded by the danger of internal coups in which the control of nuclear weapons may he the main object of the struggle and the key to political power. Under these fearful circumstances to maintain governmental authority and civil order may be impossible. The legitimacy of the state and the loyalty of its citizenry may dissolve because the state is no longer thought to be capable of maintaining external security and internal order. The first fear is that states become tyran-nical; the second, that they lose control. Both these fears may be realized, either in different states or, indeed, in the same state at different times.

What can one say? Four things primarily. First, Possession of nuclear weapons may slow arms races down, rather than speed them up, a possibility considered later. Second, for less developed countries to build nuclear arsenals requires a long lead time. Nuclear power and nuclear weapons programmes, like population policies, require administrative and technical teams able to formulate and sustain pro-grammes of considerable cost that pay off only in the long run. The more unstable a govern-ment, the shorter becomes the attention span of its leaders. They have to deal with today's problems and hope for the best tomorrow. In countries where political control is most diffi-cult to maintain, governments are least likely to initiate nuclear-weapons programmes. In such states, soldiers help to maintain leaders in power or try to overthrow them. For those pur-poses nuclear weapons are not useful. Soldiers who have political clout, or want it, are less interested in nuclear weapons than they are in more immediately useful instruments of poli-tical control. They are not scientists and tech-nicians. They like to command troops and squadrons. Their vested interests are in the military's traditional trappings.

Third, although highly unstable states are unlikely to initiate nuclear projects, such projects, begun in stable times, may continue through periods of political turmoil and suc-ceed in producing nuclear weapons. A nuclear state may be unstable or may become so. But what is hard to comprehend is why, in an inter-nal struggle for power, any of the contenders should start using nuclear weapons. Who would they aim at? How would they use them as instruments for maintaining or gaining control? I see little more reason to fear that one faction or another in some less developed country will fire atomic weapons in a struggle for political power than that they will be used in a crisis of succession in the Soviet Union or China. One or another nuclear state will experience uncertainty of succession, fierce struggles for power, and instability of regime. Those who fear the worst have not shown with any plausibility how those expected events may lead to the use of nuclear weapons.

Fourth, the possibility of one side in a civil war firing a nuclear warhead at its opponent's stronghold nevertheless remains. Such an act would produce a national tragedy. not an inter-national one. This question then arises: Once the weapon is fired, what happens next? The domestic use of nuclear weapons is, of all the uses imaginable, least likely to lead to escalation and to threaten the stability of the central balance. The United States and the Soviet Union, and other countries as well, would have the strongest reasons to issue warnings and to assert control.

Nuclear Age and Regional Stability

Nuclear weapons are not likely to be used at home. Are they likely to be used abroad? As nuclear weapons spread, what new causes may bring effects different from and worse than those known earlier in the nuclear age? This section considers five ways in which the new world is expected to differ from the old and then examines the prospects for, and the con-sequences of, new nuclear states using their weapons for blackmail or for fighting an offen-sive war.

In what ways may the actions and inter-actions of new nuclear states differ from those of old nuclear powers? First. new nuclear states may come in hostile pairs and share a common border. Where States are bitter enemies one may fear that they will be unable to resist using their nuclear weapons against each other. This is a worry about the future that the past does not disclose. The Soviet Union and the United States, and the Soviet Union and China, are hostile enough; and the latter pair share a long border. Nuclear weapons have caused China and the Soviet Union to deal cautiously with each other. But bitterness among some poten-tial nuclear states, so it is said, exceeds that experienced by the old ones. Playing down the bitterness sometimes felt by the United States, the Soviet Union, and China requires a crea-tive reading of history. Moreover, those who believe that bitterness causes wars assume a close association that is seldom found between bitterness among nations and their willingness to run high risks.

Second, some new nuclear states may have governments and societies that are not well rooted. If a country is a loose collection of hos-tile tribes, if its leaders form a thin veneer atop a people partly nomadic and with an authori-tarian history, its rulers may be freer of con-straints than, and have different values from, those who rule older and more fully developed polities. Idi Amin and

Muammar el-Qaddafi fit into these categories, and they are favourite examples of the kinds of rulers who supposedly cannot be trusted to manage nuclear weapons responsibly. Despite wild rhetoric; aimed at foreigners, however, both of these 'irrational' rulers became cautious and modest when puni-tive actions against them might have threat-ened their ability to rule. Even though Amin lustily slaughtered members of tribes he dis-liked, he quickly stopped goading Britain once the sending of her troops appeared to be a pos-sibility. Qaddafi has shown similar restraint. He and Anwar Sadat have been openly hostile since 1973. In July of 1977 both sides launched commando attacks and air raids, including two large air strikes by Egypt on Libya's el Adem airbase. Neither side let the attacks get out of hand. Qaddafi showed himself to he forbearing and amenable to mediation by other Arab leaders. Shai Feldman uses these and other examples to argue that Arab leaders are deter-red from taking inordinate risks not because they engage in intricate rational calculations but simply because they, like other rulers, are 'sensitive to costs'.

Many Westerners who write fearfully about a future in which third-world countries have nuclear weapons seem to view their people in the once familiar imperial manner as 'lesser breeds without the law'. As is usual with ethno-centric views, speculation takes the place of evidence. How do we know, someone has asked, that a nuclear-armed and newly hostile Egypt or a nuclear-armed and still hostile Syria would not strike to destroy Israel at the risk of Israeli bombs falling on some of their cities?

More than a quarter of Egypt's people live in four cities: Cairo, Alexandria, Giza, and Aswan. More than a quarter of Syria's live in three: Damascus. Aleppo, and Homs. What government would risk sudden losses of such proportion or indeed of much lesser propor-tion?

Rulers want to have a country that they can continue to rule. Some Arab country might wish that some other Arab country would risk its own destruction for the sake of destroying Israel, but there is no reason to think that any Arab country would do so. One may be impres-sed that, despite ample bitterness, Israelis and Arabs have limited their wars and accepted constraints placed on them by others. Arabs did not marshal their resources and make an all-out effort to destroy Israel in the years before Israel could strike back with nuclear warheads. We cannot expect countries to risk more in the presence of nuclear weapons than they have in their absence.

Third. many fear that states that are radical at home will recklessly use their nuclear weapons in pursuit of revolutionary ends abroad. States that are radical at home. how-ever, may not be radical abroad. Few states have been radical in the conduct of their foreign policy, and fewer have remained so for long. Think of the Soviet Union and the People's Republic of China. States coexist in a competitive arena. The pressures of com-petition cause them to behave in ways that make the threats they face manageable, in ways that enable them to get along. States can remain radical in foreign policy only if they are overwhelmingly strong—as none of the new nuclear states will be—or if their radical acts fall short of damaging vital interests of nuclear powers. States that acquire nuclear weapons will not be regarded with indifference. States that want to be freewheelers have to stay out of the nuclear business. A nuclear Libya, for example, would have to show caution, even in rhetoric, lest she suffer retaliation in response to someone else's anonymous attack on a third state. That state, ignorant of who attacked, might claim that its intelligence agents had identified Libya as the culprit and take the opportunity to silence her by striking a con-ventional or nuclear blow. Nuclear weapons induce caution, especially in weak states.

Fourth, while some worry about nuclear states coming in hostile pairs, others worry that the bipolar pattern will not be reproduced regionally in a world populated by larger numbers of nuclear states. The simplicity of relations that obtains when one party has to concentrate its worry on only one other, and the ease of calculating forces and estimating the dangers they pose, may be lost. The struc-ture of international politics, however, will remain bipolar so long as no third state is able to compete militarily with the great powers. Whatever the structure, the relations of states run in various directions. This applied to rela-tions of deterrence as soon as Britain gained nuclear capabilities. It has not weakened deter-rence at the centre and need not do so region-ally. The Soviet Union now has to worry lest a move made in Europe cause France and Brit-ain to retaliate, thus possibly setting off Ameri-can forces. She also has to worry about China's forces. Such worries at once complicate cal-culations and strengthen deterrence.

Fifth, in some of the new nuclear states, civil control of the military maybe shaky. Nuclear weapons may fall into the hands of military officers more inclined than civilians to put them to offensive use. This again is an old worry. I can see no reason to think that civil control of the military is secure in the Soviet Union given the occasional presence of serv-ing officers in the Politburo and some known and some surmised instances of military inter-vention in civil affairs at critical times. And in the People's Republic of China military and civil branches of government have been not separated but fused. Although one may prefer civil control, preventing a highly destructive war does not require it. What is required is that decisions be made that keep destruction within bounds, whether decisions are made by civil-ians or soldiers. Soldiers may he more cautious than civilians. Generals and admirals do not like uncertainty, and they do not lack patriot-ism. They do not like to fight conventional wars under unfamiliar conditions. The offen-sive use of nuclear weapons multiplies uncertainties. Nobody knows what a nuclear battlefield would look like, and nobody knows what happens after the first city is hit. *Uncertainiy* about the course that a nuclear war might follow, along with the *certainty* that destruction can he immense, strongly inhibits the first use of nuclear weapons.

Examining the supposedly unfortunate characteristics of new nuclear states removes some of one's worries. One wonders why their civil and military leaders should be less inter-ested in avoiding self-destruction than leaders of other states have been. Nuclear weapons have never been used in a world in which two or more states possessed them. Still, one's feeling that something awful will happen as new nuclear powers are added to the present group is not easily quieted. The fear remains that one state or another will fire its weapons in a coolly calculated pre-emptive strike, or fire them in a moment of panic, or use them to launch a pre-ventive war. Nuclear weapons may also back a policy of blackmail, or be set off anony-mously, or be used in a combined con-ventional-nuclear attack.

Consider blackmail first. Two conditions make for the success of nuclear blackmail. First, when only one country had nuclear weapons, threats to use them had more effect. Thus, President Truman's nuclear threats may have levered the Soviet Union's troops out of Azerbaijan in 1946. Second, if a country has invested troops and suffered losses in a conven-tional war, its nuclear blackmail may work. In 1953, Eisenhower and Dulles may have con-vinced Russia and China that they would widen the Korean War and intensify it by using nuclear weapons if a settlement were not reached. In Korea, we had gone so far that the threat to go further was plausible. The black-mailer's nuclear threat is not a cheap way of working one's will. The threat is simply incred-ible unless a considerable investment has already been made. Dulles's speech of 12 January 1954 seemed to threaten massive retaliation in response to mildly bothersome actions by others. The successful seige of Dien Bien Pbu in the spring of that year showed the limitations of such threats. Capabilities foster policies that employ them. But monstrous capabilities foster monstrous policies, which when contemplated are seen to be too horrible to carry through. Imagine an Arab state threat-ening to strike Tel Aviv if the West Bank is not evacuated by Israelis. No state can make the threat with credibility because no state can expect to execute the threat without danger to themselves.

Some have feared that nuclear weapons may be fired anonymously—by radical Arab states, for example, to attack an Israeli city so as block a peace settlement. But the state exploding the warhead could not be sure of remaining unidentified. Even if a country's leaders persuade themselves that chances of retaliation are low, who would run the risk? Once two or more countries have nuclear weapons, the response to nuclear threats, even against non-nuclear states, becomes unpredictable.

Although nuclear weapons are poor instruments for blackmail, would they not provide a cheap and decisive offensive force against a conventionally armed enemy? Some people think that South

Korea wants, and that earlier the Shah's Iran had wanted, nuclear weapons for offensive use, Yet one cannot say why South Korea would use nuclear weapons against fellow Koreans while trying to reunite them nor how she could use nuclear weapons against the North, knowing that China and Russia might retaliate. And what goals could a conventionally strong Iran have entertained that would have tempted her to risk using nuclear weapons? A country that takes the nuclear offensive has to fear an appropriately punishing strike by someone. Far from lowering the expected cost of aggression, a nuclear offence even against a non-nuclear state raises the possible costs of aggression to incalculable heights because the aggressor cannot be sure of the reaction of other nuclear powers.

Nuclear weapons do not make nuclear war a likely prospect, as history has so far shown. The point made when discussing the domestic use of nuclear weapons, however, bears repeat-ing. No one can say that nuclear weapons will never be used. Their use, although unlikely, is always possible. In asking what the spread of nuclear weapons will do to the world, we are asking about the effects to be expected as a larger number of relatively weak states get nuclear weapons. If such states use nuclear weapons, the world will not end. And the use of nuclear weapons by lesser powers would hardly trigger them elsewhere, with the US and the USSR becoming involved in ways that might shake the central balance.

THE ARMS TRADE

Unsurprisingly, the West dominates the world arms market in terms of sales. Over the last six or so years, the US has towered over the other countries in weapons sales, clocking up $49,271 million worth of sales (at 1990 prices) between 1996 and 2000. Its nearest competitor, Russia, made $15,690 million worth in the same period, but a large majority of these were of second hand weapons. According to SIPRI, just under half of all transfers (movements) of major conventional weapons between 1996 and 2000 came from the US, Russia and France each accounted for 10 per cent, and Britain and Germany each accounted for between five and 10 per cent. The seven following biggest sellers-the

Netherlands, Ukraine, Italy, China, Belarus, Spain and Israel-accounted for around 15 per cent of the world total transfers between them. So it is clear that the global arms market is controlled by just a few players. The six biggest arms selling countries-four of whom, ironically, are permanent members of the UN Security Council-accounted for almost 85 per cent of all arms transfers over the last six years.

The top 7 largest arms companies, in terms of military sales. The figures in italics represent the percentage of arms in total sales for each company. Figures for arms sales are in US $ billions at constant (1998) prices and exchange rates. Selection of top arms-purchasing countries between 1996 and 2000. Figures are trend-indicator' values expressed in US $ millions, at constant (1990) prices.

The global small arms market

Small arms require a special mention in any assessment of the global trade in armaments, simply because they are so prolific, the trade in them is so difficult to control and the devastation caused by them is so severe. Taking the definition of the UN panel of government experts on small arms, the category includes all of the following military, police and domestic weapons: revolvers and self-loading pistols, rifles and carbines, assault rifles, sub-machine guns and light machine guns, heavy machine guns, hand-held under-barrel and mounted grenade launchers, portable anti-tank and anti-aircraft guns, recoilless rifles, portable launchers of anti-tank and antiaircraft systems, and mortars of less than 100 mm caliber.

So there are plenty of them, and they are everywhere. They are used by police and security patrols, by national armies and by guerrilla and revolutionary groups, they are carried by civilians legally in a number of countries, for sport in many more, and illegally in every country. They feature in practically every armed conflict between nation-states, in internal and civil wars, in gang fighting and as status symbols.

They are so prolific because they are small and relatively cheap, easy to pass on, smuggle, hide, steal, capture from an enemy or buy over the counter. But, they are ubiquitous because of the sheer numbers they are produced in: millions of them, every day, all over the world. It is a myth that the trade in small arms is only one of recycling second-and third-hand weapons. New production merely creates more second-and third-hand guns. In 1999, 45 different countries reported to the UN that firearms, components and ammunition were legally produced in their territories for domestic or export markets. Many more countries didn't respond to the requests for information. The main producers of these little killers are China, Russia and the US. Another 20 or so countries, mainly in Europe and Asia, produce most of the rest of the world's supply. A further 29 countries produce nominal quantities mainly to meet their domestic never be accurate data on which countries have the most of them. Even if there were, accurate figures for exactly which of these were legal, illegal, military or civilian would be impossible to determine.

'The total number and global distribution of small arms remains one of the greatest enigmas in the field of international peace and security', says the Small Arms Survey. The Survey is a project of the Graduate Institute of International Studies in Geneva, which has attempted to profile and estimate the proliferation of firearms (hand-held guns and rifles, rather than hand-held missile launchers and the like), based on rough estimates and incomplete reporting by countries.

Their research estimates that there are at least 550 million legally-held firearms in the world today-at least one gun for every 11 of the world's people. Over half of all of these are privately owned. The group was unable, not surprisingly, to estimate the number of illegally-held arms in the world. The 20th century was the most violent one in human history. Not only did it witness two world wars, and 30 years of major arms-fuelled tension between the world's superpowers, it also featured hundreds of localized conflicts, armed border disputes, civil wars, military coups and counter coups, revolutionary struggles and armed invasions.

According to the Armed Conflicts Report 2000 and the State of the World Report 1999, there were 40 armed conflicts underway in 36 different countries as the 21st century was born. Even in the short time since the millennium, the world has witnessed a new 'war on terror' waged by the US and its allies against Afghanistan, with the threat of extension to Somalia, and the possibility of intensified attacks on Iraq.

Earth is a planet at war, and to a large extent this is a consequence of the legal and illicit sale of arms. In crude but plain terms, without weaponry, combat would be more limited in scale. In most conflict zones in the world, war is a way of life. Waging war is a means of generating money, exerting political power, and providing employment. In some areas of the developing world, children grow up knowing nothing else but bloodshed, dead, injured or maimed relatives, the daily risk of landmines; even bearing arms themselves. If they survive long enough to procreate, their own children will know only the same.

War today

Despite tension between India and Pakistan, the future stability of the world is probably now less at risk from an all-out nuclear catastrophe-as was thought during the Cold War era-than from a slow, insidious, systematic proliferation of small wars and local strife in mainly smaller nations, many of them in Africa. In 1998, Africa suffered 11 major armed conflicts. It is now the most war-torn region in the world. Those small wars are created and sustained in a constant battle to control territory, plunder resources and wield power. William Hartung, of the World Policy Institute, illustrates the problem. When the current Liberian president Charles Taylor invaded Liberia on Christmas Eve in 1989, he did so with just 100 irregular soldiers, armed with AK47 rifles. Within months they had seized mineral and timber resources and used the profits to purchase more light weapons: the first few turns in an ongoing vicious cycle.

According to Hartung: 'This pattern of war as plunder has been repeated with local variations in Sierra Leone, where the Liberian-backed Revolutionary United Front (RUF) has used diamond sales to fuel its campaign of terror; in Colombia, where government forces, right-wing paramilitaries and anti-government rebels have skimmed off profits, fees and bribes from the cocaine trade; in Angola, where UNITA rebel forces have raised billions of dollars through diamond sales and the Angolan Government has countered by stocking its arsenal with revenues drawn from its large offshore oil deposits."

The seizure or trafficking of drugs, diamonds and other valuable commodities produces profits for warring factions. Profits are spent not on peace, reconciliation or education, but on more weapons-bought on the illicit market, and through more 'legitimate' channels. The weapons suppliers to the perpetrators of the 1994 genocide in Rwanda included brokers and shippers in Britain, South Africa and France, working with collaborators in Albania, Belgium, Bulgaria, Egypt, Italy, the Seychelles and the former Zaire (now DR Congo/DRC). Arms and military training are also supplied to warring or revolutionary factions, both openly and secretly, by Western nations to serve their own political ambitions.

Bigger picture

But the arms trade also has a role in sustaining larger, more 'official' tensions and conflicts between states. The deadly dealing increases strains and thereby fuels wars between established nations. Here are some examples. From 1989 to 1998, the US provided over $227 million in weapons and training to African military forces. Of this, over $111 million went to governments that have been directly or indirectly involved in the war in the Democratic Republic of Congo (DRC): Angola, Burundi, Chad Namibia, Rwanda, Sudan, Uganda and Zimbabwe. The big seven arms-selling countries in the world-the US, France, Germany, Britain, Russia, China and Italy have all sold arms to states currently involved in conflict including Sri Lanka, Indonesia, Israel, China, Taiwan, India and Pakistan. And they usually show their deadly wares at arms fairs.

Military training

Military training Military training is an aspect of the industry often overlooked by campaigners and politicians working towards arms control. Yet the provision of training to foreign armies, or warring factions, is commonplace and was clearly illustrated with the allied forces' training and assistance given to the Afghan United Front forces during their reclaiming of Afghanistan at the end of 2001. Just as with the hardware, military training is used by governments to further their strategic and political objectives, as well as being a tool in international relations. But like arms sales, military training of foreign fighters can also bounce back. Since the US armed forces are among the most highly trained and best financially supported in the world, it is no surprise that the US is a major provider of military training. Here's an example. Towards the end of his presidency, Bill Clinton took a special interest in Africa. His proposed 'new partnership' was not to supply aid or help build civil society as was hoped, but apparently to establish a wide program of troop training. In 1998, the US provided $45.8 million in international military education training (IMET) for over 400 African soldiers.

UNDER THE PENTAGON'S JOINT COMBINED EXCHANGE

Training (JCET) program, US Special Forces have trained military personnel from at least 34 of Africa's 53 nations. That includes troops fighting on both sides of the DRC's 'civil' war- from Rwanda and Uganda (supporting the rebels) to Zimbabwe and Namibia (supporting DRC's Kabila regime).

Dirty dozen

The main suppliers of small arms include the same dozen governments that dominate the trade. The main government suppliers include the US, Russia, China, France and Britain, along with Belgium, Bulgaria, Germany, Israel, Italy and South Africa. Innumerable independent arms dealers, criminals, brokers and middlemen control the illicit trade. Some governments and campaigners draw a distinction between legally transferred small arms, and the illegal trade. The vast majority of small arms which infest southern Africa were originally supplied legitimately' by the USSR to 'liberation movements' there. Ukraine, Belarus and Bulgaria remain large suppliers to the region. Worldwide, the 'legal' trade makes up by far the majority of small arms sales. Transfers from established companies, within established nations, make up nearly 90 per cent of the total annual value of the trade.

The annual legal global trade in small arms and light weapons is estimated at $4-6 billion.

War in the Congo

The ongoing bloody conflict in the Democratic Republic of Congo (DRC), formerly Zaire, has been called Africa's 'first world war'. In 1965 Mobutu Sese Seko became president of Zaire with the backing of the US Central Intelligence Agency (CIA), who needed a strategic friend in Africa. Mobutu quickly became one of the continent's most brutal dictators, but was nevertheless supported by the US in weapons sales and military training. Even after the Cold War, the United States continued to supply military support to the Mobutu regime. In 1991, more than $4.5 million of military equipment was delivered to Zaire.

In 1996 and 1997, Laurent Kabila and his Alliance of Democratic Forces fought running battles with the Mobutu dictatorship, eventually ousting the despot. The US immediately offered the Kabila regime military training, even as the new president suspended human rights and banned opposition political parties. On 2 August 1998, DR Congo's current brutal conflict began, with nine African nations siding with either the Mobutu faction or Kabila regime in a fight for DR Congo's rich mineral and diamond resources. Foreign troops from Rwanda, Uganda, Burundi, Angola, Namibia, Sudan, Chad and Zimbabwe have all been drawn into the fight, along with irregular and guerrilla movements from surrounding African states. US, Britain, China, Russia, South Africa and other weapons-selling giants have gathered like vultures, gladly supplying the factions with weapons of death. Even after six of the governments involved were drawn together to sign the Lusaka peace accords in July 2000, the battling continues, supported by Western countries and their arms companies.

Despite not sharing a border with the DRC, Robert Mugabe's Zimbabwe has played a major part in the tensions since the mid-1990s in support of the Kabila regime. It is widely known that Zimbabwe sent a steady supply of North Korean weapons to Kabila's rebels before they came to power. In 2000, Zimbabwe had an estimated 13,000 troops fighting in the DR Congo. The

Government then estimated its involvement in the DRC cost $3 million a month-though leaked documents have put the figure closer to $27 million, a price the country can ill afford with unemployment at more than 50 per cent, huge debts and massive inflation. Britain has been a good friend to Zimbabwe in terms of arms sales, continuing to supply even after a June 1999 call by the Presidency of the European Union (EU) for states to observe a 'rigorous application' of the EU Code of Conduct on arms sales regarding the region.

In February 2000, the British Guardian newspaper revealed that the Prime Minister, Tony Blair, had pushed through licenses for Hawk fighter jet spare parts to Zimbabwe even though there was evidence that Hawks had been used in the Congo conflict. Only three months later was Robin Cook, the embattled 'ethical foreign policy' British Foreign Secretary, able to announce a full arms embargo on the country-after Zimbabwean white farmers had been attacked by Mugabe supporters. But by that time, many of the Hawk parts had already been exported.

Impact on human rights

'No security assistance may be provided to any country the government of which engages in a consistent pattern of gross violations of internationally recognized human rights. ' Section 502B, US Foreign Assistance Act. 'The President shall consider the following criteria...

The government of the country... was chosen by and permits free and fair elections... respects human rights... does not persistently engage in gross violations of internationally recognized human rights, including extra judicial or arbitrary executions, disappearances, torture or severe mistreatment, prolonged arbitrary imprisonment...' US International Arms Sales Code of Conduct Act 1999. 'Member States will not issue an export license if there is a clear risk that the proposed export might be used for internal repression... [including] torture and other cruel, inhuman and degrading treatment or punishment, summary or arbitrary executions, disappearances, arbitrary detentions and other major violations of human rights. '

EU Code of Conduct for Arms Exports 1998... human rights have not been a major barrier to weapons sales at any time in history. The world's worst dictators, despots, human rights abusers and anti-democratic regimes have been the customers of all of the major arms supplying countries in the world-and continue to be so.

According to the Centre for International Policy, during the fiscal year 1998 around 54 per cent of US arms transfers to the developing world went to undemocratic regimes. Between 1991 and 1994, 85 per cent of all US arms transfers were to undemocratic states. According to one calculation by William Hartung of the World Policy Institute, during the 1999 fiscal year, the US delivered roughly $6.8 billion in armaments to nations which violate the basic standards set out in the US's own International Code of Conduct on Arms Sales.

SMALL ARMS DEVELOPMENT

New production methods for weapons such as stamping, riveting, and welding came into being to produce the number of arms needed. While this had been tried before, during World War I, it had resulted in quite possibly the worst firearm ever adopted by any military for use: the French Chauchat light machine gun. Design and production methods had advanced enough to manufacture weapons of reasonable reliability such as the PPSh-41, PPS-42, Sten, MP 40, M3 *Grease Gun*, Gewehr 43, Thompson submachine gun and the M1 Garand rifle.

Other Weapons commonly found During World War II include the American, Browning Automatic Rifle (BAR), M1 Carbine Rifle, as well as the Colt M1911; The Japanese Type 100 submachine gun, the Type 99 machine gun, and the Arisaka bolt action rifle all were significant weapons used during the war. World War II saw the birth of the reliable semi-automatic rifle, such as the American M1 Garand and, more importantly, that of the first real assault rifles. The Germans essentially created and pioneered the idea of an "assault rifle" or sturmgewehr, coining the name for the species in the process. Earlier renditions that hinted at this idea were that of the employment of the Browning Automatic Rifle and 1916

Fedorov Avtomat in a *walking fire* tactic in which men would advance on the enemy position showering it with a hail of lead. The Germans first developed the FG 42 for its paratroopers in the assault and later the Sturmgewehr 44 (StG 44), the world's first true assault rifle. The FG 42 would probably hold this place but for its use of a full powered rifle cartridge making it hard to control by an unskilled operator.

Developments in machine gun technology culminated in the Maschinengewehr 42 (MG42) which was of an advanced design unmatched at the time. It spurred post-war development on both sides of the upcoming Cold War and is still used by some armies to this day including the German Bundeswehr's MG 3. The Heckler & Koch G3, and many other Heckler & Koch designs, came from its system of operation. The United States military meshed the operating system of the FG 42 with the belt feed system of the MG42 to create the M60 machine gun used in the Vietnam War.

Despite being overshadowed by self-loading/automatic rifles and sub-machine guns, bolt-action rifles remained the mainstay infantry weapon of many nations during World War II. When the United States entered World War II, there were not enough M1 Garand rifles available to American forces which forced the US to start producing more M1903 rifles in order to act as a "stop gap" measure until sufficient quantities of M1 Garands were produced.

During the conflict, many new models of bolt-action rifles were produced as a result of lessons learned from the First World War with the designs of a number of bolt-action infantry rifles being modified in order to speed up production as well as to make the rifles more compact and easier to handle. Examples of bolt-action rifles that were used during World War II include the German Mauser Kar98k, the British Lee-Enfield No.4, and the Springfield M1903A3. During the course of World War II, bolt-action rifles and carbines were modified even further to meet new forms of warfare the armies of certain nations faced e.g. urban warfare and jungle warfare. Examples include the Soviet Mosin-Nagant M1944 carbine, which were developed by the Soviets as a result of the Red Army's experiences with urban warfare e.g. the Battle of Stalingrad, and the British Lee-Enfield No.5 carbine, that were developed for British and Commonwealth forces fighting the Japanese in South-East Asia and the Pacific.

When World War II ended in 1945, the small arms that were used in the conflict still saw action in the hands of the armed forces of various nations and guerrilla movements during and after the Cold War era. Nations like the Soviet Union and the United States provided many surplus, World War II-era small arms to a number of nations and political movements during the Cold War era as a pretext to providing more modern infantry weapons. Besides seeing conflict long after World War II ended, the small arms of World War II are now considered collector's items with many civilian firearm owners and collectors around the world due to their historical nature, low cost (due to many of these firearms now appearing on the firearms market in large numbers over the past decade), and their durability.

The Atomic Bomb

The massive research and development demands of the war included the Manhattan Project, the effort to quickly develop an atomic bomb, or nuclear fission warhead. It was perhaps the most profound military development of the war, and had a great impact on the scientific community, among other things creating a network of national laboratories in the United States.

Development was completed too late for use in the European Theater of World War II. Its invention meant that a single bomber aircraft could carry a weapon sufficiently powerful to devastate entire cities, making conventional warfare against a nation with an arsenal of them suicidal.

The strategic importance of the bomb, and its even more powerful fusion-based successors, did not become fully apparent until the United States lost its monopoly on the weapon in the post-war era. The Soviet Union developed and tested their first nuclear weapon in 1949, based partially on information obtained from Soviet espionage in the United States. The competition between the two superpowers would lead to the Cold War. The strategic implications of such a massively destructive weapon still reverberate in the 21st century.

There was also a German project to develop an atomic weapon. This failed for a variety of reasons, most notably German Antisemitism. The first tier of continental high energy physicists (Einstein, Bohr, Fermi, and Oppenheimer) who did much of their early study and research in Germany, were either Jewish or, in the case of Enrico Fermi, married to a Jew. Oppenheimer, who was an American Jew, was also a Socialist by conviction, and associated with the Communist Party. When they left Germany, the only significant atomic physicist left in Germany was Heisenberg, who dragged his feet on the project. He made some faulty calculations suggesting that the Germans would need significantly more heavy water than was necessary. The project was then doomed due to insufficient resources.

The Empire of Japan was also developing an Atomic Bomb, however, it floundered due to lack of resources despite gaining interest from the government.

GATHERING THE FACTS ON THE SMALL ARMS TRADE

In late 1997, following the Oslo conference that drafted the treaty against anti-personnel landmines, many NGOs and governments began pressing for more public attention to the devastation wrought by the worldwide sale and distribution of light arms–weapons that can be carried by a person–such as assault rifles, mortars, and grenades. Such arms are believed to be responsible for the vast majority of combat deaths, including many tens of thousands of civilian deaths annually. Even after conflicts end, demobilization and reconciliation efforts are frustrated by the over-supply of these inexpensive weapons, which often flow into criminal hands.

Among the governmental and non-governmental initiatives at the time, in late December 1997, on the first anniversary of the murder of Red Cross/Red Crescent workers in Chechnya, PRIO and three other organizations in Oslo–Norwegian Red Cross, Norwegian Church Aid and the Norwegian Institute of International Affairs–banded together to form the Norwegian Initiative on Small Arms Transfers (NISAT). The database proposal here is a central part of NISAT's activities.

Need for the Project

In the past few years, the European Union, OSCE, Organization of American States, Organization of African Unity, Economic Community of West African States, and the South African Development Community all took up some aspect of small arms control. Almost every part of the UN engaged the topic, including—increasingly—the Security Council. Modeled on a 1997 OAS treaty, the UN in Vienna began negotiation of a global protocol against firearms trafficking in 1999. In addition, the UN General Assembly voted in 1999 to hold a United Nations conference in 2001 on the illicit arms trade "in all its dimensions."

Despite this high level of engagement by governments and NGOs, the knowledge base on which these efforts rest is extremely thin. There are enormous gaps in the factual record on arms production and transfers. The lack of focused research in this area leaves open fundamental questions such as whether the legal or the illegal arms trade is the leading source of supply, and which states are the largest legal exporters of small arms.

Approximately 70 states produce small arms and/or ammunition. Some production enterprises are state-owned (usually military armories), and some are private companies. From the existing reference works,

- it is not difficult to know what types of small arms the major producer states manufacture;
- it is much harder to determine production quantities; and
- it is nearly impossible to know where weapons are being exported.

The standard sources of data on the international arms trade–SIPRI, the UN Register of Conventional Arms, *World Military Expenditures and Arms Transfers*–do not include information on small arms shipments.

Few governments provide information to their parliaments on major weapons exports they have approved, and even fewer on their small arms trade. An exception to the prevailing pattern of secrecy is the US government. Since 1997, the United States openly reports in a highly specific manner all of its small arms shipments and export license approvals (with the notable exception of covert government-run arms supply, like the Iran-contra operation). Other states that have recently begun to provide more detailed public reports on their arms exports (including small arms shipments) are Belgium, Canada, the Netherlands, Norway, South Africa, Sweden and the United Kingdom. These are the eight leaders in transparency, on which the database will first concentrate in 2000-2001.

Despite this improvement in transparency, there is a need to organize the newly available data. In the above eight and other countries, the relevant information is scattered across many agencies and departments–in shipping documents at customs offices, judicial records, police records, and documents in the foreign, defense and trade ministries. No one is currently pulling this information together systematically, translating it, or presenting it to the international community in a readily useable format. That is what the database project will do.

The Need for Transparency

The information included in the database will serve as a template for the kind of governmental transparency that we will encourage the Norwegian Foreign Ministry to press for through its diplomatic contacts and on the international stage. In addition, we hope the database itself will encourage greater openness on the part of some governments, when they see the amount and types of information that the United States and – to a lesser degree – some others already make public without adverse effect.

Increased transparency and organization of the available data will also improve the ability of governments to verify the appropriate end-uses and end-users of weapons exports they are authorizing. It will allow the non-governmental community, as well as national legislatures, to play an important role in aiding governments' efforts to curb diversion of these arms by providing oversight through research, questioning and reporting. Such information is also important for the safety of aid and relief workers operating in a region where a sudden influx of guns has occurred or is anticipated.

Increased openness about weapons shipments could serve as a confidence building measure among forces within a state, or states in a region, potentially heading off some purchases spurred by 'fear of the unknown'. Finally, such information will greatly facilitate formal disarmament activities, by providing some baseline information about arms stocks and supply in the state or region.

How the Project Addresses These Needs

The centerpiece of this proposal is an on-line database of small arms production and transfers. The database addresses the need for better information on three levels:

- it provides a composite picture of the small arms trade by collecting, translating and organizing the hard-to-find data;
- it interlinks policy-relevant information so as to provide both governments and activist organizations a stronger base for argumentation, strategy and agreement on common norms; and
- it demonstrates the positive aspects of transparency.

The database will eventually contain information on virtually every country of the world. It will be a public resource, accessible to all Internet users.

We believe that the database will yield substantial results within one year of full funding, and if so we are committed to further developing and sustaining the initiative for as long as small arms control measures are required. As more governments provide public information about their light weapons shipments, the resource will grow in value (in terms of providing a fuller picture of the dynamics of the arms market).

4

Arms Races among New Nuclear States

One may easily believe that American and Russian military doctrines have set the pattern that new nuclear states will follow. One may then also believe that they will suffer the fate of the United States and the Soviet Union, that they will compete in building larger and larger nuclear arsenals while continuing to accumulate conventional weapons. These are doubtful beliefs. One can infer the future from the past only insofar as future situations may be like present ones for the actors involved. For four main reasons, new nuclear states are likely to -decrease rather than increase their military spending.

First, nuclear weapons alter the dynamics of arms races. In a competition of two or more parties, it may be hard to say who is pushing and who is being pushed, who is leading and who is following. If one party seeks to increase its capabilities, it may seem that the other(s) must too. The dynamic may be built into the competition and may unfold despite a mutual wish to resist it. But need this be the case in a strategic competition between nuclear countries? It need not be if the conditions of competition make deterrent logic dominant. Deterrent logic dominates if the conditions of competition make it nearly impossible for any of the competing parties to achieve a first-strike capability. Early in the nuclear age, the implications of deterrent strategy were clearly seen. 'When dealing with the absolute weapon', as William T. R. Fox put it, 'arguments based on relative advantage lose their point'. The United States has sometimes designed her forces according to that logic. Donald A. Quarles argued when he was Eisenhower's Secretary of the Air Force that 'sufficiency of air power' is determined by 'the force required to accomplish the mission assigned'. Avoidance of total war then does not depend on the '*relative* strength of the two opposed forces'. Instead, it depends on the '*absolute* power in the hands of each, and in the substantial invulnerability of this power to interdiction'. To repeat: If no state can launch a disarming attack with high confidence, force comparisons are irrelevant. Strategic arms races are then pointless. Deterrent strategies offer this great advantage: Within wide ranges neither side need respond to increases in the other side's military capabilities.

Those who foresee nuclear arms racing among new nuclear states fail to make the distinction between war-fighting and war-deterring capabilities. War-fighting forces, because they threaten the forces of others, have to be compared. Superior forces may bring vic-tory to one country; inferior forces may bring defeat to another. Force requirements vary with strategies and not just with the character-istics of weapons. With war-fighting strategies. arms races become difficult, if not impossible, to avoid. Forces designed for deterring war need not be compared. As Harold Brown said when he was Secretary of Defense, purely deterrent forces 'can be relatively modest, and their size can perhaps be made substantially, though not completely, insensitive to changes in the posture of an opponent'. With deter-rent strategies, arms races make sense only if a first-strike capability is within reach. Because thwarting a first strike is easy, deterrent forces are quite cheap to build and maintain. With deterrent forces, the question is not whether one country has more than another but whether it has the capability of inflicting 'unacceptable damage' on another, with unacceptable damage sensibly defined. Once that capability is assured, additional strategic weapons are useless. More is not better if less is enough.

Deterrent balances are also inherently stable. if one can say how much is enough, then within wide limits a country can be insensitive to changes in its adversaries' forces. This is the way French leaders have thought. France, as former President Giscard d'Estaing said, 'fixes its security at the level required to maintain, regardless of the way the strategic situation develops in the world, the credibility—in other words, the effectiveness—of its deterrent force'. With deterrent forces securely estab-lished, no military need presses one side to try to surpass the other. Human error and folly may lead some parties involved in deterrent balances to spend more on armaments than is needed, but other parties need not increase their armaments in response, because such excess spending does not threaten them. The logic of deterrence eliminates incentives for strategic arms racing. This should be easier for lesser nuclear states to understand than it has been for the US and the USSR. Because most of them are economically hard pressed, they will not want to have more than enough.

Allowing for their particular circumstances, lesser nuclear states confirm these statements in their policies. Britain and France are relatively rich countries, and they tend to overspend. Their strategic forces are nevertheless modest enough when one considers that their purpose is to deter the Soviet Union rather than states with capabilities comparable to their own. China of course faces the same task. These three countries show no inclination to engage in nuclear arms races with anyone. India appears content to have a nuclear military capability that may or may not have produced deliverable warheads, and Israel maintains her ambiguous status. New nuclear states are likely to conform to these patterns and aim for a modest sufficiency rather than vie with each for a meaningless superiority.

Second, because strategic nuclear arms races among lesser powers are unlikely, the interesting question is not whether they will be run but whether countries having strategic nuclear weapons can avoid running conventional races. No more than the United States and the Soviet Union will lesser nuclear states want to rely on the deterrent threat that risks all. And will not their vulnerability to conventional attack induce them continue their conventional efforts?

American policy as it has developed since the early 1960s again teaches lessons that mislead. For almost two decades, we have emphasized the importance of having a continuum of forces that would enable the United States and her allies to fight at any level from irregular to strategic nuclear warfare. A policy that decreases reliance on deterrence increases the chances that wars will be fought. This was well appreciated in Europe when we began to place less emphasis on deterrence and more on defence. The worries of many Europeans were well expressed by a senior British general in the following words: 'McNamara is practically telling the Soviets that the worst they need to expect from an attack on West Germany is a conventional counterattack'. Why risk one's own destruction if one is able to fight on the ground and forgo the use of strategic weapons?

The policy of flexible response lessened reliance on strategic deterrence and increased the chances of fighting a war. New nuclear states are not likely to experience this problem. The expense of mounting conventional defen-ces, and the difficulties and dangers of fighting conventional wars, will keep most new nuclear states from trying to combine large war-fighting forces with deterrent forces. Disjunc-tion within their forces will enhance the value of deterrence.

Israeli policy seems to contradict these prop-ositions. From 1971 through 1978, both Israel and Egypt spent from 20% to 40% of their GNPs on arms. Israel's spending on conventional arms remains high, although it has decreased since 1978. The decrease followed from the making of peace with Egypt and not from increased reliance on nuclear weapons. The seeming contradiction in fact bears out deter-rent logic. So long as Israel holds the West Bank and the Gaza Strip she has to be prepared to fight for them. Since they are by no means unambiguously hers, deterrent threats, whether implicit or explicit, will not cover them. Moreover, while America's large subsi-dies continue, economic constraints will not drive Israel to the territorial settlement that would shrink her borders sufficiently to make a deterrent policy credible.

From previous points it follows that nuclear weapons are likely to decrease arms racing and reduce military costs for lesser nuclear states in two ways. Conventional arms races will wither if countries shift emphasis from conventional defence to nuclear deterrence. For Pakistan. for example, acquiring nuclear weapons is an alternative to running a ruinous conventional race with India. And deterrent strategies make nuclear arms races pointless.

Finally, arms races in their ultimate form—the fighting of offensive wars designed to increase national security—also become point-less. The success of a deterrent strategy does not depend on the extent of territory a state holds, a point made earlier. It merits repeating because of its unusual importance for states whose geographic limits lead them to obsessive concern for their security in a world of ever more destructive conventional weapons.

The Frequency and Intensity of War

The presence of nuclear weapons makes wars less likely. One may nevertheless oppose the spread of nuclear weapons on the ground that they would make war, however unlikely, unbearably intense should it occur. Nuclear weapons have not been fired in anger in a world in which more than one country has them. We have enjoyed three decades of nuclear peace and may enjoy many more.

But we can never have a guarantee. We may be grateful for decades of nuclear peace and for the discouragement of conventional war among those who have nuclear weapons. Yet the fear is widespread, and naturally so, that if they ever go off, we may all die. People as varied as the scholar Richard Smoke, the arms controller Paul Warnke, and former Defense Secretary Harold Brown all believe that if any nuclear weapons go off, many will. Although this seems the least likely of all the unlikely possibilities, it is not impossible. What makes it so unlikely is that, even if deterrence should fail, the prospects for rapid de-escalation are good.

McNamara asked himself what fractions of the Soviet Union's population and industry the United States should be able to destroy in order to deter her. For military, although not for budgetary, strategy this was the wrong question. States are not deterred because they expect to suffer a certain amount of damage but because they cannot know how much damage they will suffer. Near the dawn of the nuclear age Bernard Brodie put the matter simply: 'The prediction is more important than the fact'. The prediction, that is, that attacking the vital interests of a country having nuclear weapons may bring the attacker untold losses, As Patrick Morgan more recently put it: 'To attempt to "compute" the cost of a nuclear is to miss the point'.

States are deterred by the prospect of suffering severe damage and by their physical inability to do much to limit it. Debate over the Soviet Union's civil defence efforts calls attention to this inability. Defensive measures can reduce casualties, but they would still be immense were either of the great powers launch a determined attack. Moreover, civil defence cannot save the Soviet Union's heavily concentrated industries. Warheads numbered in the hundreds can destroy the United and the Soviet Union as viable societies no matter what defensive measures they take. Deterrence works because nuclear weapons enable one state to punish another state severely without first defeating it. 'Victory', in Thomas Schellings words, 'is no longer a prerequisite for hurting the enemy'. Coun-tries armed only with conventional weapons can hope that their military forces will be able to limit the damage an attacker can do. Among countries armed with strategic nuclear forces, the hope of avoiding heavy damage depends mainly on the attacker's restraint and little on one's own efforts. Those who compare expected deaths through strategic exchanges of nuclear warheads with casualties suffered by the Soviet Union in World War II overlook this fundamental difference between conventional and nuclear worlds.

Deterrence rests on what countries *can* do to each other with strategic nuclear weapons. From this statement, one easily leaps to the wrong conclusion: that deterrent strategies, if they have to be carried through, will produce a catastrophe. That countries are able to annihi-late each other means neither that deterrence depends on their threatening to do so nor that they will do so if deterrence fails. Because countries heavily armed with strategic nuclear weapons can carry war to its ultimate intensity, the control of force, in wartime as in peace-time, becomes the primary objective. If deter-rence fails, leaders will have the strongest incentives to keep force under control and limit damage rather than launching genocidal attacks. If the Soviet Union should attack Western Europe,

NATO'S objectives would be to halt the attack and end the war. The United States has long had the ability to place hundreds of warheads precisely on targets in the Soviet Union. Surely we would strike mili-tary targets before striking industrial targets and industrial targets before striking cities. The intent to do so is sometimes confused with a war-fighting strategy, which it is not. It would not significantly reduce the Soviet Union's ability to hurt us. It is a deterrent strategy, resting initially on the threat to punish. The threat, if it fails to deter, is appropriately followed not by spasms of violence but by punishment administered in ways that convey threats to make the punishment more severe.

For several reasons, then, deterrent strate-gies promise less damage than war-fighting strategies. First, deterrent strategies induce caution all around and thus reduce the incidence of war. Second, wars fought in the face of strategic nuclear weapons must be carefully limited because a country having them may retaliate if its vital interests are threatened. Third, prospective punishment need only be proportionate to an adversary's expected gains in war after those gains are discounted for the many uncertainties of war. Fourth, should deterrence fail, a few judiciously delivered warheads are likely to produce sobriety in the leaders of all of the countries involved and thus bring rapid de-escalation.

A deterrent strategy promises less damage, should deterrence fail, than does the Schles-inger-Brown 'countervailing' strategy, a strat-egy which contemplates fighting a limited, strategic nuclear war. War-fighting strategies offer no clear place to stop short of victory for some and defeat for others. Deterrent strategies do, and that place is where one country threat-ens another's vital interests. Deterrent strate-gies lower the probability that wars will be fought. If wars are nevertheless fought, deter-rent strategies lower the probability that they will become wars of high intensity.

A war between the United States and the Soviet Union that did get out of control would be catastrophic. If they set out to destroy each other, they would greatly reduce the world's store of developed resources while killing mil-lions outside of their own borders through fall-out. Even while destroying themselves, states with few weapons would do less damage to others. As ever, the biggest international dangers come from the strongest states. Fearing the world's destruction, one may prefer a world of conventional great powers having a higher probability of fighting less destructive wars to a world of nuclear great powers having a lower probability of fighting more destructive wars. But that choice effectively disappeared with the production of atomic bombs by the United States during World War II. Since the great powers are unlikely to be drawn into the nuclear wars of others, the added global dangers posed by the spread of nuclear weapons are small.

The spread of nuclear weapons threatens to make wars more intense at the local and not at the global level, where wars of the highest intensity have been possible for a number of years. If their national existence should be threatened, weaker countries, unable to defend at lesser levels of violence, may destroy them-selves through resorting to nuclear weapons. Lesser nuclear states will live in fear of this possibility. But this is not different from the fear under which the United States and the Soviet Union have lived for years. Small nuclear states may experience a keener sense of desperation because of extreme vulnerability to conventional as well as to nuclear attack, but, again, in desperate situations what all parties become most desperate to avoid is the use of strategic nuclear weapons. Still, however improbable the event, lesser states may one day fire some of their weapons. Are minor nuclear states more or less likely to do so than major ones? The answer to this question is vitally important because the existence of some States would be at stake even if the damage done were regionally confined.

Looking at the situation of weaker nuclear states and at the statements of stronger nuclear states, one suspects that weak states are less likely to use nuclear weapons first than are strong ones. Many have worried about conven-tional wars between minor nuclear states becoming nuclear wars as one side loses. It is NATO, however, that plans to use nuclear weapons in battle if conventional troops can-not hold. Moreover, after the Soviet Union invaded Afghanistan in December of 1979, American officials considered using nuclear weapons in the Middle East if need be. At various times, some Americans have thought of reasons for making limited counterforce strikes—firing a few missiles at the Soviet Union to show our determination—an idea revived by James R. Schlesinger when he was Secretary of Defense. Among others, Generals Earle G.

Wheeler and George Brown, former chairmen of the Joint Chiefs of Staff, have talked of our emerging from a nuclear war with a 'relative advantage' over the Soviet Union by targeting their 'war recovery capabilities'. Presidential Directive 59, signed by President Carter in July of 1980, contemplates fighting a limited nuclear war, perhaps a prolonged one, if deterrence should fail. And some of the Soviet Union's military leaders have publicly discussed using nuclear weapons to win wars.

The United States and the Soviet Union have more readily contemplated the use of nuclear weapons than lesser nuclear states have done or are likely to do. But planning is distinct from deciding to act. Planners think they should offer Presidents a range of choices and a variety of nuclear weapons to carry them through.

In the event, Presidents, like Party Chairmen, will shy away from using nuclear weapons and will act with extreme care in dealing with situations that might get out of control, as they have done in the past. New nuclear states are likely to be even more mindful of dangers and more concerned for their safety than than some of the old ones have been. Ordinarily, weak states calculate more fearfully and move more cautiously than strong ones. The thought that fear and caution may lead insecure countries to launch pre-emptive strikes has amplified anxieties about the instability of regions populated by lesser nuclear powers and about the extent of destruction their weapons may bring. Such worries rest on inferences drawn froom the behaviour of conventional states and do not apply to nuclear ones, for reasons already discussed.

Nuclear weapons lessen the intensity as well as the frequency of war among their possessors. For fear of escalation, nuclear states do not want to fight long or hard over important interests—indeed, they do not want to fight at all. Minor nuclear states have even better reasons than major ones to accommodate one another peacefully and to avoid any fighting. Worries about the intensity of war among nuclear states have to be viewed in this context and against a world in which conventional weapons become ever costlier and more destructive.

THE ROLES AND REACTIONS OF THE GREAT POWERS

Should a great power help a lesser one improve on its force once it has shown the will and the ability to build one? Will great powers be drawn into the nuclear confrontations of lesser ones, or will they draw away from them to avoid involvement? Will small nuclear powers cut themselves adrift from the great powers and follow independent policies? Will small countries' nuclear forces trigger an arms race between the great powers? These questions suggest four ways in which big and small nuclear powers may interact.

Small and crude forces tempt pre-emption, so it is thought, and maybe used in reckless and unintended ways because of inadequate com-mand and control. These dangers can be removed by great powers assisting lesser ones in building and managing their forces. Never-theless, neither the United States nor the Soviet Union will want to help much, lest countries come to believe that they can build insufficient and unreliable forces and rely on one of the great powers to turn them into something substantial. Such hindrance is unfortunate, if improving others' forces serves wider interests. Is help required, not just for the sake of the recipient, but also to avoid nuclear imbalances between states that might prompt wars and to reduce the chances of accidents that might set them off? We saw earlier that these are minor worries. Because they are minor, the United States and the Soviet Union are not likely to be tempted to give technical help to countries entering the nuclear military business.

Nuclear weapons in the hands of six or seven states have lessened wars and limited conflicts. The further spread of nuclear weapons can be expected to widen those effects. Should the United States then promote the spread of nuclear weapons for the sake of peace, even though we need not for the sake of stability? To do so would replace one extreme policy with another. Present policy works hard to prevent additional states from acquiring nuclear weapons. My examination of the effects of nuclear weapons leads to the conclusion that our policy is wrong without supporting the proposition that true proliferation—the rapid spread of nuclear weaponry—is desirable. Rapid change may be destabilizing. The slow spread of nuclear weapons gives states time to learn to live with them, to appreciate their virtues, and to understand the limits they place on behaviour.

Will the United States and the Soviet Union be drawn into the struggles of lesser nuclear states? This question loses much of its urgency given the aversion of states to crises that raise the spectre of nuclear war and the care they take in crises that do so. Will they then draw away from other states' crises rather than being drawn in?

The United States and the Soviet Union will continue to have interests in various parts of the world for all of the old political. economic, and military reasons. In a region where nuclear powers are locked in dis-pute, the great powers will move cautiously in attempting to tend to their separate and to their common interests. We can hardly expect the United States or the Soviet Union to risk more in other people's crises than they have risked in their own. Neither the United States nor the Soviet Union want a regional nuclear confron-tation to become a global one. If that risk hangs over them, their strong mutual interest is to withdraw.

Will lesser nuclear powers want to edge away from their great-power patrons in order to be able to choose their policies more freely? To do so would be risky. A nuclear Israel, for exam-ple, may threaten to fire missiles at her attackers' cities if ever their victory in war seems likely. In the face of' possible Russian opposition, signs of American acquiescence in Israel's policy would help to make the prospect of retaliation credible. Any lesser power contemplating the use of nuclear weapons even for deterrent or defensive purposes will expect opposition from at least one of the great powers. An alliance or some other kind of connection with one of them may stay the hand of the other. This is another way of saying that even with nuclear weapons weaker states continue to depend on stronger states in various ways.

By acquiring nuclear weapons a state changes one variable in a complex equation of forces. That variable is the most important one. Nuclear weapons increase the ability of states to fend for themselves when the integrity of their legitimate boundaries is at stake. Thus an Israeli deterrent force would enable Israel to maintain her legitimate boundaries while reducing her extreme dependence on the United States.

In recent years our aid has amounted to a seventh or an eighth of Israel's GNP yearly. Such dependence will substan-tially lessen only it military security becomes less of a concern or can be more cheaply pro-vided. Nuclear weapons and strategies, how-ever, do not cover all of the military problems of new nuclear states nor are military problems the whole of their concerns.

Israeli dependence on the United States will not disappear so long as she remains a small country in a hostile world. Similarly, the deterrent effect of China's nuclear weapons makes her less dependent on others militarily, without much reducing her need for economic and technical assistance. Nuclear weapons are useful against threats to a state's territorial integrity, but most of the doings of states fall far short of this extreme. Independent nuclear forces reduce depen-dency by lesser powers on others without eliminating it.

Will the nuclear arms of lesser powers stimu-late the great powers to further exertion? And will arms control and disarmament agreements be harder to reach? Consider arms racing first. A faster race between the great powers may come about in the following way, and to some extent already has. The United States or the Soviet Union builds more missiles and more defences against missiles as she perceives a growing threat from China. The increased effort of one of the great powers prompts the other to try harder, and the effects become reciprocating causes. Action, reaction, and over-reaction by the United States and the Soviet Union have formed a pattern too familiar to disregard. The pattern is likely to repeat itself, but it need not.

Consider a historical case. In 1967, McNamara half-heartedly proposed deploying a cheap ($5-billion) ABM system designed to handle an attack by China even though, as he said, we had 'the power not only to destroy completely her entire nuclear offensive forces, but to devastate her society as well'. Whatever his political and bureaucratic reasons, be publicly argued that a light ABM system offered four advantages:

1) China might miscalculate.
2) America would be showing Asian states that she would not let China blackmail them and would thus dampen their desires to have their own nuclear weapons.
3) America would gain marginal pro-tection for *Minuteman* sites against an attack by the Soviet Union.
4) America would be safe against acci-dental launchings.

Had the United States persisted in building a 'Chinese' system, this might have prompted further efforts by the Soviet Union. The United States and the Soviet Union can react to third countries' nuclear forces in ways that stimulate their own competition in arms, but they need not do so, as is shown by examining Mc-Namara's four reasons. His fourth reason applies to any and all nuclear countries. It raises the question of the value of taking out an ABM insurance policy against accidental firings whether by third countries, by the Soviet Union, or by the United States.

His third reason applies explicitly to the Soviet Union and not to third nuclear countries. His second reason rests on a false belief about the feasibi-lity of nuclear blackmail. Only the first of McNamara's reasons applies specifically to the forces of China or of any lesser nuclear country.

It raises this question: Under any imaginable circumstances, might a lesser nuclear country's miscalculation lead it to launch an attack on the United States? The miscalculation would have to be monumental. Building missile defences against China would imply that great powers can deter each other but cannot deter minor ones. The weakness of the proposition is apparent.

Nor need more missiles be added to either great power's arsenal in order to deter lesser nuclear powers, even should the great powers fail to deter each other. In 1978, the United States had about 2,150 warheads on land-based launchers, about 5,120 on sea-based launchers, and about 2,580 in bombers. These numbers had changed little by 1980. One study estimates that the Soviet Union's best attack, launched in the mid-1980s and coming at the worst time for us with our forces only on normal day-to-day alert, would leave us with about 6,400 warheads and about 1,800 equiva-lent megatons. After such an attack, the Soviet Union would have about 6,000 warheads left and 6.000 equivalent megatons. We would still have more than we need since 1.000 *Poseidon* warheads (the force loading of some six sub-marines) 'can destroy about 75 percent of the Soviet industrial targets'. With our present force we can absorb a first strike and still destroy the Soviet Union as 'a modern industrial society', and do so with missiles to spare for counterforce attacks. And we and they would have more than enough left over to deter third countries. This plenitude of deliverable war-heads is sometimes referred to as 'sufficiency'. The great powers scarcely need get into an arms race because of what lesser powers do.

Still, the United States and the Soviet Union do race from time to time, and the racing has been fuelled in part by what third countries have done. The Soviet Union, for example, argues that many of her intermediate and medium-range ballistic missiles are needed because of the threat posed by China. Some of the NATO countries then conclude that because these missiles threaten Western Europe, cruise missiles and *Pershing IIs* must be deployed there. This then further worries the Soviet Union. No one doubts these effects.

Strategic arms races between the United States and the Soviet Union, however, are produced mainly by the strategies they follow and by the kinds of forces they build. In their strategies, dissuasion by deterrence has always been alloyed with defensive and war-fighting policies and capabilities. The number of Russian cities worth striking is finite and indeed quite low. We have long had more survivable warheads than Russian cities to strike. If only cities were aimed at, many war-heads would lack targets. The quantity of war-heads on hand and their increased accuracy constitute arguments for a counterforce strat-egy. In the last two decades, the balance between deterrent strategy and war-fighting strategy has tilted towards the latter. Available weapons affect the strategy a country adopts, and the strategy that is fashioned in turn calls for the further development of weapons. If each side views the other's strategic forces as designed for fighting wars as much as, or more than, for deterring them, then arms races become very difficult to avoid. Such percep-tions vary with changes in the strategies and forces of the great powers, not of the lesser ones. Great powers engage in arms races main-ly because of what other great powers do. That was true in a multipolar, conventional world; it remains true in a bipolar, nuclear world.

ARMS PRODUCTION, EXPORTS AND CONTROL IN THE ASEM PROCESS

Arms production and arms trade should be addressed within the political and security pillar of the ASEM process. Three of the EU ASEM countries are among the most prominent arms exporters - France, the UK and Germany. Of the top importers three countries are from East Asia: China, South Korea and Taiwan. Only China is itself a significant arms exporter. However, the flow of arms trade is like a river going one direction - towards Asia. Despite the fact that some recipient states embarked long ago on the creation of a domestic defence industry, they are still dependent on importing supplies.

There is an Asian as well as a European side to arms exports and production of the countries participating in the ASEM process, but this only tells a partial story. Significant differences exist both within and between regions. Europe is home to three of the ten biggest arms manufacturers worldwide. The Japanese Mitsubishi Heavy Industries with a military turnover of US$ 3.6 billion lies just behind the military industries from the US, the UK and France/ Germany, making it by far the biggest arms manufacturer of Asia.

Arms production within both Europe and Asia is too diverse to be analysed as one single region. For instance, weapons production in South Korea cannot be compared with Cambodia and Greece (a top ten arms importer) and Germany are playing a very different role in the arms market. Furthermore, the provision in the Japanese constitution against arms trade is not matched in any of the EU countries. These differences indicate the need for further research in establishing the significance of the arms trade and arms production in the ASEM process and for identifying the arms trade connections between the European Union and Asia ASEM countries.

Enhanced Partnerships

In the European Commission Framework document for 'Enhanced Partnerships between Asia and Europe' the latest outline of Europe's Asia policy is given. One of the few remarks on arms trade in the document identifies arms trafficking as a common concern on the level of Ministries of Justice and Home Affairs. Arms traffickers are working across boundaries and co-operation in this field is essential to tackle the illegal flow of arms. One example from 1999 illustrates how an Israeli businessman transported 40 armoured personnel carriers from Germany to Iran. The arms followed a route through the Netherlands, Britain and Singapore before reaching Iran. The Israeli businessman was in close contact with a South Korean arms dealer known to sell arms to Iran. To tackle this kind of flows concerted action between law enforcement bodies of all involved countries is essential.

The Framework document also states that co-operation should exist "for the early and comprehensive ratification of major international Instruments such as the Comprehensive Test Ban Treaty or the Conventions on small arms and anti-personnel mines." Regional and global security is certainly helped by an orchestrated implementation of those conventions. Landmines are a hidden killer and the removal of those weapons from the stocks of armies is essential for the security of those wanting to use the land for productive purposes such as agriculture, leisure and transport. Illegal small arms are causing death and destruction in all parts of the world and their wide distribution leads to killings by criminals, gangs and paramilitaries. The small arms convention is also addressing those used by resistance groups.

The killings by armies, democratically controlled or not, are outside this Convention and so its implementation is limited to law enforcement and control by the government. The scope of arms control is too limited when it stops at the level of law enforcement and nuclear testing. Such an approach uses a narrow concept of security - that is military security. Arms trade is a way of beefing-up allies, with consequences for regional balances of power and relations between nations and as such part of the conservative security debate. Moreover, major arms deals involving hundreds of millions or even billions of dollars of government expenditure cannot be left out of a genuine people's oriented security debate. Arms trade and acquisitions are part of such a security debate and for this reason should be part of the Framework document.

Finance Packages and Debt

When the EU adopted a strategy on Asia in 1994, it clearly identified the increase in the ambitious armament programmes in the Asian region as one of the factors "which could disrupt world equilibrium and thereby impinging on Europe's Common Foreign and Security Policy objectives." In the 2001 update of the Asia Strategy however, there is less attention to the security dimension of the relationship, with the exception of the issue of small arms trade and nuclear testing.

There can hardly be any justification for this omission. Although the impression exists that arms trade to the ASEM countries declined due to the economic crisis of 1997, this is not yet reflected in the figures given by SIPRI for 1999. Because the negotiations for arms deliveries in general take a long time it is possible that there will be a significant decrease visible in the near future. Another reason the economic crisis is not yet reflected in the figures, is that Arms companies made financial arrangements with governments and banks, such as low interest loans and favourable re-payment schedules to back up ongoing arms deals and negotiations. 'Buy now, Pay later' became the modus operandi of both arms exporters and importers. An official of the British Ministry of Defence explained it in this way: "In the United Kingdom, we view innovative financing packages as a key factor in any likely success". The Defence business was not willing to let existing deals collapse and used financial flexibility to secure additional new deals. Sales did not stop and some were merely postponed. This of course has led to further public debt. Conveniently, the international attention on the burden of debt on state budgets was put aside in order to continue arms trade.

Growing Demand

Besides, the long term effects of the crisis will be downplayed by new developments. Analysts see a growing demand for arms in South East Asia. The Malaysian Defence Minister Najib Razak told the well attended Defence Services Asia (DSA) arms fair: "With the economy of most of these countries back on track there will be a projected increase in the defence expenditure to procure platforms, weapon systems and solutions to meet national requirements." Defence companies likewise felt rewarded for participating in the DSA 2002. Malaysia alone ordered weapons valued US$ 958 million in April 2002. According to an Australian analyst, the process will go more rapidly in Southeast Asia than in the nineties: "Those that haven't started to move with new fighters, new surface combatants, new subs, are very quickly going to."

Issues raised in the nineties are very much back in the debates on arms trade in Asia. Is an arms race ongoing or not?. Do the acquisitions find their logic in modernisation, overhaul or refurbishment? Is it old shopping lists which now materialise? All these questions which had been set aside for five years are once again on the agenda.

However, there are also new issues with the turmoil in Indonesia being an important new factor. What is not yet very much back in the discussion is the ASEAN Regional Forum (ARF) or any other initiative on genuine regional security co-operation. Military exercises with the US and Australia are the most developed forms of regional military co-operation at present. The absence of a multilateral framework for regional security co-operation seriously hampers confidence among the countries in the region and arms acquisitions of one country are followed by similar acquisitions by neighbouring countries.

9/11 Becomes a New Sales Pitch

According to Malaysia's Defense Minister Razak when he defended the Malaysian arms acquisitions during the DSA arms fair "The 9/11 attack drastically changed the outlook toward national security". By invoking the 9/11 terrorist attacks, he was joining those government leaders who have used the 9/11 events to popularize a new sales pitch for arms acquisitions.

The strike on the World Trade Center and Pentagon is a weak rationale for placing submarines and fighter aircraft on the shopping list of many East and Southeast Asian countries. These are not the best weapons in the fight against terrorism.

The current weapons acquisitions are high-tech buys demonstrated during the Second Gulf War on Iraq (1990-91). Furthermore, the latest orders and wish lists follow the images of US technology shown on the Afghan battlefield: the integration of remote operation, new observation techniques, state of the art Information Technology, improved precision guided munitions, and lasers. According to an Australian expert, "we will see increasing sophistication, not only of the platforms, the ships, tanks and aircraft, but of the weapon systems that go with them."

The 9/11 attacks and the creation of US led coalition against terrorism provided the rationale for lifting arms embargoes and relaxing arms export policies on more advanced weapon systems as a reward to countries for their participation.

This applied to the Middle East, South Asia, and also in Southeast Asia e.g. Indonesia. The restrictions on military co-operation between Jakarta and Washington (developed between 1994 and 2000) have been under pressure ever since. Likewise the Philippines has received 100 million US$ in military assistance, and has allowed the intervention of US Special Forces in Mindanao.

An additional factor for further militarisation in the region is Missile proliferation and the re-emergence of the US Star Wars programme - pushing military budgets ever higher.

According to John Chipman, Director of the International Institute for Strategic Studies in London, " The nature of missile proliferation in the region holds in prospect the kind of arms race that was not seen in the first half of the 1990s"

Defence Industry in East and Southeast Asia

The economic crisis of 1997 did change the picture of the defence industry in Asia. Domestic defence industries in Southeast

Asia are opening their firms to foreign investment to build equity and market links with Western nations for capital, technology and markets. Malaysia recently indicated that it wants to become a regional hub to help international defence firms to penetrate Asian markets and most of the ASEAN defence industries are eager to find a foreign partner to attract market access as well as capital.

This path is also followed by South Korea. The French Thales company has a joint venture with Samsung. Taiwan wants to build the submarines offered by the US in 2001 at the China Shipbuilding Corp. as well as import the technology from abroad. All this is underlining dependence on Western funds and weapon technology, developed with large sums on Research & Development programmes (R&D) -estimated at US$ 39.3 billion in the US and at US$ 9.1 billion in Europe annually.

Singapore Technologies follows another route similar to what Western firms do - buying what it needs mainly in the US.

This excludes the real state-of-the-art technology because this is prevented from foreign participation even by key allies. Of the six ASEAN countries which are producing small arms at home, only Singapore Technologies has a sound economic policy and export record. It exported ordnance, machine guns and assault rifles to a wide range of regions of tension. Other countries produce arms against higher market prices - which has more to do with national pride than with sound economics and the rule of the market.

The Chinese defence industry still produces obsolete weapon systems. It is not yet able to start the reorganisation process demanded to generate the capacity needed for the technological advanced weapon systems which the Chinese military want to possess. There has been little change in the Japanese weapons industry. However, as a result of the economic recession the Japanese car industry was opened up to foreign investment. Renault took this opportunity and its investment in Nissan resulted in the sale of the military division of Nissan Motor Corp. to Ishikawajima-Harima Heavy Industries. This reflects the imperative to keep arms production in Japanese hands.

GATHERING THE FACTS ON THE SMALL ARMS TRADE

In late 1997, following the Oslo conference that drafted the treaty against anti-personnel landmines, many NGOs and governments began pressing for more public attention to the devastation wrought by the worldwide sale and distribution of light arms–weapons that can be carried by a person–such as assault rifles, mortars, and grenades. Such arms are believed to be responsible for the vast majority of combat deaths, including many tens of thousands of civilian deaths annually. Even after conflicts end, demobilization and reconciliation efforts are frustrated by the over-supply of these inexpensive weapons, which often flow into criminal hands.

Among the governmental and non-governmental initiatives at the time, in late December 1997, on the first anniversary of the murder of Red Cross/Red Crescent workers in Chechnya, PRIO and three other organizations in Oslo–Norwegian Red Cross, Norwegian Church Aid and the Norwegian Institute of International Affairs–banded together to form the Norwegian Initiative on Small Arms Transfers (NISAT). The database proposal here is a central part of NISAT's activities.

Need for the Project

In the past few years, the European Union, OSCE, Organization of American States, Organization of African Unity, Economic Community of West African States, and the South African Development Community all took up some aspect of small arms control. Almost every part of the UN engaged the topic, including—increasingly—the Security Council. Modeled on a 1997 OAS treaty, the UN in Vienna began negotiation of a global protocol against firearms trafficking in 1999. In addition, the UN General Assembly voted in 1999 to hold a United Nations conference in 2001 on the illicit arms trade "in all its dimensions."

Despite this high level of engagement by governments and NGOs, the knowledge base on which these efforts rest is extremely thin. There are enormous gaps in the factual record on arms production and transfers. The lack of focused research in this area leaves open fundamental questions such as whether the legal or the illegal arms trade is the leading source of supply, and which states are the largest legal exporters of small arms.

Approximately 70 states produce small arms and/or ammunition. Some production enterprises are state-owned (usually military armories), and some are private companies. From the existing reference works,

- it is not difficult to know what types of small arms the major producer states manufacture;
- it is much harder to determine production quantities; and
- it is nearly impossible to know where weapons are being exported.

The standard sources of data on the international arms trade–SIPRI, the UN Register of Conventional Arms, *World Military Expenditures and Arms Transfers*–do not include information on small arms shipments. Few governments provide information to their parliaments on major weapons exports they have approved, and even fewer on their small arms trade. An exception to the prevailing pattern of secrecy is the US government. Since 1997, the United States openly reports in a highly specific manner all of its small arms shipments and export license approvals (with the notable exception of covert government-run arms supply, like the Iran-contra operation). Other states that have recently begun to provide more detailed public reports on their arms exports (including small arms shipments) are Belgium, Canada, the Netherlands, Norway, South Africa, Sweden and the United Kingdom. These are the eight leaders in transparency, on which the database will first concentrate in 2000-2001.

Despite this improvement in transparency, there is a need to organize the newly available data. In the above eight and other countries, the relevant information is scattered across many agencies and departments–in shipping documents at customs offices, judicial records, police records, and documents in the foreign, defense and trade ministries. No one is currently pulling this information together systematically, translating it, or presenting it to the international community in a readily useable format. That is what the database project will do.

The Need for Transparency

The information included in the database will serve as a template for the kind of governmental transparency that we will encourage the Norwegian Foreign Ministry to press for through its diplomatic contacts and on the international stage. In addition, we hope the database itself will encourage greater openness on the part of some governments, when they see the amount and types of information that the United States and – to a lesser degree – some others already make public without adverse effect. Increased transparency and organization of the available data will also improve the ability of governments to verify the appropriate end-uses and end-users of weapons exports they are authorizing. It will allow the non-governmental community, as well as national legislatures, to play an important role in aiding governments' efforts to curb diversion of these arms by providing oversight through research, questioning and reporting. Such information is also important for the safety of aid and relief workers operating in a region where a sudden influx of guns has occurred or is anticipated.

Increased openness about weapons shipments could serve as a confidence building measure among forces within a state, or states in a region, potentially heading off some purchases spurred by 'fear of the unknown'. Finally, such information will greatly facilitate formal disarmament activities, by providing some baseline information about arms stocks and supply in the state or region.

How the Project Addresses These Needs

The centerpiece of this proposal is an on-line database of small arms production and transfers. The database addresses the need for better information on three levels:

- it provides a composite picture of the small arms trade by collecting, translating and organizing the hard-to-find data;
- it interlinks policy-relevant information so as to provide both governments and activist organizations a stronger base for argumentation, strategy and agreement on common norms; and
- it demonstrates the positive aspects of transparency.

The database will eventually contain information on virtually every country of the world. It will be a public resource, accessible to all Internet users. We believe that the database will yield substantial results within one year of full funding, and if so we are committed to further developing and sustaining the initiative for as long as small arms control measures are required. As more governments provide public information about their light weapons shipments, the resource will grow in value (in terms of providing a fuller picture of the dynamics of the arms market).

NUCLEAR STATES IN CONFLICT : INDIA AND PAKISTAN

When the British withdrew from the Indian subcontinent after the second world war, it was divided, primarily on religious grounds, into the two states of India and Pakistan. At that time Kashmir was included in India, but the issue of which state it should belong to has been contested ever since, largely because Kashmir's population is predominantly Muslim. In 1947 a United Nations resolution called for a referendum in Kashmir to settle the issue on the basis of what the people wanted. It was, however never carried out and it is generally assumed that the reason for this is because the Indian government feared the popular vote would support unification with Pakistan on religious grounds. Many in Kashmir campaign for independence, a position that neither India nor Pakistan supports.

Around 30,000 people have died in Kashmir in the last 11 years. What happens in Kashmir is at the heart of the continuing tension between India and Pakistan. The possibility of the world's first direct war between two nuclear-armed states occurring is very real. The history of the conflict over Kashmir is well documented with three India/Pakistan wars taking place since 1947. But this time it would be with both sides having access to nuclear weapons. Since the attack on the Indian Parliament building in December 2001, the tension and rhetoric have grown considerably. India accused Pakistan of supporting terrorist groups. Pakistan, in turn, pledges its support for Kashmiri freedom fighters. One state's terrorist is another's freedom fighter. Since the attack in December, Pakistan has arrested around 1500 'militants' and banned five groups, two said to be sectarian, one pro-Taliban and two who have been fighting Indian rule in Kashmir. However, Gen Musharraf has pledged continued support for Kashmir.

Many people living along the border close to Kashmir have fled the area due to the large military presence being built up by both sides. From the end of 2001 there were clashes virtually every night in that border region, with sometimes one or two people being shot. There are claims that large numbers of military silos have been destroyed. In an atmosphere of increased tension and sabre-rattling rhetoric on both sides, this led to the situation in May 2002 where upwards of a million troops were gathered near the border. Any mistake or small incident runs the risk of setting off something far, far worse.

Nuclear Numbers

Estimates on actual warhead numbers vary wildly with reports that India has anywhere between 50-150 warheads and Pakistan 10-100. There is a bit more clarity, however, regarding the missile systems that would deliver them.

India:

Agni (Intermediate Range Ballistic Missile), nuclear capable and tested.

Range: 1,500 miles.

Could reach Karachi in about 14 minutes.

Prithvi (Surface to Surface Missile), nuclear capable and deployed.

Range: 90-220 miles.

Could reach Islamabad or Lahore within three minutes.

Trishul (Surface to Surface Missile), nuclear capable.

Range: 6 miles.

Pakistan:

Ghauri (Intermediate Range Ballistic Missile), nuclear capable in production.

Range: 930 miles

Could reach Bombay in 10 minutes.

One medium-range and one short-range missile, both nuclear capable, were tested in May 2002.

The Current Situation

All this, of course, is fuelled by the continuing rhetoric on both sides. Officials in both countries claimed that they would not use nuclear weapons first, but they seem remarkably keen to use them second. Given the proximity of the two states, it is clear that millions of their own people would die along with millions of their nearest neighbours. India has said that it would not use nuclear weapons first, while Pakistan has clearly stated that it would. Whilst a 'no first use' policy is an important step towards disarmament, it is all too often used as an excuse to build a large 'second use' capacity. Eventually, of course, the 'second use' becomes indistinguishable from the 'first use'. As the tension mounts, the temptation grows to get your retaliation in first.

But what are the immediate reasons for the current increasing tension and the risk of war? India appears to be escalating events but its argument is that it is following the lead of the US and the west by zero tolerance of terrorist attacks. It has identified what it sees as terrorists being harboured by another state so it threatens military retaliation.

Both sides have had internal problems as well. In Pakistan, Musharraf has been promising a democratic election ever since the army took control, but there has been only a referendum. Though it was boycotted by many political parties, Musharraf claimed it as a mandate for him to continue. Meanwhile in India, the ruling BJP has lost every state election for over a year, so now uses the well-known tactic of uniting the country against an outside 'threat'. Whatever the reasons for the tensions, the crucial aim is to avoid the devastation of nuclear war.

The British Prime Minister, Tony Blair, visited the region in January 2002 to try to persuade both sides that a war was not a good idea. This took place against the background of the bombing in Afghanistan, in which Britain was an enthusiastic participant. His approach raised concerns about Western hypocrisy, as if war is fine for some countries but not others. The sincerity of Blair's mission was also in question after it transpired that his plea for peace preceded two British trade missions to Delhi in February, both designed to sell weapons to India. Defexpo is an arms fair whose promotional material pushes the weaponry on sale, with everything from small arms to missile systems. India and Pakistan have long been valuable markets for British arms manufacturers. So this arms fair, combined with the resumption of arms sales to Pakistan, as a result of its support for the war in Afghanistan, means that Britain will be arming both sides in any future war. This is, of course, not unique. A similar thing happened during the Iraq-Iran war.

So, what's the answer? The situation in south Asia shows the importance of nuclear disarmament. A war even with conventional weapons would be an appalling waste of life. But this would be turned into a complete disaster on an unimaginable scale if nuclear weapons were used. In the short term there must be more diplomatic language and there must be proper international negotiations at the UN to resolve the problem of Kashmir.

Our own politicians could do more to help. How can the British Government's attempts to calm the situation be taken seriously when the Defence Minister, Geoff Hoon, appears on television saying that he would use nuclear weapons against any state if necessary?

In the long term, the declared nuclear weapon states (NWS)-US, UK, France, Russia and China-must carry out their obligations under the nuclear Non-Proliferation Treaty (NPT) and get rid of their nuclear weapons. The NPT was drawn up in 1968, giving the definition of a NWS as one that tested nuclear weapons before then.

Because India was preparing its nuclear programme at that time, it would not sign. Because India would not sign, neither would Pakistan. Therefore, they cannot sign the NPT as NWS and, since the nuclear testing by both sides in 1998, they cannot sign as non-nuclear weapon states. The NWS made statements at the time of the tests saying how appalled they were at this development. But after 11 September, the US lifted sanctions imposed on both sides, in order to boost its coalition in the 'War on Terrorism'.

If the NWS put the words of the NPT into action, they would be in a position to push India and Pakistan to sign the NPT themselves. After all, part of the excuse given by India and Pakistan for the 1998 nuclear tests was that those nuclear weapon states had done nothing about their NPT commitments, so if nuclear weapons were good enough for them...

Both sides need to be persuaded that nuclear weapons make the world a more dangerous, not a safer, place and to take a step back and realise that peaceful resolutions to conflict are the best way forward. This should happen through the UN. But the UN also needs to look at the continuing nuclear policies of the NWS.

There are peace activists in both India and Pakistan working hard to get their views across. Their work has been particularly difficult since the nuclear tests carried out by both countries in 1998. They have the entire might of the government and military propaganda machine ranged against them. We should do all we can to support them.

5

Conventional Operations under Nuclear Overhang in South Asia

NUCLEAR WEAPONS NOT FOR WAR

"Nuclear weapons are not for war fighting. Let's be quite clear on it," Singh said Jan 15 on the sidelines of the Army Day parade when asked about the nuclear postures and arsenals of Pakistan and China. "They've got a strategic significance and that's where it should end. Me and my army are not bothered about who has nuclear weapons. We have our task cut out and we will progress along that," he said. India maintains a credible minimum deterrence and its nuclear doctrine consists of, among other things, No First Use (NFU) as a matter of policy. Gen Singh's comments came a day before India hosts the meeting of officials of the Nuclear Security Summit that will focus on issues relating to nuclear terrorism and the safety of atomic materials and facilities.

Artillery Modernisation is Gathering Momentum

After a long spell of keeping the power dry, action on modernization of the Indian artillery is livening up once again. Since January 2008, the Ministry of Defence has issued three global tenders for 155MM howitzers for the mountains, the plains and self-propelled guns for the deserts. Summer and winter trials are expected to be held over the next year one year and, red tape permitting contracts may be awarded as early as in the first half of 2010. Artillery firepower had paved the way for victory during

Kargil conflict. Despite, the lessons learnt in Kargil, modernization of artillery has continued to lag behind.

The last major acquisition of towed gun-howitzers was that of about 400 pieces of 39 calibre-155mm FH-778 Howitzers from Bofors of Sweden in the mid 1980s. This gun had proved its mettle in the Kargil conflict. Just when a contractor for 120 tracked and 180 wheeled self-propelled (SP) 155mm guns was about to be concluded after years of protracted trials, South African arms manufacturer Denel, a leading contender for the contract, was alleged to have been involved in corruption scam in an earlier deal for Anti-Material Rifles (AMRs). The other two howitzers in contention, Soltam of Israel and BAE systems (which own Bofors of Sweden) did not meet the laid down criteria and the Army HQ recommended fresh trials. This set the programme back at least three to four years. A key issue was that the howitzers that had been offered were technology demonstration models and not guns that were in actual service with the home country armies. The probability of the next conventional war breaking out in the mountains is far higher than that of a war in the plains.

With this in view, the artillery recently conceptualised a requirement for a light-weight towed howitzer of 155mm calibre for employment in the mountains. Neither the present Bofors howitzer nor its 52-calibre replacement will be capable of effective operations in the mountains. A light-weight 45-calibre 155mm howitzer weighing less than 5,000 kg, with a light but adequately powered prime mover, is ideal for the mountains. The gun-train should be capable of negotiating sharp road bends without the need to unhook the gun from the prime mover. The two British 45-calibre 155mm howitzers that competed for the US contract for a similar howitzer some years ago – the UFH (Ultralightweight Field Howitzer) and the LTH (Light-weight Towed Howitzer) – or others that have now been developed could be considered for licensed production with transfer of technology. In January 2008, the MoD floated a Request for Proposal (RfP) for 140 pieces of ultra-light 39 calibre 155mm towed howitzers for use by the Indian Army's mountain formations. Presumably, these will also be employed by its rapid reaction divisions – as and when these are raised – as these howitzers will be easy to transport by air. 140 howitzers will be adequate to equip seven medium artillery regiments and will cost approximately ₹ 3,000 crore.

The RfP had been reportedly issued to UK's BAE Systems (which now owns Bofors), for the M777 howitzer claimed to be the lightest in the world at under 4,220 kg, and to Singapore Technologies for the Pegasus SLWH, also an excellent gun. India has floated a global tender for the purchase of 400 155mm towed artillery guns for the Army, to be followed by indigenous manufacture of another 1,100 howitzers, in a project worth a whopping ₹ 8,000 crore. The RFP was issued to eight prospective bidders including BAE Systems, General Dynamics, Nexter (France), Rhinemetall (Germany) and Samsung (South Korea). An RfP has also been issued for 180 wheeled self-propelled guns for around ₹ 4,700 crore for employment by mechanised forces in the plains and semi-desert sectors.

Since the Bofors 155mm Howitzer was introduced into service, the indigenously designed and manufactured 105 mm Indian Field Gun (IFG) and its (not so) light version, the Light Field Gun (LFG), have joined the 75/24 Indian Mountain Gun, the 100mm Russian field gun and the 122mm Russian howitzer on the obsolescence list. Approximately 180 pieces of 130mm M46 Russian medium guns have been successfully "up-gunned" to 155mm calibre with ordnance supplied by Soltam of Israel. The new barrel length of 45 calibre has enhanced the range of the gun to about 40 km with extended range ammunition. A contract for the acquisition of two regiments of the 12-tube, 300mm Smerch multi-barrel rocket launcher (MBRL) system with 90 km range was reported to have been signed with Russia's Rosoboronexport in early-2006.

This will be a major boost for the long-range.repower capabilities of the army. If this weapon system had been available during the Kargil con.ict, Pakistan's brigade HQ and forward airfield at Skardu and other targets deep inside POK could have been hit with impunity. Extended range (ER) rockets are being introduced for the 122 mm Grad MBRL that has been in service for over three decades. The ER rockets will enhance the weapon system's range from 22 to about 40 km. A ₹ 5,000 crore contract has also been signed for the serial production of the Pinaka MBRL weapon system, another DRDO project plagued by time delays and completed with help from Larsen and Toubro and the Tatas. And it has now a precision capability to one metre. Counter-bombardment (US term counter-.re) capability is also being upgraded, but at a slow pace.

At least about 40 to 50 Weapon Locating Radars (WLRs) are required for effective counter-bombardment, especially in the plains, and only a dozen have been procured so far. In addition to the 12 AN-TPQ 37 Fire.nder WLRs acquired from US military technology leader Raytheon, under a 2002 contract worth US $200 million, Bharat Electronics Limited is assembling 28 WLRs. These radars will be based on both indigenous and imported components and have been approved for induction into service after extensive tests.

The radar is expected to match the capabilities of the Firender system and will have a detection range of about 40 km. The chassis is Tatra, made indigenously by BEML The modernisation plan of tube artillery alone is likely to cost ₹ 13,000 crores, or USD 3 billion-plus, going possibly to $ 4 billion. The major acquisitions will be of the initial lots of 400 towed howitzers of 155mm calibre, with a barrel length of 52 calibre, costing about ₹ 4,000 crore, 140 ultra-light weight 155mm towed howitzers, with a barrel length of 45 calibre, costing ₹ 3,000 crore and 180 SP 155mm howitzers costing ₹ 5,000 crore. The "Shakti" project for a command and control system for the artillery, called Artillery Combat Command and Control System (ACCCS), has reached the stage of maturity and is now being fielded up to the regimental level. The BrahMos supersonic cruise missile (Mach 2.8 to 3.0), with a precision strike capability, very high kill energy and range of 290 km, was inducted into the army in July 2007.

It is a versatile missile that can be launched from TATRA mobile launchers and silos on land, aircraft and ships and, perhaps in future, also from submarines. Fifty BrahMos missiles are expected to be produced every year for the Army, and further development towards a Block II version to increase its strike range and lethality. BrahMos Aerospace has orders worth ₹ 3,500 crore from the Indian Army and the Navy, with the latter having opted for the anti-ship as well as the land attack cruise missile (LACM) versions. These terrain hugging missiles are virtually immune to counter measures due to their high speed and very low radar cross section and are far superior to subsonic cruise missiles like Pakistan's Babur.

Chile, Kuwait, Malaysia and South Africa have shown interest in acquiring this missile. It is often not realised that the Regiment of Artillery of the Indian Army is also its strategic arm as it mans the nuclear-tipped Prithvi, Agni-I and Agni-II ballistic missiles and will soon be equipped with the Agni-III. Surely when the Surya project is completed and India gets its first ICBM, the honour of manning that too is likely to go to the Gunners.

As a fighting arm that straddles the operational scenario from the tactical to the strategic, and as an arm that holds the bulk of the Indian Army's surveillance and target acquisition equipment, the Regiment of Artillery is a force to reckon with – a force that will contribute extensively to guiding the manner in which the next conventional war will be prosecuted and how victory will be measured. Hence, it is in the national interest to ensure that that the modernisation of the artillery proceeds apace without let or hindrance.

DEALING WITH TWO FRONTS NEEDS MATCHING CAPABILITIES

Given the known lacuna in higher military management in India of lack of a Chief of Defence Staff (CDS), coping with this imperative is difficult. The assumption is that a CDS could help resolve any inter-service matters. However, if Clausewitz's principle precept that if the nature of the conflict being embarked upon is done correctly, then this problem is reduced considerably.

At the outset, it must be pointed out also that India wants and needs peace for its own economic development. Shiv Shankar Menon, as Foreign Secretary, told a select gathering at the Institute for Defence Studies and Analyses (IDSA) that "peace within and around India is imperative for India's own development and that of the countries around it for everyone's benefit." But that unfortunately is not a view shared particularly in Islamabad which attacks India through proxy and terrorism. In the first, the outbreak of conflict in the immediate aftermath of another 26/11-type attack may be with the aim of inflicting decisive punishment on the adversary. In such a case the weight of the effort will be with the Air Force launching 'surgical strikes'.

The Army in such a case would posture for deterrence purposes, so as to preclude escalation. To this end, a repeat of the mobilisation like Op Parakram would not be required. However, the Army may make precautionary troop inductions into vulnerable areas so as not to lose them to enemy pre-emption. Air action will be to reinforce a diplomatic offensive to coerce Pakistan to finally acceding to India's long standing demand of an about-turn on its policy of supporting terrorists as 'strategic assets'.

In fact, even foreign strategists say that it is time that India made it clear that 'Enough is Enough.' The Second scenario could involve resorting to pre-emption as part of policy of active defence emanating from a deliberate decision taken at the highest level. This may be a considered response to prior provocative 'Kargils' and '26/11s'.

The scenario's probability increases in case of any implosion in Pakistani polity resulting in the seizure of power by religious extremists. In such a case, the military objectives of the three Services in the war effort acquire significance. The respective positions of the Air Force and the Army, on occasion at variance, have been reflected in many papers written on the subject since early last decade.

The general consensus is that the lead service in the various phases of the conflict may shift depending on the conflict circumstances. In the early stage, the Air Force taking advantage of its flexibility would be the lead Service, as it is only an air force which can take the battle to an enemy territory or an area of hostilties. The Army and Navy would chip in with offensive forces immediately available while the remainder is mobilised. The Army's early offensives being launched under the air cover should be adequate. With additional resources becoming available to support the Indian Air Force (IAF), it would also be possible for it to address its own and Army's concerns simultaneously. The Navy would mount pressure in the Arabian Sea to address Pakistan's economy, war potential in terms access to fuel and bring about the incidental political effect of disruption of life in its largest city. The Army promises to be off-theblocks in double quick time in its Cold Start doctrine as reported in a recent newspaper report: 'The (Cold Start) plan now is to launch selfcontained and highly-mobile 'battle groups', with Russian-origin T-90S tanks and upgraded T-72 M1 tanks at their core, adequately backed by air cover and artillery fire assaults, for rapid thrusts into enemy territory within 96 hours.'

The Air Force's doctrine is known to have been formed by study of the emerging pattern of war over the past two decades. Therefore, gaining air dominance along with destruction of enemy infrastructure, particularly of military significance such as transport, communication and power, would be its primary objective in the opening phases. Demands of net-centric and information war, where India has made considerable progress, would be fulfilled in a tri-service offensive in respective domains. IAF has quietly worked for the past few years to achieve air dominance capability.

The third scenario is one that was averred to by the Army Chief as a 'two- front' one. The mediainduced controversy around this misses the point that this has been a preoccupation with the Army dating to the Thorat report on organising defences on the China front of the 1950s.

It was central to the defining engagement in India's civil-military relations in which the political head deferred to General Sam Manekshaw's persuasive case in avoiding a two-front situation by attempting to liberate East Pakistan while the passes towards China were open. In the mid-1990s also, the threat was acknowledged by one of India's leading defence analysts, Air Commodore Jasjit Singh, Director IDSA, who had advised in the context of the times of straitened financial circumstance that China be managed till the capability to cope is built up. Anticipating the demands of a 'twofront' situation, capabilities are, if slowly but steadily, being put in place.

But a lot needs to be done in double quick time if this two-front doctrine is to become credible to our competitors and even likely allies. And that means building up strength dissipated after 1989 following allegations of corruption in Bofors gun acquisition. The major difference in this conflict scenario is that the national effort would have to be of a higher order. This would require recourse to the Blue Book, which was avoided even during Op Parakram. So as to prevent simultaneous strain on two fronts, a call by the political head informed by the military-strategic perspective would need to be taken early. Sticking with the choice thereafter would fulfil the requirement of selection and maintenance of aim, the foremost principles of war. The resulting sequencing of effort would help increase the military weight being brought to bear. The lessons from the two World Wars may be worth a recall on this score. The Germans, the British and the US had to make a grand strategic decision early on in the war. The failure of the Germans to stick with their decision, due to leadership and organisational deficiencies of Hitler and his Reich, led in substantial measure to their loss. The nuclear overhang is now a permanent presence in South Asia.

While in Scenario One, it does not come to the fore, it serves as a backdrop to Scenario Two. Every effort of Pakistan would be stay India's conventional hand through foregrounding its nuclear card. As earlier in Op Parakram with posturing in relation to strike corps, the conflict will throw up new lessons in nuclear signaling for their exists no precedence yet of a wider, yet limited, conflict between two nuclear states. The earlier such episodes along the Ussuri and at Kargil are instructive, but not very much so. The third scenario would require a deliberate effort at decreasing the visibility of the nuclear card even as it is not hobbled. The Chief's reference to 'two-front' possibilities has only and actually served a purpose in initiating this discussion.

Building Capabilities

But then it is the delays in building up of capabilities all across the Services which would have a telling effect on realisation of both the single front or two-front scenarios. The Army continues to suffer from delays especially in artillery modernisation and to an extent in armour modernisation. Acquisition of network centric capabilities in the Army has also not kept pace. Since January 2008, the Ministry of Defence has issued three global tenders for 155MM howitzers for the mountains, the plains and self-propelled guns for the deserts. Summer and winter trials were expected to be completed last year but they are still to commence. It was hoped that with commercial negotiations proceeding smoothly, contract/s could have been completed by the first half of 2010.

The artillery modernization includes off-the-shelf purchase of 200 155mm/52-calibre mounted gun systems to be followed by indigenous manufacture of another 614 such howitzers under transfer of technology (ToT). The 17-tonne motorized howitzers will arm 40 regiments. Another major project includes the purchase of 100 155mm/52-calibre self-propelled tracked guns for five artillery regiments. India is also looking to finalize the ₹ 8,000 crores project to buy 400 155mm/52-calibre towed artillery guns, which is to be followed by indigenous manufacture of another 1,180 howitzers. The major contenders are the BAE Systems, ST Kinetics of Singapore and Israeli Soltam. However, the bottlenecks in procurement may not be cleared even by the new procedure promulgated in 2009.

Another negative feature of procurement process has been the inordinate delay in acquisition through Fast Track Procedure (FTP). This was introduced for the first time in DPP-2002 to meet the urgent requirements emanating from operational imperatives. Under FTP, the stages of procurement like issue of Request for Proposal (RFP), technical evaluation and trial evaluation were to be skipped to provide a tested and established product. A system under this procedure was to be provided within the maximum time limit of 12 months. But a performance audit of Army has revealed that at least in eight cases, it has taken much more time than mandated. For instance, weapons and equipment for Para Security Forces, the demand for which was initiated in September 2003 under FTP, took almost 29 months to sign the contract for the same in February 2006.

Similarly, Electronic Warfare System for the Army approved in the wake of Kargil conflict took 75 months for the signing of contract under FTP. In case of acquisition of Extended Range Rockets it took over 40 months for the FTP to be completed. In the case of Remotely Operated Vehicle, Thermal Imaging Stand Alone Sights for T-72 tanks and UAVs purchased through FTP, the CAG's audit report has pointed out that there was no need to adopt the FTP, and that normal procedure would have sufficed. The need for acquisition of these items existed since long and these could have been procured without resorting to FTP. UAVs have been under indigenous development since the 1990's but have had to be imported by the three Services from Israel since 1996.

FTP not only compromised on competitiveness but in the instant case, failed the intended purpose of acquiring the capability within the shortest possible time. The new DPP-2006 and 2008, which has been modified again in November 2009, mandates that the application of FTP will be approved by the Defence Acquisition Council (DAC) and that contract should be signed within five months of intimation and delivery should be completed within three to 12 months.

Hopefully, with these timelines, FTP would live up to its terminology and fulfill the purpose of its formulation. Some of the ills pointed out by the Comptroller and Auditor General in our procurement system, especially in case of the Naval equipment, are illustrative of the lack of capacities and capabilities for forging a modern force required to deal with a two front situation. CAG has noted that "the objective of inducting an aircraft carrier – Gorshkov – in time to fill the gap in Indian Navy has not been achieved. The cost of acquisition has more than doubled to USD 2.3 billion in four years. At best, the Indian Navy would be acquiring, belatedly, a second-hand ship with a limited life span by paying significantly more than what it would have paid for new ship."

Further, despite Indian Navy's depleting force level, the Ministry of Defence took nine years to conclude a contract for the construction of six submarines. The inordinate delay led to enormous increase in the project cost to the extent of ₹. 2,838 crore. And perhaps more. The procurement procedure has had problems and the technical evaluation conducted for a particular type of submarine including the missile to be fitted on-board was not comprehensive and reportedly "biased" in favour of the vendor. Contractual provisions have resulted in undue financial advantage to the vendor to the minimum extent of Euro 58.20 million (Rs. 349 crore) besides other unquantifiable benefits. In addition, "five radars imported at a cost of ₹ 24.88 crore could not be installed for more than three to five years after their acquisition. In the process the radars have not only lost 50 per cent of their life but also remained unavailable for operational purpose. The Navy failed to persuade a foreign firm to replace unsuitable items supplies.

As a result, the expenditure of ₹ 385 crore on their import was yet to yield any operational benefit to the Navy." Similarly, for the IAF the long pending acquisition of MMRCA and then bringing up the required strengths of number of Air Force squadrons to the sanctioned level will not be achieved in a hurry. Therefore the conclusion is inescapable that talking about two-front situations requires strong capabilities, inducted timely, clarity of purpose and a strong political leadership. So far diplomacy and wisdom have prevented the eventuality of a twofront scenario. But the geo-political and geo-strategic environment is under flux and the glacial pace of developing such force capabilities would leave gaping holes in our security shield. An extensive political-military interaction that this necessitates in peace needs now to be pursued.

SOUTH ASIA AND HORIZONTAL PROLIFERATION

As a starting point, it is helpful to focus on cases of horizontal proliferation elsewhere that are connected to South Asia. This includes potential WMD supply routes as well as entities that might be involved, some of whom may be operating outside state control. In particular, the focus is on connections between entities in Pakistan and proliferation dynamics in other regions. Three major issues need to be addressed-(i) the North Korean nuclear program, and in particular the impact of the October 2006 nuclear test on South Asia; (ii) the current state of the A.Q. Khan network and its implications for WMD supply trends; and (iii) proliferation links between South Asia and the Middle East.

The North Korean Nuclear Test and South Asia

As expected, North Korea's nuclear test put renewed focus on the dangers of nuclear proliferation, and policymakers in India assumed it would lead to more stringent criticism of its nuclear agreement with the United States. Indian experts expected the North Korean test to impact especially on any nuclear test-related provisions of the nuclear agreement with the United States. Consequently, New Delhi swiftly condemned the test and indirectly highlighted Islamabad's contribution to Pyongyang's nuclear test. Some Indian officials even stated that Pyongyang's illegal acquisition of nuclear technology would actually spur reluctant supplier countries (such as Australia) to legitimately sell nuclear fuel to India, especially since it would be used for civilian purposes.

On the other hand, Islamabad refuted any suggestion that the activities of the A.Q. Khan network had contributed to Pyongyang's test, stating that North Korea's nuclear program is based on plutonium while Pakistan relies on uranium. In this manner, both India and Pakistan tried to ensure that proliferation in South Asia was not equated with proliferation in Northeast Asia. To a certain extent, the Bush administration obliged the subcontinental nuclear powers, as senior officials dismissed any parallels between North Korea's path to nuclear weapons to those of India and Pakistan. However, while Pakistan denied any links to the test, it did not help Islamabad's case when Japanese sources stated that days before Pyongyang's test, several Pakistani nuclear technicians arrived in North Korea through China. This augmented the suspicions that Pakistani agencies may have had some role in the test, perhaps through data sharing before or after the explosion.

The A.Q. Khan Network and Proliferation Dynamics

The A.Q. Khan network, which provided nuclear assistance to North Korea and Iran, has represented the most serious proliferation problem in recent years. Since Khan's public confession in February 2004, the Musharraf regime has consistently asserted that this network was the work of a rogue scientist and that the Pakistani government and its military leaders were not involved in these activities. However, it is not clear to what extent this assertion is accurate. Analysts and officials in Pakistan as well as in the United States have expressed skepticism over Khan's confession as well as the implicit professed innocence of the Pakistani political and military establishment. A highly publicized report released in April 2007 by the London-based International Institute for Strategic Studies, also stated that individuals and entities involved in the network could still be dormant and can conceivably be reactivated in the future.

So far, Islamabad has refused to allow foreign interrogators to question Khan even though the U.S. government has regularly expressed dissatisfaction over information released by Pakistan. >Furthermore, most individuals connected to the network are still at large, including important figures such as B.S.A. Tahir, while others, such as Henk Slebos, have been given light sentences. Moreover, the Khan claimed in a signed statement that successive army chiefs in the 1990s (Generals Mirza Aslam Beg and Jehangir Karamat) had authorized the sales of nuclear technology. While this could be taken as Khan's attempts to remove the burden of guilt, it is true that the military was closely associated with the nuclear and missile programs. In fact, in 1990, Gen. Beg warned U.S. government officials that Pakistan would be forced to provide nuclear technology to Tehran if Washington did not offer support to Pakistan.

Other circumstantial evidence, such as visits by the Pakistani military leadership to North Korea throughout the nineties, suggests that there was a barter deal between Pyongyang and Islamabad (uranium enrichment technology in exchange for missiles). Additionally, in August 2005, Gen. Musharraf conceded that Khan had transferred centrifuge machines to North Korea through which uranium hexafluoride (which was also transferred) can be enriched for eventual processing into civilian reactors fuel or for military purposes.

Shipping out such large centrifuge machines without the military's knowledge would have been impossible. Therefore, it would have been highly unlikely that these activities were carried out without the military's acquiescence. On a side note, it is possible that Washington's attitude was colored by the need to retain

Islamabad's support in the anti-Taliban/Al Qaeda campaign in Afghanistan.

Additionally, for a country to acquire a nuclear delivery system (such as the No Dong missiles transferred to Pakistan), the decision-making process incorporates several factors, as well as the opinions of numerous government agencies to ensure compatibility among the various systems. It is therefore not very plausible that a nuclear-missile barter deal with such serious and risky international consequences could have been approved without cooperation from senior levels of the political-military establishment in Pakistan. The issue of the Pakistani military-scientific establishment's involvement (or endorsement) in the Khan's network activities is crucial due to its implications for contemporary proliferation routes and processes. If these elements within and outside Pakistan (including non-Pakistani nationals) and their methods and routes remain undiscovered, it has two broad consequences for proliferation in South Asia.

First, it allows Islamabad to potentially procure missile and nuclear technology in the future, in an attempt to catch up with India. In this regard, a Pakistani national, Mohammed Aslam, working at the Tabani Corporation's Moscow office, was named by the Russian government in 2006 as having attempted to acquire dual-use technology and other materials for Pakistan's nuclear and missile development programs. This example demonstrates that elements of the network are still active, though it is unclear if they are directly connected to Pakistani nuclear and missile development programs. Given Islamabad's need to construct a secure deterrent against India (especially long-range missiles that can reach southern and eastern India), it is possible that the above case is an instance of continuing efforts to exploit non-state networks to procure prohibited equipment. As one analyst noted, due to Pakistan's apparent inability to acquire nuclear weapons components legally, it is encouraged to look toward illegal sources. Furthermore, according to some experts, apart from Pakistan, other countries can easily utilize the same supply networks. The Iranian government has made use of these networks for its nuclear and missile programs. As the previously mentioned IISS report states, Tehran controls a clandestine nuclear materials network comparable to the one run by Khan, and in the past has procured technology from some of the same suppliers used by Khan. In context of nuclear proliferation networks, a further concern is that if North Korea dismantles its nuclear weapons program, it will create a potential source of unwanted nuclear materials in the process. Such discarded, but nevertheless lethal technology, could be bought by illegal nuclear supply entities that may or may not have had any connection to the Khan network.

Second, the continued existence of the kind of middlemen that the network generated increases the possibility of nuclear technology leakage out of Pakistan in the event of a coup or widespread instability from radical groups. Since 9/11, there have been periodic fears of internal upheavals in Pakistan, especially from groups linked to the Taliban. Recent reports have also stated that two nuclear scientists from the Pakistan Atomic Energy Commission (PAEC) were kidnapped by the Taliban in late 2006, and as of March 2007 remained in captivity in the Waziristan area. > Soon after that kidnapping, there was an aborted attempt to capture six more PAEC officials in the North West Frontier Province of Pakistan in January 2007. While it is not clear if the officials and scientists were targeted specifically because of their links to Pakistan's nuclear program, these incidents demonstrate the potential danger of non-state actors' participation in the illegal market in nuclear technology. In order to demonstrate to the international community that it is a responsible nuclear power, Islamabad has decided to set up a "Strategic Export Control Division" in its foreign ministry that will ostensibly prevent prohibited WMD-related technology from being exported. However, this does not necessarily address the problem of possible involvement of government entities and officials that have remained under the radar even after the network was uncovered. In general, the proliferation-related fear for U.S. policymakers is twofold-first, that nuclear technology could be transferred to a terrorist organization; and second, that the Musharraf regime could be overthrown, resulting in uncertainty for the counter-terrorism as well as nonproliferation campaigns.

The case of Pakistan demonstrates the difficulty that arises when nonproliferation goals collide with other strategic imperatives such as counter-terrorism. While the Khan network problem is one of the reasons why Washington has refused to offer a nuclear cooperation agreement to Pakistan, the perceived tilt toward India (through the Indo-U.S. nuclear agreement) can also be a reason why Washington has not pressured Islamabad any further on the A.Q. Khan issue. Nevertheless, in January 2007, in a proactive step, the U.S. Congress under the Democratic leadership passed the Nuclear Black Market Counter Terrorism Act, which authorizes the administration to implement "punitive actions" against states condoning or cooperating with entities actively engaged in nuclear proliferation.

INDIA - NUCLEAR NEIGHBOURHOOD: CHALLENGES FOR INDIA

An excellent civilian perspective on the aspect of Limited wars against a Nuclear backdrop. India is perhaps the only country that faces the challenges arising from having two nuclear neighbours, who closely cooperate with each others' nuclear programmes and who maintain adversarial relations with her. A nuclear-weapon enabled terrorist threat is supported by strong and consistent denials of culpability for any such 'non-state' attack and a reliance on its 'protector' and mentor, China, to handle the inevitable diplomatic furore that is bound to rise if the taboo on nuclear weapons is broken with however limited an application.

It would appear that Pakistan has adopted a policy of battlefield use of its nuclear weapons, a likely escalation of a conventional confrontation to a nuclear level, arrangements for rapid deployment which could entail pre-delegation to unit commanders in the event of a loss of communications, (which is what apparently happened at Salala recently when 24 Pakistani soldiers were killed in an ISAF air attack on two border posts). She asserts that there is a need to slightly tweak our nuclear doctrine; the objective would be not to change our No First Use policy, but to revert to the language of the Draft doctrine on the question of retaliatory strikes - these should be 'punitive' rather than 'massive' as now exists. Lastly, she makes the very bold assertion that in order to disillusion the adversary of our intent to retaliate, the control of the weapons should be placed squarely with the Strategic Forces Command. Recent developments in India's neighbourhood have led to an increase in the instability in the region with particular implications for India's security. Pakistan's foolhardiness - or as the Pakistanis view it, their boldness - in challenging the international community by deciding to not attend - and to not allow its surrogates, the Taliban - to attend the just concluded Bonn Conference on Afghanistan, in taking actions which could see a military confrontation with the US and the ISAF forces on its western border and when it is such a parlous situation at home, can only arise from their assurance that at least politically and diplomatically, if not militarily, they can depend on the support of China.

Despite India's own efforts to manage her prickly relations with China, such unqualified support of Pakistan, particularly in the military and nuclear areas, must inevitably raise concerns in India. India is perhaps the only country that faces - or has ever faced - the challenges arising from having two nuclear neighbours, who closely cooperate with each others' nuclear programmes and who maintain adversarial relations with her.

To be sure, during the Cold War, the Soviet Union faced several hostile nuclear neighbours, which were bound together in an alliance and from 1971, another nuclear neighbour that formed a formidable challenge to its security. China, too, till 1971 and for about a decade before that, faced both the United States and the Soviet Union in adversarial positions. It was in the context of the Cold War that theories of limited conventional wars under a nuclear overhang - usually on different continents - has been developed by scholars, mainly in the West. Whether such theories are applicable to the dual challenge facing India is a question that needs to be carefully considered.

Unique Scenario

The situation that India faces today is unique; firstly, it shares common and disputed borders with both hostile neighbours; China has, according to several knowledgeable commentators and intelligence sources (of the West) built-up Pakistan's nuclear arsenal almost from scratch - providing designs, material, including fissile material, technology, delivery vehicles (either directly or through North Korea) and even conducted a weapons test in 1990 on its Lop Nor Test site, for Pakistan. Today it is supplying reactors, which it claims will be under IAEA safeguards; but given the short shrift it has given the Nuclear Suppliers' Group, not to mention its obligations under the NPT in arriving at the agreement to do so, it is unlikely that the material from these reactors will remain for civilian purposes only.

Thirdly and most dangerously, Pakistan has been using its growing nuclear arsenal as an umbrella under which it appears to feel that it can use sub-conventional attacks against India with little or no danger of (conventional) retaliation. None of the above has been seriously disputed by either party; nor has the vague but ominous 'red lines' that Pakistan seems to have evolved regarding its stated doctrine of first use of nuclear weapons. It appears to have in mind the escalation of any conventional response from India to even an armed attack on Indian soil by its nationals, to a nuclear counter-response.

The theories of deterrence would seem to not be applicable in a situation if there is a 'failure of rationality' on one side. Of course, it could very well be that the intention is to indeed give an impression of irrationality, to act as a deterrent to any action on India's part for fear that Pakistan would react 'irrationally'. This stand, of what has been termed 'a nuclear-weapon enabled terrorist threat' is supported by strong and consistent denials of culpability for any such 'non-state' attack and a reliance on its 'protector' and mentor, China, to handle the inevitable diplomatic furore that is bound to rise if the taboo on nuclear weapons is broken with however limited an application. India's doctrine calls for 'massive retaliation' in the event of a nuclear first strike; that would entail attacking counter-value targets, which could include cities and other population centres.

There would inevitably be calls for restraint on India's part, despite the enormity of the action by Pakistan and there is also likely to be some domestic resistance to attacks on cities or towns.

In this, perhaps, worst-case but not improbable, scenario, what are India's options?

There are some facts which are needed to be factored in to any consideration of the issue

Difference between a 'declaratory' doctrine and an operational one; the latter can only be deduced from the information available on acquisitions and capabilities, statements of policy by albeit retired senior military men from Pakistan and such Western sources, presumably from intelligence inputs. On the basis of these, it would appear that Pakistan has adopted a policy of battlefield use of its nuclear weapons, a likely escalation of a conventional confrontation to a nuclear level, arrangements for rapid deployment which could entail predelegation to unit commanders in the event of a loss of communications, (which is what apparently happened at Salala recently when 24 Pakistani soldiers were killed in an ISAF air attack on two border posts)

Sino-Pak Nexus

Firstly, we need to take China's support of Pakistan for granted, even the use by the latter of non-state groups as a part of their foreign and security policy. This has been demonstrated repeatedly and not only in the UN Security Council, where China has blocked any forward movement on the naming of specific Pakistani nationals and sponsored groups as terrorists. Secondly, while the state of the internal instability in Pakistan is probably exaggerated in the media, Indian, Pakistani and the Western, there is no doubt that there is a considerable rise in religiosity with strong sectarian and intolerant strains in Pakistani society in general; this would have an inevitable impact on all state institutions, including the military. At the same time, the military has not yet abjured its support for specific non-state groups as 'assets' in the furtherance of its foreign policy objectives.

Some of the groups may well be out of control of the military, though there is little apparent effort to control them in any effective way, though some other groups, targeting the Pakistani state, are being attacked or negotiated with, according to press reports.

Thirdly, while like many other developing countries, Pakistan's economy is currently in a very fragile condition, the worsening of relations with the US may adversely affect the budgetary support that Pakistan has been used to receive - China usually restricts itself only to project and commodity aid and does not give budgetary support to any of its allies, however close.

Notwithstanding these developments, the ambitions of Pakistan's military remain vaulting. Given these facts, it is clear that the situation is such that in the event of any crisis, or with the intention of creating one, India could face nuclear threats at multiple levels from Pakistan - it is not unlikely that these would be supported by China, which, however, will ensure that it is not directly involved.

The Pakistani nuclear doctrine, at least our knowledge of it, is today based on an interview given by Lt General Khalid Kidwai (retd), Director General of Pakistan's Strategic Plans Division to Paolo Cotta-Rassmussen and Maurizio Martinelli published by Pugwash International in 2002. There is, however, as has been noted elsewhere, a difference between a 'declaratory' doctrine and an operational one; the latter can only be deduced from the information available on acquisitions and capabilities, statements of policy by albeit retired senior military men from Pakistan and such Western sources, presumably from intelligence inputs.

On the basis of these, it would appear that Pakistan has adopted a policy of battlefield use of its nuclear weapons, a likely escalation of a conventional confrontation to a nuclear level, arrangements for rapid deployment which could entail predelegation to unit commanders in the event of a loss of communications, (which is what apparently happened at Salala recently when 24 Pakistani soldiers were killed in an ISAF air attack on two border posts) and increasing risks of inadvertent or accidental launch. Ashley Tellis in his 2000 book on India's Emerging Nuclear Posture has written of the 'uncertainties' which arise from "The severe motivational and cognitive biases that have historically afflicted Pakistan's higher decision making institutions on matters of war and peace (which) raise fears about the prospect of extreme responses that might be precipitated in a crisis ... These failures of rationality ... could be compounded by exigencies of domestic politics, civil-military discord and biased and unreliable intelligence ... "This posture is one which appears to be based on the assumption that India will not permit the situation to escalate, by considering a limited and targeted use of, for example, air strikes.

Non-state Actors

At another level, non-state groups could be used either to provoke a military response from India, or, more dangerously, nuclear material could become available to these groups through theft or through insider linkages. The attack on Pakistan's Mehran naval base was apparently enabled by insider collusion. At the same time the already friable situation could be exacerbated to intolerable levels if the state itself, following the trends within Pakistani society, becomes a theocratic intolerant state, bent on the establishment of a Caliphate in the region. The military and non-state groups are certain to have been emboldened by India having been 'deterred' in 1999, following the Kargil attack, in 2001 after the attack on Parliament and Operation Parakram and more so, after 2008, after the attack on Mumbai.

Would India react differently in the event of another Mumbai-type attack? *There is a need to slightly tweak our nuclear doctrine; the objective would be not to change our No First Use policy, but to revert to the language of the Draft doctrine on the question of retaliatory strikes - these should be 'punitive' rather than 'massive' as now exists. Massive retaliation would imply counter-value strikes and would lead to incorrect assumptions on the part of the adversary, whereas a punitive strike would retain the flexibility of options. In addition, in order to disillusion the adversary of our intent to retaliate, the control of the weapons should be placed squarely with the Strategic Forces Command* There is no doubt that the current dialogue with Pakistan helps us to buy some time, though given the political instability in Pakistan and the split polity in India, the chances of it being sustainable or effective remain slight unless other signals are sent.

There is a need to use this time to formulate other tools to reinforce the message behind the talks; a need for example, to start serious discussions with Pakistan on nuclear doctrines. It will be more difficult to get this accepted by the Pakistanis, particularly as the Pakistani military is at the moment more preoccupied with consolidating its somewhat frayed image within the country and dealing with the immediate challenges of dealing with the US and Pakistan's ambitions in Afghanistan. Nonetheless this objective has to be followed with persistence and patience, with as much importance given to this objective as to our overall military preparedness. So far, there have been some discussions on nuclear CBMs with Pakistan, mainly at the Track II level, but they have been over-modest efforts and at the official level, the steps have been faltering and weak. Pakistan sees its nuclear weapons not only as essential to their security but as their 'crown jewels' almost as a symbol of their nationhood.

Without disputing their possession of these weapons, however, an increase in efforts to prevent any nuclear misadventure is urgent. At the same time, discussions on nuclear issues with China too, need to be started and again it will be a difficult task. The discussions need to be at high political levels or even with trusted back channels. Some Track II discussions have indeed taken place with China, but they remain sporadic and with little substance or follow-up.

Retribution

Within our own establishment, there is a need to slightly tweak our nuclear doctrine; the objective would be not to change our No First Use policy, but to revert to the language of the Draft doctrine on the question of retaliatory strikes - these should be 'punitive' rather than 'massive' as now exists. Massive retaliation would imply counter-value strikes and would lead to incorrect assumptions on the part of the adversary, whereas a punitive strike would retain the flexibility of options. In addition, in order to disillusion the adversary of our intent to retaliate, the control of the weapons should be placed squarely with the Strategic Forces Command.

The Pakistani and Chinese militaries have the 'advantage' of greater coherence and congruence in their weapons policies, as the military is in full control of the nuclear weapons programme, whereas our weapons remain under civil control even while the delivery vehicles may be with the military. *India is perhaps the only country that faces - or has ever faced - the challenges arising from having two nuclear neighbours, who closely cooperate with each others' nuclear programmes and who maintain adversarial relations with her.* To emphasise, these are signals to the adversary in this interim period, without any other change in our nuclear posture. There are bound to be many who will see this as too hawkish and too dangerous; they should then propose less dangerous methods of signalling. Others might see it as too little in terms of preparedness for retaliation, but the hope is to try and avoid the necessity of nuclear retaliation.

The ultimate objective must always be to ensure that the chances of adversarial nuclear incidents are minimised and that nuclear weapons are never actually used in a war. *The already friable situation could be exacerbated to intolerable levels if the state itself, following the trends within Pakistani society, becomes a theocratic intolerant state, bent on the establishment of a Caliphate in the region. The military and non-state groups are certain to have been emboldened by India having been 'deterred' in 1999, following the Kargil attack, in 2001 after the attack on Parliament and Operation Parakram and more so, after 2008, after the attack on Mumbai. Would India react differently in the event of another Mumbai-type attack?*

INDIA'S RESPONSE OPTIONS TO PAKISTANI NUCLEAR FIRST USE

In the event, India's conflict strategy for its western borders would unfold as per options selected. One among other options is possibly in accord with the much written about Cold Start doctrine. Nevertheless, the conflict strategy can be expected to be offensive, taking advantage of the changed mindset and organisations enabling this over the past decade. The services are conscious that these operations would be under the nuclear overhang. No doubt this would find reflection in the manner political aims are translated into strategic and in turn operational objectives. Reflection in the early part of last decade on Limited War doctrine indicates that proverbial nuclear thresholds would be respected. In effect Pakistan's nuclear deterrent would have worked but only partially. Its leveraging of the nuclear deterrent to deter conventional war would have failed.

But, the nuclear backdrop would help preserve it from any expansive Indian war aims. Since, as Peter Lavoy informs, Pakistan would largely rely on conventional forces to counter Indian offensives, the nuclear card would have political utility. Brandishing the same for nuclear signalling so as to bring war termination pressures from the international community can be expected. This may be in the form of rhetoric, nuclear tests or a demonstration strike. A hypothetical case of highly provocative nuclear first use with the purpose of nuclear signalling for war termination is defensive use on own territory against insignificant tactical targets.

A favoured example in strategic literature is a solitary nuclear strike on an advancing column in the desert. It has been estimated that such a strike would cause just a few Indian casualties. Such a strike would be twin edged for Pakistan. One is that it would breach the professed Indian nuclear threshold of 'any Indian casualties any where' resulting in 'assured retaliation' of proportions exacting 'unacceptable damage'. The second, in Pakistan's favour as intended, is in focussing international attention on to restricting the manner of Indian reaction. India's nuclear deterrent doctrine is explicit that the counter would be 'massive'. Since this is for deterrence, in case of deterrence breakdown, response strategy could well be different.

'Unacceptable damage' can be caused by less than 'massive' levels of nuclear retaliation. In the event, the political leadership would have its nuclear decision making informed by doctrine, but not restricted by it. In effect, nuclear employment doctrine may be different from nuclear deterrent doctrine. The latter is known, while the former is not known. India's conventional offensives are likely to exploit the existing space between sub-conventional and perceived nuclear thresholds. While Pakistan can be expected to self-servingly project these thresholds as 'low', a realistic appreciation may indicate that enough space exists for measured force application.

This being within the capability of Pakistani conventional counter action, risk of war escalation is minimised. Nevertheless, contingency planning being the measure of a professional military, India's counter options to Pakistani nuclear first use can be expected. This commentary makes some suggestions in this direction. Firstly, in the pre-conflict stage, India needs to make its military doctrine transparent. It needs to indicate a pronounced inclination towards the Limited War concept. This has not been explicitly spelt out thus far in the Army doctrine in the open domain. The Navy doctrine is somewhat hazy. It takes General or Total War as 'involving nearly all resources of the nation, with few, if any, restriction on the use of force, short of nuclear strike/retaliation.' Two problems arise. One is that this formulation appears to suggest that Total War aiming for 'annihilation or total subjugation of the opponent' can yet occur below the nuclear threshold. Second, there is no category in the 'Spectrum of Conflict' in the doctrine in which it accommodates nuclear use, since the definition of Total War recounted here seems to place it outside into some separate, undefined, category. The issue that arises is that minimalist resort to nuclear weapons such as in the example given does not automatically place the war into the Total War domain since 'annihilation' is not being sought. The overall impression is that the military is undecided to weigh in on the side of Limited War unambiguously.

It needs to do so in order to raise the nuclear threshold. Maintaining the threshold at a high level during conflict so as to gain military objectives without flirting with it requires explicitly conveying to Pakistan at the outset of the conflict through multiple channels that war aims do not seek regime change or state extinction. This would require not only information operations but also be conveyed by the threat perception in Pakistan stemming from its reading of troop deployment and dispositions. There is a paradox that requires to be lived with here. Operational transparency to indicate limited war aims is to the detriment of the heightened threat that serves to deter conventional conflict escalation. In case the enemy gets to know that limited aims are to be achieved, he can throw in much more than he otherwise would to deny these. But the problem of withholding from transparency is that in case the enemy is not able to match professions of limited war with actions on the ground, he may be inclined to a 'worst case' judgement. This builds in avoidable dynamism in lowering the nuclear threshold. In the hypothetical case of lower order nuclear first use, the first consideration for retaliation is consequences for political aims of the conflict.

The original limited political aim is threatened with expansion since nuclear weapons have been introduced into the conflict changing its nature and dimensions. In which case can original limited war aims be sustained? If not, is revision necessary? Such thinking needs be done prior. That an expanded nuclear war needs to be avoided is selfevident. This can at best be in order to degrade a continuing nuclear threat under the logic of 'limiting damage' (Hermann Kahn) that may be sustained in further nuclear exchanges. The logic informing 'massive' nuclear retaliation seems to be precisely this. Taking out enemy nuclear capability along with punishing it would preserve oneself from his counter strikes. Nevertheless, this is ruled out by the second strike capability available with Pakistan in terms of an expanded arsenal. Since both sides share a common interest in limiting damage, continuation of the nuclear threat would be dependent on the counter. Therefore, the considerations on the nature of the counter would need to factor in the implications of escalation. It being undesirable, retaliation would be designed not so much to punish but also to enable exchange termination. Doing so at the lowest levels of nuclear retaliation would place the onus of escalation on the enemy. Since the exchange can get out of hand and result in spasmic retaliation, in-conflict deterrence based on Schelling's concept of 'threat that leaves something to chance' is heightened. Such deterrence also exists to deter first use, but it is now more consequential since a nuclear war is an entirely new environment and would serve to focus minds more acutely on the threatening possibilities.

What then are Limiting Options?

Firstly, the mistaken impression that Indian resolve may be weak, needs to be dispelled in Pakistani thinking. The propensity towards this may be more in Pakistan corresponding to the levels of ideological penetration by extremism of the Establishment and the military mind there. The Army can generally be reckoned as a rational organisation and its nuclear decision making system more so. Transparency has been resorted to over the last decade by Pakistan to influence perceptions that its nuclear capability lacks safety and control. It has taken steps in streamlining systems and these contribute to rational decision making. Irrationality projected is for deterrence purposes. This circumstance lends itself to Indian planning for conventional war, albeit a limited one. However, in case a mistaken impression on Indian resolve were to inform Pakistani thinking then, the propensity to lower the nuclear threshold would be greater.

Therefore, either tests or better still a demonstration strike may both reinforce Indian resolve and impress Pakistani decision makers of its credibility. The action would require prior communication to Pakistan in order that it is not mistaken for a nuclear strike. Unstated possibilities this evokes would bring the international community to bear down on events compelling Pakistan to concede India's reasonable self-evidently demands without further 1 affray. Secondly, as discussed, nuclear first use by Pakistan may be with the political aim of conflict termination through influencing both Indian minds and the international community. Despite this intent and the low provocation levels of such a strike, this would place Pakistan inevitably and irreversibly on the political defensive. Nuclear resort may be sustainable in international law in the extreme case of threat to existence of the state. This would patently not be the case in light of broadcast limited war aims of India and the progress of the war. Therefore, India could profit politically from a measured response including a non-nuclear one. Such responses could be more violent conventional strikes against value targets of Pakistan that were originally kept off the scope of the war due to the intent of limitation.

These could include political and military leadership, symbolic targets such as politically significant structures, expanded infrastructure degradation and heightened attrition on conventional forces. The nuclear threshold having already been crossed, restrictions would no longer apply. Therefore, keeping going conventionally would enable greater attrition on the Pakistani state and it's military. This would have political dividend post war in that the military not only would be blamed for provoking the punishment but would be too weak to regain its political salience in internal politics. Indian restraint in contrast to military adventurism in Pakistan would heighten calls for accountability, both internally in Pakistan and externally in a war crimes court. Therefore, a better peace post-conflict is possible through negotiations with a civilian regime.

The point is that a non-nuclear counter deserves to be considered. Continuing restraint has advantages that current calls for scaling down Indian restraint and prudence seem to neglect. The counter argument would be that restraint at this stage of a war gone nuclear may give the impression of pusillanimity to the enemy and embolden further, possibly more provocative, strikes. This is based on the logic that deterrence requires capability, resolve and communication of possession of both to the enemy. While capability exists, resolve may require communication. This can only be through striking back, deterring him from further strikes and limiting damage thereby. It would be useful for in-conflict deterrence, broadcasting unambiguously worse to come in case of continuation of the exchange by Pakistan. Internally political pressures would only be satisfied by nuclear punishment for Pakistan's temerity.

The sustainability of the argument can best be seen in light of the changed conflict environment; one that has transited speedily from a limited war to a nuclear one, but has not acquired Total War portents. What would be the mental condition of decision makers in a nuclear war scenario? Would they be amenable to being deterred as this logic indicates or would they be emotionally so charged as to be incapable of the self-restraint on which deterrence is predicated? Here, an answer is not attempted, but it is suggested that any risk of the latter is enough to bring the non-nuclear response route back into the reckoning, particularly in case of militarily inconsequential, non-provocative lower order nuclear use by Pakistan. The promise of 'massive' nuclear retaliation may prove inadequate in staying Pakistani nuclear hand in face of Indian offensives. Inflicting 'unacceptable damage' may appear disproportionate to its leadership if in response to lower order nuclear first use. Therefore, nuclear retaliation could well be of quid pro quo or quid pro quo plus levels with damage not amounting to an 'unacceptable' order. Nevertheless, there is a case for considering the nonnuclear measures covered here since the advantage would be a better post conflict peace and at a lower cost.

INDIA AND PAKISTAN: ON THE NUCLEAR THRESHOLD

This briefing book contains material from the National Security Archive's project on U.S. policy toward South Asia, which is documenting nuclear developments in India and Pakistan from the 1950s to the present. The archive is collecting U.S. government records that illustrate American policies and perspectives. Information is being collected from the National Archives and the presidential libraries, and through Freedom of Information Act (FOIA) and Mandatory Review requests, used to obtain the declassification of now-secret materials. A selective and focused collection of documents will be made available to researchers.

The project is creating a comprehensive history of nuclear developments in South Asia, including weapons programs in India and Pakistan, as well as international efforts to curtail proliferation in the region. Information about factors that influenced nuclear issues, such as the unresolved enmity between India and Pakistan, and India's perception of China as a security threat, will also be incorporated. The U.S. has generally opposed nuclear proliferation in South Asia, while seeking to preserve good relations with both India and Pakistan. At times, however, its commitment has been questioned, because it has seemed to subordinate nonproliferation policy to other concerns. During the Soviet occupation of Afghanistan, for instance, the U.S. provided massive levels of economic and military aid to its ally, Pakistan. The assistance was widely criticized, because Pakistan was demonstrably importing nuclear-related material, from China and other nations. Few doubted that it was engaged in an active nuclear weapons development program.

China's role as a leading provider of sensitive technology to Pakistan has repeatedly strained U.S.-China relations, and has complicated efforts to expand U.S.-China trade. The Archive's

South Asia project is using the FOIA to seek the declassification of documents discussing this issue, and other contemporary and controversial topics. Materials collected for this project will, of course, reflect a U.S. perspective. As noted, nonproliferation policy is influenced by other concerns, including competition among the major powers. The Archive's efforts are directed toward enhancing understanding of U.S. decisions and the issues that influenced policy formulation. The analyst for the South Asia nuclear project is Joyce Battle, who prepared this briefing book. She is also the analyst for the Archive's documentation projects on the Persian Gulf and U.S. policy toward Iraq. Materials collected for the latter project were published in a document set, Iraqgate: Saddam Hussein, U.S. Policy and the Prelude to the Persian Gulf War, 1980-1994.

BRIEFING BOOK DOCUMENTS

The documents in the briefing book date from 1961 to 1983. In 1961, India had an advanced civilian nuclear program, while Pakistan's was in its early stages. In 1983, nine years had elapsed since India's explosion of a nuclear device, and Pakistan's nuclear weapons program was well under way. During the early 1960s, India under Prime Minister Jawaharlal Nehru strongly advocated global disarmament, but was apprehensive about China's nuclear weapons program. India's concern increased following its October 1962 territorial war with China. The stakes were raised by China's first nuclear weapons test in October 1964. Many observers thought it increasingly likely that India would respond to China's actions by seeking its own weapons capability. War with Pakistan in 1965 further alarmed India: it was angered by China's outspoken support for Pakistan during the conflict, and disappointed by what it viewed as insufficient Western attention to its security needs. The U.S. considered various options that might dissuade India from developing nuclear weapons, including scientific cooperation aimed at enhancing India's national prestige. It also joined in cooperative arrangements with both India and Pakistan to monitor nuclear and missile developments in China and the Soviet Union. India, for its part, launched a campaign seeking security guarantees to shield it from Chinese nuclear attack, arguing that such assurances might make a nuclear weapons program of its own unnecessary. Various options were proposed: U.S. guarantees, joint U.S.-Soviet guarantees, guarantees from all the nuclear states, British guarantees, or guarantees in conjunction with the nuclear nonproliferation treaty, then being negotiated. U.S. policy makers seriously considered these proposals, although some doubted that they would deter India from developing a bomb.

The Embassy in New Delhi viewed India's overtures sympathetically, while the Defence Department opposed any commitment to India that would alienate Pakistan, a U.S. military ally. In 1967, both President Lyndon Johnson and Defence Secretary Robert McNamara supported the concept of guarantees during meetings with a visiting Indian representative. Later that year, U.S. and Soviet officials were still discussing security guarantees, hoping to induce India to sign the nuclear nonproliferation treaty. No agreement was ever reached, however, in part because India itself concluded that such commitments would not guarantee its security in the event of actual nuclear conflict. In May 1974, India tested a nuclear device, although it called the event a "peaceful nuclear explosion."

Its terminology did not forestall censure, both within the international community and from domestic critics. The test had serious consequences: India lost much of the foreign technical assistance that had till then sustained its civilian nuclear program. A Pakistani reaction to India's test of a nuclear explosive was predicted, and confirmed within a few years. By the mid-1970s, intelligence reports indicated that Pakistan had an active nuclear weapons program, and in 1983 the State Department noted that it had "unambiguous evidence" of this fact. Documents in this briefing book illuminate aspects of the internal debate among U.S. officials, as they attempted to formulate effective policies toward nuclear proliferation in South Asia while protecting sometimes conflicting interests and objectives.

INDIA'S PROPAGANDA AGAINST PAKISTAN AND CHINA

Although Indian officials and media have always implicated Pakistan and China on various issues, now with the help of

American media, they have started a new phase of propaganda against these two countries in respect of Gilgit-Baltistan. In this respect, Indian writer B. Raman has already been maligning both Beijing and Islamabad, while Selig Harrison, former correspondent of the "Washington Post" in New Delhi has left no stone unturned in this regard.

On August 27, 2010, the "New York Times" carried an article by Selig Harrison who wrote, "While the world focuses on the flood-ravaged Indus River valley, a quiet geopolitical crisis is unfolding in the Himalayan borderlands of northern Pakistan, where Islamabad is handing over de facto control of the strategic Gilgit-Baltistan region in the northwest corner of disputed Kashmir to China. The entire Pakistan-occupied western portion of Kashmir stretching from Gilgit in the north to Azad (Free) Kashmir in the south is closed to the world...but reports from a variety of foreign intelligence sources reveal, "two important new developments in Gilgit-Baltistan: a simmering rebellion against Pakistani rule and the influx of an estimated 7,000 to 11,000 soldiers of the People's Liberation Army."

The report caused considerable sensation in India. The Government of India, while expressing its concern, ordered a verification of it by its agencies. A strong denial of the report came from the Pakistani Embassy in Beijing. "A senior Pakistani official on August 31 denied recent reports that Chinese troops are stationed in the area of Pakistan-controlled Kashmir to build a high-speed rail and road there. Masood Khan, ambassador of Pakistan to China told the Global Times, "The story is not true," and "It is totally fabricated."

Selig Harrison, in his article referred to the Gilgit-Baltistan region as "Pakistan-controlled Kashmir". On the other hand, Chinese Government officials and journalists describe Jammu and Kashmir as "Indian-controlled Kashmir." On the September 1, 2010, the Government-controlled Xinhua news agency disseminated the report: "China rejected reports of the presence of over 11,000 Chinese troops in northern Pakistan, saying that such "groundless reports" were made with "ulterior motives." Chinese Foreign Ministry spokesperson Jiang Yu remarked, "We believe the attempts of some people to fabricate stories to provoke China-Pakistan are doomed to fail." The comment came in response to recent reports of some American and Indian press that China had deployed more than 10,000 troops in the Gilgit-Baltistan region of Pakistan.

The next day, during the regular briefing of Bejing-based journalists including some from India, Jiang Yu reportedly used the expression "northern Pakistan" while referring to Gilgit-Baltistan in context of the article of Selig Harrison.

As Pakistan's close neighbour and all-weather friend, China has been helping Pakistan for its severe natural disaster. The Chinese Government has offered several instalments of humanitarian relief supplies worth more than RMB 100 million. An international relief team sent by the Chinese Government has arrived in the hardest-hit southern part of Pakistan and set up a mobile hospital which is in operation now.

Beijing has provided sincere and timely assistance to Pakistan without any strings attached. According to reliable sources, China recently refused to grant a visa to Lieutenant General Jaswal, head of Indian Army's Northern Command, and the Indian side said that the refusal was about the Kashmir issue. China's visa policy towards the residents of Indian-held Kashmir is consistent and remains unchanged. Unlike the western countries, Beijing more strongly holds that the Kashmir issue should be properly handled through dialogue and consultation between India and Pakistan.

The fact of the matter is that the Chinese reference to northern Pakistan could have been the result of the use of a similar expression by Selig Harrison who has referred to Gilgit-Baltistan as "Himalayan borderlands of northern Pakistan." Nevertheless, it is evident that the Chinese, while sticking to the decisions to issue stapled visas to residents of Jummu and Kashmir and to assist Pakistan in the development of its infrastructure in Gilgit-Baltistan have irked the Indian eyes—whose high officials and journalists have misperceived the close ties of Beijing with Islamabad.

As regards Beijing's contention that their troops were present in the Gilgit-Baltistan region only for humanitarian relief work, the Chinese have made two humanitarian interventions in the area this year. The first was in January last. On January 4, a landslide created a huge artificial lake in the Hunza area, which subsequently burst submerging a large number of villages in the Gojal Tehsil. About 22 KMs of the Karakoram Highway were submerged under water totally disrupting road communications with Xinjiang in China and with the rest of Gilgit-Baltistan. The Pakistan Army was able to go to the assistance of the affected villages only in the downstream area. It was not able to reach the affected villages in the upstream area for want of helicopters. The Pakistan Government appealed to the Chinese for assistance. Workers of the Chinese Red Cross and engineers of the People's Liberation Army entered the Hunza area for relief.

In that connection, The Xinhua reported: "On January 19, at the request of the Pakistani government, the Chinese side made special arrangements to open the Kunjirap border and facilitate the purchase of relief goods from China and its clearance. The second humanitarian intervention at the request of Islamabad was made after the recent floods.

It is mentionable that during the visit of President Zardari, under Memorandum of Understanding (MoU) officials of the two Governments signed—that China will build the 165-km long Jaglot-Skardu road and the 135-km long Thakot-Sazin road. Under another MoU to be jointly executed by Chinese company Datang and Norwegian company EBT—500 MW electricity would be produced through wind power.

China and Pakistan plan on building a rail link, which would pass through Gilgit-Baltistan near the Karakoram Highway. This has sparked a debate in India. In this regard, Indian Minister of State for Defence M M Pallam Raju said, "It is definitely a matter of concern." Besides, the two leaders of Pakistan and China discussed a host of issues relating to strategic partnership. The most prominent area of this bolstering of ties—especially for the world is the Sino-Pak civilian nuclear deal which is now beginning to see complete formalisation and initiation. It is unfortunate that the US and India have expressed their concerns about this deal, where the main goal is to address the acute power crisis in Pakistan.

While rejecting particularly US objections, China has once again clarified that it will supply two nuclear reactors to Pakistan under the old nuclear deal.

It is also regrettable that, until now, we have been denied the same right to civil nuclear technology that India was granted by the US in 2008. It provides the precedent, and in fact, has opened the door for any similar sort of nuclear deal in the future. Indeed, after setting precedent by themselves, both India and the US have no legal and moral grounds to challenge the legality of the Pak-China nuclear deal. In fact, Pakistan's province, Balochistan where China has invested billion of dollars to develop Gwadar seaport that could link Central Asian trade with rest of the world, irritates both Washington and New Delhi. It has even shifted the central gravity of the Great Game to Pakistan.

6

India and Weapons of Mass Destruction

India possesses nuclear weapons and maintains short- and intermediate-range ballistic missiles, nuclear-capable aircraft, surface ships, and submarines under development as possible delivery systems and platforms. Although it lacks an operational ballistic missile submarine, India has ambitions of possessing a nuclear triad in the near future when INS Arihant the lead ship of India's *Arihant* class of nuclear-powered submarines formally joins the Indian Navy in 2011 after undergoing extensive sea-trials. Though India has not made any official statements about the size of its nuclear arsenal, recent estimates suggest that India has between 80 and 100 nuclear weapons, consistent with earlier estimates that it had produced enough weapons-grade plutonium for up to 75–110 nuclear weapons. Production of weapons-grade plutonium is believed to be taking place at the Bhabha Atomic Research Centre, which is home to the CIRUS reactor, acquired from Canada and shut down in 2010, to the indigenous Dhruva reactor, and to a plutonium separation facility.

India is not a signatory to the 1968 Nuclear Non-Proliferation Treaty (NPT), which India argues entrenches the status quo of the existing nuclear weapons states whilst preventing general nuclear disarmament. India tested a nuclear device in 1974 (code-named "Smiling Buddha"), which it called a "peaceful nuclear explosion." The test used plutonium produced in the Canadian-supplied CIRUS reactor, and raised concerns that nuclear technology supplied for peaceful purposes could be diverted to weapons purposes. This also stimulated the early work of the Nuclear Suppliers Group. India performed further nuclear tests in 1998 (code-named "Operation Shakti").

India has signed and ratified both the Biological Weapons Convention and the Chemical Weapons Convention.

Brief Historical Overview

As early as 26 June 1946, Jawaharlal Nehru, soon to be India's first Prime Minister, announced:

"As long as the world is constituted as it is, every country will have to devise and use the latest devices for its protection. I have no doubt India will develop her scientific researches and I hope Indian scientists will use the atomic force for constructive purposes. But if India is threatened, she will inevitably try to defend herself by all means at her disposal. "

India's first nuclear test occurred on 18 May 1974. Since then India has conducted another series of tests at the Pokhran test range in the state of Rajasthan in 1998.

India has an extensive civil and military nuclear program, which includes at least 10 nuclear reactors, uranium mining and milling sites, heavy water production facilities, a uranium enrichment plant, fuel fabrication facilities, and extensive nuclear research capabilities.

In 1998, as a response to the continuing tests, the United States and Japan imposed temporary economic sanctions on India.

Some nuclear experts have speculated that India obtained nuclear enrichment from illicit proliferation through the A.Q. Khan Network from Pakistan.

Current arsenal and estimates of inventory

- In 2005, it was estimated that India had between 40 and 50 warheads.
- In November 2008, the Bulletin of the Atomic Scientists estimated that India has about 70 assembled nuclear warheads, with about 50 of them fully operational.

- A report by David Albright, published by the Institute for Science and International Security in 2000, estimated that India at end of 1999 had 310 kilograms of weapon grade plutonium, enough for 65 nuclear weapons. He also estimated that India had 4,200 kg of reactor grade plutonium which is enough to build 1,000 nuclear weapons. By the end of 2004, he estimates India had 445 kilograms of weapon grade plutonium which is enough for around 85 nuclear weapons considering 5 kg of plutonium required for each weapon.
- As of February 2011, the Federation of American Scientists estimated that India had a stockpile of 80-100 weapons.
- Former R&AW official J.K. Sinha, claimed that India is capable of producing 130 kilograms of weapon grade plutonium per year from six "unsafeguarded" reactors not included in the nuclear deal between India and the United States.

Doctrine

India has a declared nuclear no-first-use policy and is in the process of developing a nuclear doctrine based on "credible minimum deterrence." In August 1999, the Indian government released a draft of the doctrine which asserts that nuclear weapons are solely for deterrence and that India will pursue a policy of "retaliation only". The document also maintains that India "will not be the first to initiate a nuclear first strike, but will respond with punitive retaliation should deterrence fail" and that decisions to authorize the use of nuclear weapons would be made by the Prime Minister or his 'designated successor(s).'"

According to the NRDC, despite the escalation of tensions between India and Pakistan in 2001-2002, India remains committed to its nuclear no-first-use policy.

Indian National Security Advisor Shri Shivshankar Menon signaled a significant shift from "No first use" to "no first use against non-nuclear weapon states" in a speech on the occasion of Golden Jubilee celebrations of National Defence College in New Delhi on October 21, 2010, a doctrine Menon said reflected India's "strategic culture, with its emphasis on minimal deterrence."

Command and control

India's Strategic Nuclear Command was formally established in 2003, with an Air Force officer, Air Marshal Asthana, as the Commander-in-Chief. The joint services SNC is the custodian of all of India's nuclear weapons, missiles and assets. It is also responsible for executing all aspects of India's nuclear policy. However, the civil leadership, in the form of the CCS (Cabinet Committee on Security) is the only body authorized to order a nuclear strike against another offending strike: In effect, it is the Prime Minister who has his finger "on the button."

International treaties

India is not a signatory to either the Nuclear Non-Proliferation Treaty (NPT) or the Comprehensive Test Ban Treaty (CTBT), but did accede to the Partial Test Ban Treaty in October 1963. India is a member of the International Atomic Energy Agency (IAEA), and four of its 17 nuclear reactors are subject to IAEA safeguards.

India announced its lack of intention to accede to the NPT as late as 1997 by voting against the paragraph of a General Assembly Resolution which urged all non-signatories of the treaty to accede to it at the earliest possible date.

India voted against the UN General Assembly resolution endorsing the CTBT, which was adopted on 10 September 1996. India objected to the lack of provision for universal nuclear disarmament "within a time-bound framework." India also demanded that the treaty ban laboratory simulations. In addition, India opposed the provision in Article XIV of the CTBT that requires India's ratification for the treaty to enter into force, which India argued was a violation of its sovereign right to choose whether it would sign the treaty. In early February 1997, Foreign Minister I.K.Gujral reiterated India's opposition to the treaty, saying that "India favors any step aimed at destroying nuclear weapons, but considers that the treaty in its current form is not comprehensive and bans only certain types of tests."

In August 2008, the International Atomic Energy Agency (IAEA) approved safeguards agreement with India under which the former will gradually gain access to India's civilian nuclear reactors. In September 2008, the Nuclear Suppliers Group granted India a waiver allowing it to access civilian nuclear technology and fuel from other countries. The implementation of this waiver makes India the only known country with nuclear weapons which is not a party to the NPT but is still allowed to carry out nuclear commerce with the rest of the world.

Since the implementation of NSG waiver, India has signed nuclear deals with several countries including France, United States, Mongolia, Namibia, and Kazakhstan while the framework for similar deals with Canada and United Kingdom are also being prepared.

Delivery systems

Below is the list of missiles currently in India's inventory or under development that can carry Nuclear Warheads. Information on the missiles is given below.

AAD and PAD

Under former president Dr. Abdul Kalam India pursued the Integrated Guided Missile Development Program (IGMDP) which was an Indian Ministry of Defense program for the development of a comprehensive range of missiles, including the intermediate range Agni missile (Surface to Surface), and short range missiles such as the Prithvi ballistic missile (Surface to Surface), Akash missile (Surface to Air), Trishul missile (Surface to Air) and Nag Missile (Anti Tank). Other projects such Indian Ballistic Missile Defense Program have derived from the IGMDP. In 2005, India became only the fourth country to have Anti Ballistic capability when India tested two systems the AAD and PAD.

India has methodically built an indigenous missile production capability, using its commercial space-launch program to develop the skills and infrastructure needed to support an offensive ballistic missile program. For example, during the 1980s, India conducted a series of space launches using the solid-fueled SLV-3 booster.

Most of these launches put light satellites into near-earth orbit. Elements of the SLV-3 were subsequently incorporated into two new programs. In the first, the new polar-space launch vehicle (PSLV) was equipped with six SLV-3 motors strapped to the PSLV's first stage. The Agni IRBM technology demonstrator uses the SLV-3 booster as its first stage.

Prithvi

The Prithvi (Sanskrit: "Earth") I is mobile liquid-fueled 150 kilometer tactical missile currently deployed with army units. It is claimed that this missile is equipped only with various conventional warheads (which stay attached to the missile over the entire flight path).

The missile is of particular interest to the United States (and potential buyers) in that has the capability of maneuvering in flight so as to follow one of several different pre-programmed trajectories. Based on the same design, a modified Prithvi, the Prithvi II, is essentially a longer-ranged version of the Prithvi I except that it has a 250-kilometer range and a lighter payload. It is suspected that any nuclear missions will be executed by the Prithvi II. Currently, the Prithvi II has completed development and is now in production. When fielded, it will be deployed with air force units for the purpose of deep target attacking maneuvers against objectives such as air fields.

- Prithvi I – Army Version (150 km range with a payload of 1,000 kg)
- Prithvi II – Air Force Version (250 km range with a payload of 500 kg)
- Prithvi III – Naval Version (350 km range with a payload of 500 kg)

The Prithvi missile project encompassed developing 3 variants for use by the Indian Army, Indian Air Force and the Indian Navy. The initial project framework of the Integrated Guided Missile Development Program outlines the variants in the following manner. in October 2009 India conducted 2 simultenous user trials of 350 km extended range Prithvi II to be used for strategic purposes.

Dhanush

Dhanush (Sanskrit: Bow) is a naval variant of the Prithvi missile. It can fire either the 250 km or the 350 km range missiles. Supposedly it is a customised version of the Prithvi and that the additional customizations in missile configuration are to certify it for seaworthiness. Dhanush has to be launched from a hydraulically stabilized launch pad. Its low range acts against it and thus it is seen a weapons either to be used to destroy an aircraft carrier or an enemy port. Indian Navy's K-15 Sagarika submarine-launched ballistic missile is reported to be a variant of the Dhanush missile.

The ship launched Dhanush Ballistic Missile was tested from INS Subhadra of the Sukanya class patrol craft in 2000. INS Subhadra is a vessel which was modified and the missile was launched from the reinforced helicopter deck. The 250 km variant was tested but the tests were considered partially successful. In 2004, the missile was again tested from the INS Subhadra and was this time successful. Then the following year in December the missile's 350 km version was tested from the INS Rajput and hit the land based target.

Agni

The Agni (Sanskrit: Fire) missile system comprises five missiles:

- Agni I
- Agni II
- Agni III
- Agni IV
- Agni V

There are some reports about one other variant of Agni missile:

Agni VI

Agni-I uses the SLV-3 booster (from India's space program) for its first stage and a liquid-fueled Prithvi for its second stage.

Nuclear-capable Agni-II missiles have a range of up to 3,000 km and can carry a payload of 1,000 kg. Unlike the Agni-I, the Agni-II has a solid-fueled second stage.

In July 2006, India successfully test-fired Agni-III, a two-stage nuclear-capable ballistic missile with a range of 3,000 km. Both stages of the Agni-III utilizes solid-fuel propellants and its range can be extended to 4,000 km. The missile is capable of carrying a nuclear payload within the range of 600 to 1,800 kg including decoys and other anti-ballistic counter-measures.

India's DRDO is also working on a submarine-launched ballistic missile version of the Agni-III missile, known as the Agni-III SL. This missile is expected to provide India with a credible sea-based second strike capability. According to Indian defense sources, Agni-III SL will have a range of 3,500 km. In addition, the 5,000 km range Agni-V ICBM is expected to be tested by 2010-11.

Surya

The report of Surya ICBM (Sanskrit: Sun) has not been confirmed by officials of the Indian government and have repeatedly denied the existence of the project.The Surya ICBM is an ICBM program that has been mentioned repeatedly in the Indian press. Surya (meaning Sun in Sanskrit and many other Indian languages) is the codename for the first Intercontinental Ballistic Missile that India is reported to be developing. The DRDO is believed to have begun the project in 1994.

As the missile is yet to be developed, the specifications of the missile are not known and the entire program continues to remain highly speculative. Estimates of the range of this missile vary from 5,000 km to 10,000 km.

It is believed to be a three-stage design, with the first two stages using solid propellants and the third-stage using liquid. In 2007, the *Times of India* reported that the DRDO is yet to reveal whether India's currently proposed ICBM will be called Agni-V (or Surya-1). As of 2009 it was reported that the government had not considered an 8,000-km range ICBM.

Four decades of investments in a missile-related design, development, and manufacturing infrastructure have also made this sector less vulnerable to long-term disruption by technology denial regimes. More significantly, India's sophisticated civilian satellite launch capability makes it one of the few developing states theoretically capable of building an intercontinental ballistic missile (ICBM).

Shaurya

The Shaurya missile (Sanskrit: Valour) is a short-range surface-to-surface ballistic missile developed by DRDO of India for use by the Indian Army. It has a range of 600 km and is capable of carrying a payload of one-tonne conventional or nuclear warhead. The Shaurya missile provides India with a significant second strike capability. Shaurya Missile is considered a land version of the Sagarika. This missile is stored in a composite canister just like the BrahMos supersonic cruise missile. The composite canister makes the missile much easier to store for long periods without maintenance as well as to handle and transport. It also houses the gas generator to eject the missile from the canister before its solid propellant motors take over to hurl it at the intended target. Shaurya missiles can remain hidden or camouflaged in underground silos from enemy surveillance or satellites till they are fired from the special storage-cum-launch canisters. DRDO Defence scientists admit that given Shaurya's limited range at present, either the silos will have to be constructed closer to India's borders or longer-range missiles will have to be developed. The Shaurya system will require some more tests before it becomes fully operational in two-three years. Moreover, defense scientists say the high-speed, two-stage Shaurya has *high maneuverability* which also makes it *less vulnerable* to existing anti-missile defense systems. When Anti-Ballistic Missile Systems Advanced Air Defence (AAD) and Prithvi Air Defence (PAD) are to be tested again, the Shaurya invulnerability to anti-missile systems will be tested. The DRDO scientists also have said that if Shaurya is successful and manages to avoid anti ballistic missile radars then the missile can even be used to improve the AAD and PAD systems.

Sagarika

Sagarika (Sanskrit: Wave / Born from the Ocean) is a nuclear capable submarine-launched ballistic missile with a range of 750 km. This missile has a length of 8.5 meters, weighs seven tonnes and can carry a pay load of up to 500 kg. The development of this missile started in 1991. The first confirmation about the missile came in 1998. The development of the underwater missile launcher known as the Project 78 (P78) was completed in 2001. This was handed over to the Indian Navy for trials. The missile was successfully test fired thrice. The Indian Navy plans to introduce the missile into service by the end of 2010. Sagarika missile is being integrated with the Arihant class submarine that is expected to begin sea trials by 2009. Sagarika will form part of the triad in India's nuclear deterrence and will provide with retaliatory nuclear strike capability.

Sagarika has already been test-fired from an underwater pontoon, but now DRDO is planning a full-fledged test of the missile from a submarine and for this purpose may use the services of a Russian sub-marine. Eventually it could be introduced into as many as 5 ballistic missile submarines.

CRUISE MISSILES

Nirbhay

Nirbhay (Sanskrit "Fearless") is a long range, subsonic cruise missile being developed in India. The missile will have a range of 1,000 km and will arm three services, the Indian Army, Indian Navy and the Indian Air Force. The Nirbhay will be able to be launched from multiple platforms on land, sea and air. The first test flight of the missile is expected in the year 2009. Nirbhay will be a terrain hugging, stealth missile capable of delivering 24 different types of warheads depending on mission requirements and will use inertial navigation system for guidance. There are plans to arm the IL-76MDs with the aerial version of the missile.

3M-54 Klub

India has acquired around 200 3M-54 Klub for arming Talwar class frigate, Shivalik class frigate, Kolkata class destroyer and Sindhughosh class submarine. The Russian 3M-54 Klub is a multi-role missile system developed by the Novator Design Bureau (OKB-8) with a range of 250 km-300 km and an average speed of.8 Mach with a maximum of 2.9 Mach. India has both the Klub-N and Klub-S variant to be used for Ships and Submarines respectively. Both the Klub-N and Klub-S have been tested successfully. India currently has the 3M-54E, 3M-54E1, 91RE1 and 91RE2 variants. In addition the Navy has plans to arm the Tu-142 and Tu-22M with an air-launched version. Due to Klub's longer range than BrahMos it may also be used in the Mirage 2000 and Su-30 MKI too. The Navy has shown interest in buying more Klubs which would be incorporated on to the S-1000 submarine if bought by India. India is also keen on other Former Soviet cruise missile such as the P-700 Granit and P-500 Bazalt.

P-70 Ametist

India has Soviet P-70 Ametist submarine-launched cruise missiles. The missile were mostly probably bought in the early 90s and may be used today as canistered launched land based cruise missiles instead of submarine launched cruise missiles. The missiles can carry nuclear warheads and have a range of 50–65 km. Although they are extremely old and incompetent due to their low range and speed, there are still reports that they are kept in reserve and can still be used due to their upgrades in the late 90s.

Moskit

India has a number of operational Moskits. The P-270 Moskit is a Russian supersonic ramjet powered cruise missile capable of being launched from land and ships. India has most probably bought both land and ship variants which have a range of 120 km. India bought around 200 Klub missiles and now it is believed that the Moskit have been kept in reserve but can still be used.

Brahmos

BrahMos is a supersonic cruise missile that can be launched from submarines, ships, aircraft or land. It is a joint venture between India's Defence Research and Development Organisation (DRDO) and Russia's NPO Mashinostroeyenia who have together formed the BrahMos Aerospace Private Limited.

The acronym BrahMos is perceived as the confluence of the two nations represented by two rivers, the Brahmaputra of India and the Moskva of Russia. It travels at speeds of Mach 2.5 to 2.8 and is the world's fastest cruise missile. It is about three-and-a-half times faster than the U.S.A's subsonic Harpoon cruise missile. A hypersonic version of the missile is also presently under development (Lab Tested with 5.26 Mach Speed). BrahMos claims to have the capability of attacking surface targets as low as 10 meters in altitude. It can gain a speed of Mach 2.8, and has a maximum range of 290 km. The ship-launched and land-based missiles can carry a 200 kg warhead, whereas the aircraft-launched variant (BrahMos A) can carry a 300 kg warhead. It has a two-stage propulsion system, with a solid-propellant rocket for initial acceleration and a liquid-fueled ramjet responsible for sustained supersonic cruise. Air-breathing ramjet propulsion is much more fuel-efficient than rocket propulsion, giving the BrahMos a longer range than a pure rocket-powered missile would achieve.

The high speed of the BrahMos likely gives it better target-penetration characteristics than lighter subsonic cruise-missiles such as the Tomahawk. Being twice as heavy and almost four times faster than the Tomahawk, the BrahMos has almost 32 times the initial kinetic energy of a Tomahawk missile (although it pays for this by having only 3/5 the payload and a fraction of the range despite weighing twice as much, suggesting a different tactical paradigm to achieve the objective).

Although BrahMos is primarily an anti-ship missile, it can also engage land based targets. It can be launched either in a vertical or inclined position and is capable of covering targets over a 360 degree horizon. The BrahMos missile has an identical configuration for land, sea, and sub-sea platforms. The air-launched version has a smaller booster and additional tail fins for added stability during launch. The BrahMos is currently being configured for aerial deployment with the Su-30MKI as its carrier. India has produced more than 110 Brahmos by March 2011 as per SIPRI, inducted 1 regiment of Brahmos Type-I GLCM with 67 missiles.

SURFACE TO AIR MISSILE

Akash

Akash (Sanskrit: Sky) is India's medium range surface-to-air missile defense system The missile can target aircraft up to 30 km away, at altitudes up to 18,000 m. Akash can be fired from both tracked and wheeled platforms. Akash is said to be capable of both conventional and nuclear warheads, with a reported payload of 60 kg. A nuclear warhead could potentially give the missile the capability to destroy both aircraft and warheads from ballistic missiles. The missile is described as being able to strike several targets simultaneously, which could mean either separate, independently targetable warheads, or a sufficient blast to destroy a number of them.

Along with India, a limited number of other countries including the US and Russia have developed operational multi-target handling surface-to-air missile systems capable of carrying a nuclear warhead.

Delivery mechanisms

Nuclear submarines

According to some accounts, India plans to have as many as 25 nuclear submarines capable of carrying missiles with nuclear warheads. Currently, India has built one and is building two more nuclear submarines under the Arihant class submarine plan. India currently maintains six submarines of the Sindhughosh Class that can launch the nuclear-capable 3M-54 Klub cruise missiles.

- Former Leasing of Soviet submarines: In 1988 INS *Chakra* (Sanskrit: Wheel), a Charlie-class submarine was leased by the Indian Navy for three years from the Soviet Union, until 1991. The submarine was leased to India between 1988 and 1991 mainly for India to gain experience in the operations of a nuclear submarine. It was later decommissioned in 1991.
- Arihant class submarine: The Arihant class submarines (Sanskrit: Slayer of Enemies) are a class of nuclear-powered Ballistic Missile submarines being constructed for the Indian Navy at Visakhapatnam, India under the Advanced Technology Vessel (ATV) Project The ATV is an SSBN and will be armed with ballistic missiles.

The first of these, INS Arihant was launched on 26 July 2009. The vessel, which will undergo sea-trials for up to two years, will then be equipped with an unknown number of K-15 Sagarika SLBMs.

The second and third submarines of the class may incorporate the Nirbhay as well. As of July 2007, the Sagarika missile as well as Dhanush had undergone three successful tests each.

- INS Cruise Missile Submarines: The INS Sindhuraj (Sanskrit: King of the Ocean), INS Sindhuvir(Sanskrit: Warrior of the Ocean), INS Sindhuratna(Sanskrit: Gem of the Ocean), INS Sindhushastra (Sanskrit: Weapon of the Ocean), INS Sindhukesari(Sanskrit: Lion of the Ocean) and INS Sindhuvijay(Sanskrit: Conqueror of the Ocean) are capable of launching 3M-54 Klub and BrahMos nuclear-capable cruise missiles. India bought 10 Kilo class (in India known as Sindhughosh Class) submarine of which 6 have been refitted by the Russian Navy so that the they can launch cruise missiles such as nuclear capable 3M-54 Klub.
- Leasing of Russian Akula and Amur submarines: In 2000, negotiations between India and Russia were conducted into the leasing of two incomplete *Akula* class. The Akulas were to be delivered to the Indian Navy in 2008 on a lease of at least seven years and up to ten years, in which at the end of the lease, it has an option to buy them. The acquisition was to help the Indian Navy prepare for the introduction of the ATV. The cost to India of acquiring two Akula submarines and their support infrastructure along with training of the crews had been estimated at $2 billion. The Indian version was reportedly armed with the 300 km range 3M-54 Klub nuclear-capable missiles. Supposedly on 9 November 2008 one of the two submarines was conducting tests, when an accident on board killed 20 sailors but no damage occurred to the submarine. Though this deal fell apart for some time due to the Indians demanding an upgrade/improvement in some of its safety features, Russia's President Dmitry Medvedev on his official trip to New Delhi said that the deal was back on track and that "The talk is not about selling submarines into India's property, but about their rent by India's navy". However,

unlike the earlier deal the modified deal states that India can only rent and not buy the subs, but defence experts state that the so-called lease agreement is only to divert international attention and that it would be eventually modified and India would inevitably keep the subs. The first submarine will be named INS Chakra.. Home voyage under Indian control from the Russian port of Vladivostok to its Indian base Visakhapatnam commenced January, 2012.

Russia has also offered the advanced Amur Class Submarine, known as the S1000. According to GlobalSecurity India is already building the S1000 cruise missile submarines in Mazagaon Docks. The Amur will be most probably fitted with P-700 Granit or the Klub cruise missile capable of carrying nuclear warheads.

Frigates, destroyers and aircraft carriers

Other than submarines, India also maintains ships such as destroyers, modified patrol crafts and frigates which can launch nuclear capable ballistic and cruise missiles.

Talwar class frigate and Shivalik class frigate are frigates of the Indian Navy that can fire nuclear capable cruise missiles. INS Tabar and INS Trishul are Talwar class vessel armed with supersonic nuclear 3M-54 Klub cruise missiles while INS Shivalik was the first vessel of the Shivalik class to incorporate the 3M-54 Klub. Other vessels of the Shivalik Class and Talwar Class are to be armed with the BrahMos and 3M-54 Klub missiles by 2009 and 2010 respectively. All these frigates are also equipped with Barak 1 missiles or other SAMs and harbour helicopters such as the HAL Dhruv. In years to come, the Nirbhay missile is also to be incorporated into Talwar class frigates and Shivalik class frigates.

Rajput Class, Kolkata Class and Delhi Class are Destroyers of the Indian Navy that may be armed with nuclear capable missile-Nirbhay. In addition Kolkata Class will also incorporate the Russian nuclear 3M-54 Klub cruise missile.

The ship launched Dhanush Ballistic Missile was tested from INS Subhadra of the Sukanya class patrol craft in 2000. INS Subhadra is a patrol vessel which was modified and the missile was launched from the reinforced helicopter deck. The 250 km variant was tested but the tests were considered partially successful. In 2004, the missile was again tested from the INS Subhadra and was this time successful. Then the following year in December the missile's 350 km version was tested from the INS Rajput and hit the land based target.

INS Vikramaditya Aircraft Carrier (formerly known as Admiral Gorshkov) was fitted with P-500 Bazalt nuclear capable cruise missiles of the range of 550 km. The Vikramaditya could still be armed with this after its refit. India is also a potential customer for a Slava class cruiser which also incorporates the P-500 Bazalt.

Nuclear-capable aircraft

India currently has fourth generation jet fighters capable of launching nuclear weapons. Nuclear-capable aircraft are also seen as a less expensive way of dropping nuclear warheads as well as being as effective.

- Fighter jets: The Sukhoi Su-30MKI, Dassault Mirage 2000, and MiG-29 serve in the Indian Air Force and are also seen as a means to deliver nuclear weapons. In addition India maintains SEPECAT Jaguar and MiG-27M which can be used to drop gravity bombs. On the other hand, the Su-30MKI, capable of carrying nuclear weapons and tailor-made for Indian specifications, integrates Indian systems and avionics. is one of the best air superiority fighters and also consists of French and Israeli subsystems. The MKI variant features several improvements over the basic K and MK variants and is classified as a 4.5 generation fighter. Due to similar features and components, the MKI variant is often considered to be a customized Indian variant of the Sukhoi Su-35. The Mirage 2000Hs were heavily customised during the Kargil War and is the only other version, other than the French 2000N, to be able to be armed with nuclear weapons. Though the MiG-29 like the HAL Tejas after many test flights have not been tested to use nuclear weapons, they have the capacity to be armed with them. Both the HAL Tejas and Su-30MKI can travel excess of 3,000 km without refueling; this allows India to attack targets far away in an effective manner only using planes rather than delivery systems such as the Agni. The HAL Tejas is India's only indigenous plane to be armed with nuclear weapons, thus making India less dependent on Russia.

India has leased four Russian Tupolev Tu-22M3 bombers, which could carry air-launched cruise missiles. India has reportedly upgraded its Russian-built Tu-142 maritime patrol aircraft to carry air-launched cruise missiles. India is expected to buy up to 200 Sukhoi T-50 stealth fighter jets, developed jointly by Russia and India.

Ballistic missile defense

India has an active ABM development effort using indigenously developed and integrated radars and locally designed missiles. In November 2006, India successfully conducted the PADE (Prithvi Air Defence Exercise) in which an Anti-ballistic missile, called the Prithvi Air Defense (PAD) an *Exoatmospheric* (outside the atmosphere) interceptor system intercepted a Prithvi-II ballistic missile. The PAD missile has the secondary stage of the Prithvi missile and can reach altitude of 80 km. During the test the target missile was intercepted at an 50 km altitude. India became the fourth nation in the world to acquire such a capability and the third nation to develop it through indigenous effort. On 6 December 2007 the Advanced Air Defence (AAD) missile system was tested successfully. This missile is an Endo atmospheric interceptor with an altitude of 30 km. According to scientist V K Saraswat of DRDO the missiles will work in tandem to ensure a hit probability of 99.8 percent. Induction of the system into services is expected to be in 2010. Two new anti ballistic missiles that can intercept IRBM/ ICBMs are being developed. These high speed missiles (AD-1 and AD-2) are being developed to intercept ballistic missiles with the range of 5,000 km.

India also has Russian S300 PMU-2 and it is used as an interceptor for ballistic missiles. An indigenous nuclear tipped surface to air missile, Akash Missile is used to destroy low range missiles and is capable of destroying various targets and is one of the few of its kind systems in the world. India has also shown interest in the Russian S-400, the most advanced anti-ballistic missile.

Chemical weapons

In 1992 India signed the Chemical Weapons Convention (CWC), stating that it did not have chemical weapons and the capacity or capability to manufacture chemical weapons. By doing this India became one of the original signatories of the Chemical Weapons Convention [CWC] in 1993, and ratified it on 2 September 1996.

According to India's ex-Army Chief General Sunderji, a country having the capability of making nuclear weapons does not need to have chemical weapons, since the dread of chemical weapons could be created only in those countries that do not have nuclear weapons. Others suggested that the fact that India has found chemical weapons dispensable highlighted its confidence in the conventional weapons system at its command.

In June 1997, India declared its stock of chemical weapons(stockpile of 1044 tonnes of sulphur mustard).

By the end of 2006, India had destroyed more than 75 percent of its chemical weapons/material stockpile and was granted extension for destroying (the remaining stocks by April 2009) and was expected to achieve 100 percent destruction within that timeframe. India informed the United Nations in May, 2009 that it had destroyed its stockpile of chemical weapons in compliance with the international Chemical Weapons Convention. With this India has become third country after South Korea and Albania to do so. This was cross-checked by inspectors of the United Nations.

India has an advanced commercial chemical industry, and produces the bulk of its own chemicals for domestic consumption. It is also widely acknowledged that India has an extensive civilian chemical and pharmaceutical industry and annually exports considerable quantities of chemicals to countries such as the United Kingdom, United States, and Taiwan.

Biological warfare

India has a well-developed biotechnology infrastructure that includes numerous pharmaceutical production facilities bio-containment laboratories (including BSL-3 and BSL-4) for working with lethal pathogens. It also has highly qualified scientists with expertise in infectious diseases. Some of India's facilities are being used to support research and development for BW defense purposes. India has ratified the BWC and pledges to abide by its obligations. There is no clear evidence, circumstantial or otherwise, that directly points toward an offensive BW program. New Delhi does possess the scientific capability and infrastructure to launch an offensive BW program, but has chosen not to do so. In terms of delivery, India also possesses the capability to produce aerosols and has numerous potential delivery systems ranging from crop dusters to sophisticated ballistic missiles.

No information exists in the public domain suggesting interest by the Indian government in delivery of biological agents by these or any other means. To reiterate the latter point, in October 2002, Indian President A.P.J. Abdul Kalam asserted that "we [India] will not make biological weapons. It is cruel to human beings..."

AGNI MISSILE TESTING IN INDIA

On 19 February 1994 Agni took its third test flight at the Indian missile test range at Balasore, this time successfully with its range extended to 1200 km. The third flight marked the end of the first phase of Agni development program. The program went into a period of dormancy while the new Agni II began development, a longer range version that replaced the liquid fuel upper stage with a solid fuel version to make an all solid fuel missile India became a nuclear weapon state in reality in May 1994, though most observers thought that this milestone had been passed years before. It was then that India completed its development of a fully combat ready system for delivering nuclear weapons by successfully conducting acceptance tests. The ARDE developed bomb case, and the TBRL developed implosion system were mated with a modified Mirage 2000 and successfully test dropped at Balasore. The bomb, complete except for its plutonium core, was fuzed for an airburst and released over the ocean. If it been required due to national crisis, no doubt the system could have been pushed into service at an earlier date as a stop gap, but in May the fully mature reliable and safe system entered service. India now had an arsenal of at least a couple of dozen operational nuclear bombs.

The years 1995-1996 proved to be watershed in the history of South Asia, and in nuclear proliferation efforts world-wide. The Non-Proliferation Treaty (NPT) came up for review and extension in 1995. Since its original drafting in 1968 the NPT had steadily gained adherents until by the mid-90s the vast majority of states in the world had signed it (by 2000 only 4 states out of 191 had not signed it - with India and Pakistan being half of the four). India had endorsed the NPT in principle, but had refrained from signing because it objected to the establishment of "legitimate" nuclear weapon states limited to the 5 nuclear armed nations then in existence. The NPT committed these nuclear states to good faith efforts at eliminating their arsenals but in the nearly 30 years since no effort in that direction could be discerned. India refused to sign the NPT unless the nuclear states committed themselves to a specific timetable to accomplish disarmament, an approach they unanimously refused to consider. As the NPT extension date approached the nuclear states began pressing for making the NPT permanent so that it would never expire again, while the non-nuclear signatories to the treaty began insisting on a firmer commitment to arms limitation from the nuclear powers in return. In lieu of an actual disarmament commitment, the nuclear powers pushed two treaties that provided for restrictions on specific proliferation activities - the Comprehensive Test Ban Treaty (CTBT) to prohibit all nuclear tests, and a treaty to cut-off the production of fissile materials for weapons. Neither of these treaties would seriously inconvenience the states already possessing extensive stockpiles of tested weapons, but they would have serious effects on states with less well developed arsenals - like India.

This situation presented India with the worst of all worlds. They found themselves under intense pressure, particularly from the U.S., to assent to these treaties which would lock them in to a permanent status of a "second tier state", sharply constrain or wholly foreclose their nuclear capabilities developed at great expense and now at a stage of advanced development, while exacting a negligible price from the nuclear weapon states. To add further insult, two of the nuclear states - China and France - embarked on a new round of nuclear tests to add still more sophisticated designs to their arsenals before the CTBT shut down all testing. The dilemma was strongly reminiscent of the 1980s when developing international restrictions on ballistic missile technology induced India to push ahead with its missile program before the door could be shut on them. The new international push for limiting the spread of nuclear weapons (but not reducing those already held by the major powers) created pressure in India to breakout of its closet status, test its new weapons, and openly deploy them.

The linkage between U.S. pressure on the NPT and India's decision to move ahead aggressively on its strategic programs seems to have been quite direct. The full court press for the NPT began in January 1995, PM Rao responded by meeting with Chidambaram and authorized him to prepare to conduct a series of tests, including a hydrogen bomb test device and sub-kiloton devices to provide data for post-CTBT weapon simulations. Rao even specified that the scientists should be ready to conduct a test on 10 days notice, after the Prime Minister's decision to do so. Later, on 13 April 1995, Rao authorized 6 billion rupees for the development of the Agni II. Kalam was directed to intensify work on setting up a sophisticated command and control system for India's nuclear weapons, and to build additional weapon storage sites around the country (up to that point they nuclear components for weapons were all stored at BARC in Trombay).

It was after Rao's meeting with him that Chidambaram authorized Satinder Kumar Sikka at BARC to begin the development and preparation of a thermonuclear test device - a hydrogen bomb. BARC had developed some designs for thermonuclear weapons in the 80s, but these had languished without any serious effort to move forward with device fabrication although important work in the basic physics and in producing many of the essential materials like enriched lithium-6 and tritium provided a sound foundation. Sikka began developing a new design — a sophisticated one intended for deployment on ballistic missiles (with a weight thus limited to 1000 kg) and using a boosted fission bomb primary.

The NPT extension passed overwhelmingly on 11 May, four days later on 15 May China conducted another nuclear test, and the next day PM Rao announced that India was considering deploying the Prithvi missile in the near future. In August K. Santhanam, DRDO's chief technical adviser, was appointed mission director for the planned test series. That month U.S. intelligence satellites observed water being pumped out of the test shafts at Pokhran, which had become flooded in the intervening years. Construction also began on a new shallower test shaft.

In October 1995, 20 pre-production models of the initial Prithvi SS-150 (with a 150 km range) were secretly delivered to the Army to form the 333rd Missile Regiment based in Secunderabad. At this time the Prithvi was not yet equipped with a nuclear warhead. Rao had never actually authorized tests though, simply preparations for them to keep his options open. Unlike in 1974, PM Rao conducted an extensive series of reviews to determine involving political, foreign policy, and economic advisers (but, in keeping with long-standing Indian practice, not the military) in addition to the nuclear scientists and engineers to determine whether tests should be conducted. Although the nuclear scientists, and members of the "strategic enclave" (like Sundarji and Subrahmanyam) strongly advocated tests, the net result of the reviews were negative, by the fall Rao had decided not to conduct tests. The principle reason for not testing were again economic, Rao recognized the principle source of China's international clout was its economic strength and that India needed to focus its energies on its economy to compete. Thus when the news that the U.S. had detected test preparations broke in the press in December, actual tests were no longer under consideration and test devices had never been transported to Pokhran. The shift of Indian public opinion towards favoring tests is illustrated by an *India Today* survey of 2000 adults on 5 December 1995 showing that 62 percent of the respondents would approve if India exploded an atom bomb to develop its nuclear weapons capability.

The disclosure created a storm of controversy booth inside and outside of India. Pres. Clinton called PM Rao soon after the disclosure to ask him not to test. Rao responded that India would not act "irresponsibly" but gave no other assurances. On 18 December the government declared that it would not succumb to external pressure, but the next day Foreign Minister Pranab Mukherjee denied that tests were planned.

But Rao's term in office was drawing to a close. Elections were held in April-May 1996, and the Congress Party was voted out of office. The balance of power in the Lok Sabha was indecisive - the BJP won the largest seats with 186. Congress and its allies won only 138 seats, and the National Front took 113 and remaining 95 split among smaller parties. A governing coalition required 273 seats and it was not clear what part could assemble a sufficiently large coalition. Since the BJP had gained the largest share of seats President Shankar Sharma asked the BJP led by Atal Behari Vajpayee to form a government on 15 May. Vajpayee was faced with the challenge of marshalling at least another 75 votes within 15 days to win a vote of confidence and remain in power.

Vajpayee had supported open nuclearization of India for 30 years, since the first Chinese nuclear test, as had the BJP for its entire existence, and as had its predecessor, the Jana Sangh before that. One of the planks in the campaign platform for the BJP had been "to exercise the option to induct nuclear weapons". So it should have been to no one's surprise that one of the first actions taken by Vajpayee upon taking office would be to set in motion the test operations that Rao had ordered to be made ready. That it appears to have actually been *the* very first issue acted upon by Vajpayee though is notable.

According to Chengappa, Vajpayee's attempt to order nuclear tests was delayed until the day after his inauguration due to problems in contacting Abdul Kalam to receive the order. Three test devices were brought to Pokhran and emplaced in the test shafts:

- a lightweight pure fission bomb (12 kt);

- a boosted fission bomb; and
- a sub-kiloton experimental test device.

The site preparations at Pokhran came within about a day of being completed, when it became apparent that Vajpayee's government was not going to be able to win the upcoming vote of confidence. Although he had the authority to order the test, Vajpayee recognized that it would be improper to saddle a successor government with dealing with the consequences of a test with which it had no involvement. So Vajpayee rescinded his authorization until after the vote was held. On 28 May the BJP lost the vote of confidence and Vajpayee's government was dissolved. Vajpayee's aides felt that without the one day delay in locating Kalam the tests would have been conducted in 1996. Within several months information about Vajpayee's initial authorization of nuclear tests leaked out, and although it did not become widely known this was undoubtedly picked up by U.S. intelligence - making the later admission of "surprise" by the U.S. when Vajpayee took office in 1998 and conducted tests soon after difficult to justify.

The delay in testing brought about the hesitance of Rao and Vajpayee was actually a boon to the weapons scientists. The thermonuclear device was not ready yet, and the delay gave them time to prepare additional devices - two sub-kiloton experiments, and a boosted fission device using reactor-grade plutonium to enable India to draw upon its very large inventory of power reactor produced material if desired.

DELIVERY SYSTEMS

Agni-I

Thermonuclear warhead (200-300 kt)?, fission/boosted fission warhead (>15 kt)? "Agni" is Hindi for "fire" and is also the name of the Hindu deity of fire. There is some question as to the operational status of the Agni-I. For many years the Agni-I program has been described as a "technology demonstration", which was consistent with the design varaitions that were tried, and the employment of a solid/liquid fuel two stage design that would be undesirable for operational use. However in August 2000 the U.S. defense industry weekly *Defense News* quoted an unnamed senior scientist at DRDO as stating that India had 10 Agni-I missiles in service. He added that the unit cost of the Agni-I is about $5 million.

Agni-I awaiting launch (17 K)

Developed by the Defense Research and Development Laboratory (DRDL) of Hyderabad. The first member of the Agni family was successfully launched on 22 May 1989 from the Chandipur test facility about 250 km southwest of Calcutta at Balasore. The two-stage missile impacted 800 km downrange in the Bay of Bengal. The Agni-I has been tested at a maximum range of 1400 km.

The Agni-I first stage was based on the Indian Satellite Launch Vehicle (SLV-3) used in satellite launches since 1979. The first stage motor was 10 meters long and capable of delivering about 45 tons average thrust with a 50 second burn duration. The second stage was a shortened version of the two chamber liquid fuel motor from the Prithvi. Second stage control was achieved through engine gimballing by its hydraulic actuation system.

Agni-II

The medium range Agni-II system is the first true strategic missile (in the Indian context) deployed by India. The Agni-II is designed to be mobile. It was originally developed in a road-mobile configuration but its deployment is being conducted using a rail-mobile version. The strap-down (limited degree of freedom) inertial guidance system may be replaced in the future with a full inertial system. The RV is reported to have an optical terminal guidance, and speculation has been made about the possible use or future use of a external positioning reference system. The Agni-II is an indigenously developed system, descended from the SLV-3 space launch vehicle via the Agni-I technology demonstrator. A pre-production road mobile Agni-II (Agni-I?) is said to have been made operational during the 1999 Kargil War. The Agni-II costs approximately Rs.400 million per missile and is manufactured by a partnership of the DRDO and Bharat Dynamics Limited (BDL) in Hyderabad. It is expected that BDL will be manufacturing 10-12 missiles every year.

The Agni-II was test fired in April 1999 with a range of 2300 km; on its second test on 17 January 2001 it travelled 2200 km. When the missile system is inducted, India will have the capability to strike at targets at least 2500 km away (up to 3000 km using specific payloads, according to some estimates).

Although the government has on several occasions stated that nuclear weaponization was now complete, the fact remains that the second Agni-II test occurred almost two years after the first and by all accounts more must take place before a true deployable arsenal is available.

In August 2000 Defence Minister George Fernandes stated that the Agni-II had "reached the point of operationalization". A DRDO scientist quoted in *Defense Weekly* reported in August 2000 at that time two pre-production Agni-II missiles were fully operational. He added that the unit cost of the Agni-II about $8 million and that, if required, DRDO's missile research laboratory could produce, in collaboration with Bharat Dynamics Limited, up to 18 Agni-IIs a year. Following the second successful test of Agni-II, on 17 January 2001, Scientific Advisor to the Defence Minister V.K. Aatre said that the Agni-II missile would be inducted into the Indian Air Force by year's end. This test was the first time the Agni-II was test-fired in its final operational configuration.

The Agni-II can be launched in 15 minutes, as opposed to half a day for the Agni-I. It uses far more accurate navigational and guidance systems and is designed to operate on a highly mobile platform which lends flexibility and reduces vulnerability to strikes.

Given its range and India's geopolitical situation, most observers say that the Agni-II was developed as a deterrent against China (it has far more range than is required to cover Pakistan). If that is the case, India has some way to go since with its current range, the Agni-II can at best cover Chinese territory as far as the western cities of Chengdu and Kunming, if based in the central plateau of Bihar. Even if based in Assam, a somewhat improbable scenario, the missile would not be able to reach either Shanghai or Beijing. For this purpose, India is developing the Agni-III, a longer-range missile capable of reaching targets out to 3500 km and beyond. The first test of this vehicle, which will feature entirely new first and second stages, is likely to take place in 2001. Speaking to the Lok Sabha in February 2001 Defence Minister George Fernandes gave the time frame for induction as 2001-2002.

Agni-III

A follow on version to the Agni-II, to be called Agni-III, with a range of 3500 to 5000 km and a 1000 kg payload, is under development. This is expected to be the final variant in the Agni family. According to DRDO sources two approaches are under consideration - an enlarged solid fuel first stage with a 1.8 meter diameter and 36 tonnes of propellant, or an added third stage to the existing Agni-II. The principal objective of the Agni-III would be to develop a missile capable of reaching China's capital of Beijing. The *Deccan Chronicle* reported on 23 September 2000 that Defence Minster George Fernandes had disclosed that the Agni-III had almost completed the development stage and was ready to be test fired soon. *Yahoo India News* reported a senior defence department official as saying India plans to build the third version of the Agni IRBM, but is yet to set a deadline for the project (8 February 2001). "Agni-III will obviously be of a higher range and better capabilities than its predecessor," said the official, who did not want to be identified. "But we have not set a date to test it," the official said on the sidelines of an aerospace conference in Bangalore.

Suriya

A higher performance missile in the ICBM class (the Suriya or Surya) with a range of over 6000 km has been discussed. It would be an entirely new development effort. Dr. APJ Abdul Kalam, Principal Scientific Adviser to the Prime Minister, was quoted in the *Hindustan Times* on 18 September 2000 as saying that "All technologies and industrial complexes are available for an ICBM. It'll not take much time, should India decide on it." He discounted speculation that the ICBM will be the derivative of the

GSLV, India's latest space launch vehicle. "Cryogenic engines (used for the GSLV) are good for satellite launch vehicles, not missiles. They require huge fuelling facilities, which can be detected by satellite."

Prithvi

Prithvi (Hindi for "Earth") is a single stage, road-mobile, short-range ballistic missile (SRBM). The missile's corrosive liquid fuel must be loaded immediately prior to launch, which is a serious disadvantage in the field. On the other hand the ability to control the liquid fuel motor, including throttling it or shutting it down (difficult or impossible with solid fuel) gives it great flexibility in range and trajectory, including in-flight maneuvering. The liquid propellant also has higher performance than solid propellants, giving the Prithvi an unusually high payload for its size and range. The inertial navigation system has been reported to have a CEP (Circular Error Probability) equal to.01% of its range, or 15 m for the Army version and 25 m for the Air Force version at maximum range (this is roughly comparable to an ICBM having a 1.5 km accuracy). The missile uses its maneuvering capability to follow up to six different trajectories so as to avoid ABM interception, and confuse launch system counter targeting. Another defense measure the Prithvi has is the use of radar absorbing paint to reduce its radar signature.

The fact that both the Indian Army and the IAF operate versions of the Prithvi is the result of a turf war over control of ballistic missile systems, a scenario that has played out in many other nations. The outcome of this struggle was that the Army controls land based missiles with a range of 150 km or less (a limit that was set by the initial range of the Prithvi) while longer range missiles belong to the Air Force. The DRDO is attempting to increase the payload of the IAF version to 1000 kg, by using higher performance liquid propellants to generate more thrust-to-weight ratio. The missile carries both nuclear warheads and a variety of conventional payloads. A family of warheads have been developed, including high-explosive (HE), pre-fragmented unitary HE, incendiary, cluster munitions (bomblets), sub-munitions, and fuel-air explosives (FAE).

For field operations, Prithvi is transported on an all-terrain, eight wheel Kolos Tatra 4x4 truck. The missile is deployed off this vehicle and fired from a simple launcher. Each battery of four Prithvi carrier vehicles is accompanied by a missile re-supply and loading vehicle, a propellant tanker and a command post vehicle to provide target data to the missile's guidance system before launch. In addition, a variety of other support support vehicles and equipment are used to support the batteries in the field.

Prithvi SS-150 which has been in serial production by Bharat Dynamics Limited in Hyderabad since 1997, following a development program that included 12 test flights.

Due to the limited strategic space of Pakistan (the Indus river valley where most major Pakistani cities are located runs close to the Indian frontier) the Prithvi has significant strategic value despite its short range. If it is deployed in states like Kashmir, Punjab and Gujrat which border Pakistan, it would place the capital of Islamabad, as well as the principal cities of Lahore and Karachi in range, as wells as many of Pakistan's strategic military installations.

In September 2000 *Defense News* reported that India would go ahead with full production of about 300 Prithvis for all three branches of the Indian defense forces. The decision, taken by Defence Minister George Fernandes on 25 August, was prompted by Pakistan's test-firing of its Ghauri-III IRBM 10 days earlier, on Independence Day, a senior Indian ministry official, who was not named, was quoted as saying. The production of 300 Prithvis was estimated to cost $200 million. The state-owned Bharat Dynamics in Hyderabad would invest $100 million to ready itself for production. According to company sources, the Army required 150 Prithvis with a range of 150 km while the Navy needed 100 missiles of equal range. 50 Prithvi missiles with a longer range of 250 km, known as Prithvi-II, have to be produced to meet the requirement of the Air Force, the company said.

The Prithvi is a descendant of an earlier program called "Project Devil", an attempt to reverse engineer the Soviet SA-2 liquid fuel surface-to-air missile by the Defense Research and Development Laboratory (DRDL) at Hyderabad. This latter project, initiated under the leadership of Dr. Basanti Dulal Nag Chaudhuri, was a failure and was cancelled in 1978; nonetheless valuable experience and technical skill was obtained which provided the basis for Prithvi.

Development was initiated in 1983 as part of the Integrated Guided Missile Development Programme (IGMDP) under the leadership of Dr. Avil Pakir Jainulabdeen Abdul Kalam, the project manager for the successful SLV-3 program. The Prithvi was intended to be a 150 km tactical missile and was first tested at Sriharikota on 22 February 1988..

In October 1995, 20 pre-production models of the initial Prithvi SS-150 (with a 150 km range) were secretly delivered to the Army to form the 333rd Missile Regiment based in Secunderabad. At this time the Prithvi was not yet equipped with a nuclear warhead. The first deployment of Prithvi missiles (numbering less than a dozen) was at Jalandhar, about 200 km from the Pakistani border in May 1997 prior to its formal operational adoption. Integration and testing of a nuclear warhead was completed in 1997 on the Prithvi SS-150 before these were formally deployed in September 1997. Significantly in December 1998, the Army deployed the Prithvi in a major military exercise code named Shiv-Shakti for the first time since its induction. According to Dr. Sanjay Badri-Maharaj during the 1999 Kargil War four nuclear armed Prithvis were actually deployed for retaliatory strikes. Some units are reported to have been moved to at least two northern locations close to the Pakistani border.

The fourth test flight of the extended range SS-250 was launched on 16 June 2000 at the Interim Test Range (ITR) at Chandipur-on-Sea on the east coast of India. The liquid-propellant weapon carried multiple warheads over a range of 250 km. At this point the SS-250 had not yet been inducted into service.

There is some question whether the Dhanush is really a Prithvi variant, or simply a new missile design in the same size class.

Jane's Missiles and Rockets reported on 9 August 2000 that John Pike of the Federation of American Scientists (FAS) has detected what it believes is the storage site for Indian's Prithvi missiles. An image of the Research Centre Imarat complex taken earlier this year by the Ikonos imaging satellite revealed an installation which Pike says "is probably the primary Prithvi garrison". The Imarat centre is associated with research and development of technologies for missiles and other advanced weapons. "Although it is reported that the 333rd Missile Group is headquartered in Secunderabad, it is evident that the military cantonment would be an inappropriate location for the actual missiles, given the urban congestion of the area," said Pike. The facility at the Imarat centre consists of three pairs of garages, each of which the FAS estimates to be large enough to house four vehicles, which suggests that each pair is used to house a battery of four launchers plus four support vehicles. The facility is surrounded by a security perimeter which incorporates a series of objects which may be guard houses. A nearby complex of buildings could be an administrative support facility for the Prithvi missiles, but "this complex is devoid of functional signatures that would support this interpretation, and is enclosed within a separate security perimeter that is suggestive of institutional associations unrelated to the Prithvi complex."

Dhanush

The Dhanush (Bow, as in "bow and arrow") is a derivative of the Prithvi program, adapted to naval use and given extended range. The first test firing was conducted on 10 April 2000 from the modified Sukanya class off-shore patrol vessel (OPV), INS *Subhadra* in the Bay of Bengal 20 km off Orissa state. It was a only partially successful with, the missile splashing down 25-30 km from its launch point. The launch platform used was a hydraulically-stabilized, rail-mounted platform built on the helicopter deck of the *Subhadra*. Dhanush is probably intended for deployment on a specialized ballistic missile submarine, either conventionally powered or the nuclear powered Advanced Technology Vessel (ATV). Neither is likely in the near future due to technical and financial constraints.

Sagarika

There have been conflicting reports about this program since Clinton administration officials in the United States reported on

27 April 1998 that India was developing a sea-launched ballistic missile with a 200 mile range intended for submarine deployment. More recent reports describe Sagarika as submarine-launched cruise missile (SLCM) intended for the nuclear-powered submarine known as the Advanced Technology Vessel (ATV). The initial description of Sagarika as a ballistic missile may have been due to confusion with the Dhanush. Sagarika had been expected to enter service by 2002, but the program has been troubled as has the ATV submarine itself. Work on an Indian nuclear powered submarine has proceeded fitfully and unsuccessfully for nearly 25 years.

Nuclear Facilities

The centre piece of India's nuclear weapons program is the Bhabha Atomic Research Centre (BARC) in Trombay near Mumbai (Bombay) which is the centre for nuclear weapons associated work. BARC was founded as the Atomic Energy Establishment, Trombay (AEET) on 3 January 1954 by Dr. Homi Jehangir Bhabha. Bhabha was the also the founder India's entire nuclear industry and infrastructure, and India's first Secretary of the Department of Atomic Energy (DAE) when it was created on 3 August 1954. In its early years BARC was already a very large, but primarily civilian-oriented nuclear research laboratory. When India's first nuclear device was designed and fabricated at there, the work was conducted surreptitiously (often at night) to hide it from the rest of the laboratory. But in May 2000 a watershed was reached in this tension between civilian and military work when the civilian Atomic Energy Regulatory Board (AERB) which had been exercising regulatory oversight was split off from BARC. As S. Rajagopal oberved, an expert on nuclear affairs and a professor of the Bangalore-based National Institute of Advanced Studies, this decision effectively reclassified BARC as a nuclear weapons laboratory - a laboratory with a primarily military function though also conducting civilian oriented work in a model similar to the U.S. weapons labs. But without much of the civilian oversight and management that the U.S. labs have.

BARC is the site of the two reactors used for weapons-grade plutonium production: the 40 MW CIRUS (Canadian-Indian-U.S.)

reactor, and the 100 MW reactor named R-5, but usually called "Dhruva". Both of these are heavy water moderated and cooled natural uranium reactors.

CIRUS was supplied by Canada in 1954, but uses heavy water supplied by the U.S. (hence its name). The reactor is not under IAEA safeguards (which did not exist when the reactor was sold), although Canada stipulated, and the U.S. supply contract for the heavy water explicitly specified, that it only be used for peaceful purposes. Nonetheless CIRUS has produced much of India's weapon plutonium stockpile, as well as the plutonium for India's 1974 Pokhran-I nuclear test. India argued in 1974 that the contract allows its use in producing peaceful nuclear explosives, which is how it characterized this explosion, though in recent years the project director Raja Ramanna has conceded that this was a sham. CIRUS reactor achieved criticality on 10 July 1960. It can produce 6.6-10.5 kg of plutonium a year (at a capacity factor of 50-80%).

In 1977 work began on the larger Dhruva plutonium production reactor, which was developed indigenous but based on the Canadian supplied technology. It was commissioned on 8 August 1985 but startup problems caused by resonance vibrations from the cooling system damaged fuel assemblies soon required shutdown. After modifications were made (spring clips to damp fuel rod vibration) it began operating at one-quarter power in December 1986 and reached full operation in mid-January 1988. It operates at 100 MW and is capable of producing 16-26 kg of plutonium annually (at a capacity factor of 50-80%).

An additional possible source of plutonium are a number of unsafeguarded CANDU power reactors, including Madras Atomic Power Stations (MAPS, known as Madras I and II, or MAPS-I and MAPS-II); the Narora Atomic Power Stations (NAPS, known as NAPS-I and NAPS-II), and the Kakrapar Atomic Power Station (KAPS). Like CIRUS and Dhruva, the CANDU reactors are heavy-water moderated natural uranium reactors that can be used effectively for weapon-grade plutonium production.

The possible production by MAPS is much larger than CIR and Dhruva combined, although the fuel burnup in power reactors of this type normally produces lower grade plutonium that is less desirable for weapons. Each power station reactor could produce up to 160 kg/yr (at a 60% capacity factor). It is uncertain how practical it is to operate MAPS for weapons grade plutonium production, although even the reactor-grade output has weapons potential. If supergrade plutonium were produced at BARC by short irradiation periods, it could be mixed with MAPS plutonium to extend the plutonium supply. As of November 1998 India had a total of 10 small power reactors operating, with 4 under construction and due to begin operation in 1999, but with 12 more planned or under construction that would boost electrical output by another 5100 MW. Nuclear power supplied 2.65 percent of India's electricity in 1999 and this is expected to reach 10 per cent by 2005. Expectations for nuclear power growth have consistently fallen far short of goals for over 30 years, so this percentage is likely to continue to grow slowly. India's nuclear power program proceeds almost entirely without fuel or technological assistance from other countries.

Partly as a result its power reactors have been among the worst-performing in the world (with regard to capacity factors), reflecting the technical difficulties of the country's isolation, but are apparently now improving significantly. Its industry is largely without IAEA safeguards, though a few plants are under facility-specific safeguards.

In February 2001 India had 14 small nuclear power reactors in commercial operation, two larger ones under construction and ten more planned. The 14 operating ones comprise:

- two 150 MWe BWRs from USA, started up in 1969, now using locally-enriched uranium and are under safeguards,
- two small Canadian PHWRs (1972 & 1980), also under safeguards; and
- ten local PHWRs based on Canadian designs, two of 150 and eight 200 MWe.

The separated plutonium for the 1974 test was produced at the separation plant in Trombay, near to Bombay, capable of processing 50 tonnes of heavy metal fuel/yr. Construction on the first facility there began in the 1950s, and began operating in 1964.

In 1974 it was shut down for repair and expansion and reopened in 1983 or 1984. Trombay handles the fuel from both the Cirus and Dhruva reactors. India also can separate plutonium in the Power Reactor Fuel Reprocessing (PREFRE) facility. This plutonium separation plant was built at Tarapur, north of Bombay, and began operating in 1979. The plant has encountered operating problems, but India reports having overcome these by 1990. The nominal annual capacity is given as 100-150 tonnes of CANDU fuel. A much larger plant is now under construction at Kalpakkam sufficient to handle all existing reactors.

Given its immense thorium resources, India is actively interested in developing the thorium/U-233 fuel cycle. India is known to have produced kilogram quantities of U-233 by irradiating thorium in CIR, Dhruva, and MAPS reactors. Substantial production of U-233 is not practical though with natural uranium fueled reactors. The thorium cycle requires more highly enriched fuel to have an acceptable breeding ratio with the non-fissile thorium blanket. Reactor-grade plutonium from MAPS could serve as start-up fuel for U-233 plants in the future. If available U-233 is as effective a weapon material as plutonium.

India has been developing the capability to produce heavy water domestically to provide the moderator load for future reactors. The heavy water for almost all existing reactors was imported however. The 110 tonnes of unsafeguarded moderator for Dhruva and Madras I and II were ironically provided by China.

India has acquired and developed centrifuge technology and built centrifuge enrichment plants in Trombay and Mysore in the 1980s. The larger Rare Metals Plant (RMP), as it is called, at Mysore has a cascade capable of producing 30% enriched uranium in kilogram quantities, beginning in 1992-93, although reliability has been a problem. These enrichment plants appear to have no role in India's power reactor development plans, so they may be intended to offset the prestige of Pakistan's enrichment capability, or to provide additional standby weapons production capability. India has reported that it plans to build an enriched uranium reactor, and a domestically fueled nuclear submarine.

India's interest in light weight weapon design can be surmised from BARC's acquisition in the 1980s of a vacuum hot pressing machine, suitable for forming large high-quality beryllium forgings, as well as large amounts of high purity beryllium metal. India is known to manufacture tritium, and may have developed designs for fusion-boosted weapons.

India is not a signatory to NPT and has opposed the treaty as discriminatory to non-weapons states. India has previously taken the position that a worldwide ban on nuclear testing, and the production of fissionable material for weapons is called for. Except for China, which continues testing, there is now a de facto halt to testing worldwide, as well as the production of weapons grade plutonium and uranium by the US and Russia. India has shown no interest so far in restricting its own activities despite these changes in the world situation. India has also rejected offers at bilateral negotiation with Pakistan, but in December 1988 the two nations signed an agreement prohibiting attacks on each other's nuclear installations and informing each other of their locations (though not their purposes).

NUCLEAR ESTABLISHMENT (BARC AND THE DRDO)

The nuclear establishment (BARC and the DRDO) also spent the rest of 1996 in mating the existing fission weapon to the Prithvi and Agni missile delivery systems and preparing the necessary command, control and security measures for the warhead (arming codes, security inter-locks, and an authentication and authorization system for use by the Prime Minister). On 1 April 1996, Anil Kakodkar became the new Director of BARC. The BJP government was succeeded by a coalition of 13 parties supported by the Congress Party from the outside. A regional politician named H.D. Deve Gowda became Prime Minister. Soon after taking office Gowda was also faced with the decision to proceed with nuclear tests (the devices that had been placed in the test shafts had not been removed). The same economic considerations that had concerned Rao militated against it. While the matter was under consideration the U.S. detected additional activity around Pokhran and Warren Christopher questioned Foreign Minister Inder Kumar

Gujral about it. Finally at the end of July or early August the devices were removed from the shafts and sent back to BARC.

The summer of 1996 was the "summer of the CTBT" for India's foreign policy. The negotiations on the Comprehensive Test Ban Treaty were drawing to a close, and although India had supported the treaty in principle for many years, as the debate on the final draft moved toward a conclusion India became increasingly critical of it. The treaty conference had been structured to require unanimous consent and on 14 August India announced that it opposed to treaty, blocking its adoption. A parliamentary maneuver subsequently side-stepped India's obstruction when the draft treaty was introduced directly into the UN General Assembly on 9 September 1996 by Australia and approved by voice vote the next day. It was adopted by a vote of 158 to 3, only India, Bhutan and Libya voted against it. Pakistan, which had said that it would sign the CTBT only if India did, abstained from voting. As one of the 44 nations possessing nuclear reaçtors, the CTBT cannot go into effect without India's signature however.

Many observers had concluded by this time that it had become inevitable that India would resume testing in the near future and inevitably declare itself a nuclear power. U.S. Defense Secretary William Perry later reported coming to this conclusion after visiting India in January 1995 and finding virtually no receptivity to avoiding nuclear development. Curiously enough, two strong long-time advocates of a nuclear armed India - Raja Ramanna and K. Subrahmanyam - argued in the fall of 1996 that testing was not necessary for India, that India's existing fission weapons were an adequate deterrent without it.

During Gowda's term in office Foreign Minister Gujral conducted a very active and successful foreign policy under Gowda - improving Indian relations with China, Pakistan, the minor states bordering India, and last but not least the United States. In part Gujral's success was due to taking advantage of the possibilities created by the end of the Cold War, which had tended to isolate India from China, Pakistan, and the United States as a quasi-client of the USSR. Also India's growing strength commanded greater attention by all parties, and there was a synergistic effect -

improving ties with one party tended to raise India's status with others.

But also important factors with regard to Pakistan's interest in improving ties with India were the fact that it was again (temporarily) under the civilian rule of Prime Minister Nawaz Sharif, and Pakistan's both relative and absolute decline. Since the end of the Cold War, and the Afghanistan War, Pakistan had lost its strategic importance to both the U.S. and China and with it some or all of their financial and technical support. While India's economy had been growing robustly since 1992 and had a positive trade balance, Pakistan's economy had deteriorated seriously and was running massive deficits both in trade and in government spending. Pakistan had also failed to establish a stable social order - the military existed outside of civilian control (when civilian control even existed), the bulk of the Pakistani economy was under the control of a small number of wealthy families that exercised near feudal control over large areas of Pakistan, and radical Islamic fundamentalist sects formed yet another independent state-within-the-state. This last independent power arose as a result of the Afghanistan War, when the increasing Islamicized Pakistani military granted considerable autonomy and funding to Mujaheedin training camps in Paksitan. After the end of the war, these Islamic factions increasingly turned their attention to radicalizing Muslim ethnic groups inside China, quickly alienating Pakistan's erst-while patrons. China's disenchantment with Pakistan accordingly raised its interest in a rapprochement with India. In the spring of 1997 PM Gowda authorized two operations that brought India closer to an open declaration of its nuclear status. The first was deploying Prithvi missiles (numbering less than a dozen), which had by this time gone into series production, at Jalandhar about 200 km from the Pakistani border. The second was to authorize the construction of two additional test shafts 50 m deep at Pokhran to accommodate the sub-kiloton test devices in March. It appears that Gowda may have decided to conduct nuclear tests at this point, a question that remains unresolved at this writing. Construction on the shafts began on 1 April and were completed on 11 April. Anil Kakodkar, BARC's director, travelled to the site on 15 April from to inspect the shafts and possibly to prepare for moving the devices. But two days later Gowda was forced by a vote of no confidence to resign.

In an article entitled "Nuclear India's Status" in the *Indian Defence Review* in 2000, Dr. Sanjay Badri-Maharaj, author of *The Armageddon Factor* said that during 1996-97 the Gowda government gave clearance so that India "actually began work on mating nuclear warheads to missiles." "This was confirmed to me in 1997 by a former artillery officer. This required modifications in safety locking systems and validating the mechanism's ability to withstand high-G (gravitation) forces," he said. Two tests for the mechanism to mount and trigger warheads were done on Prithvi SS-250 missiles before these were formally deployed in September 1997."

The deployment of the Prithvi was detected by U.S. intelligence in June, during Gujral's term in office, and brought about a diplomatic protest. Gujral downplayed its significance, pointing out that Pakistan had stored Chinese-made M-11 missiles of similar range at Sargoda, about 200 km from the Indo-Pak border. Gujral opposed nuclear tests and never approved them. Curiously enough though he did allow additional test preparations at Pokhran by authorizing a sixth shaft to be dug there in July.

August marked the fiftieth anniversary of India's independence. Widespread celebrations were held, but the occasion found the nation in an uncertain and reflective mood. Certainly much of the promise of the new nation had yet to be realized, and many were anxious for India to emerge as a major player on the world stage. A most telling (and often quoted) exchange between PM Gujral and Pres. Clinton occurred on 22 September 1997 at the occasion of the U.N. General Assembly session in New York. Gujral later recounted telling Clinton that an old Indian saying holds that Indians have a third eye. "I told President Clinton that when my third eye looks at the door of the Security Council chamber it sees a little sign that says 'only those with economic power or nuclear weapons allowed.' I said to him, 'it is very difficult to achieve economic wealth'."

According to then Defense Minister Mulayam Singh Yadav in October 1997 the BARC scientists had completed assembly of the test devices ("[they] had even tightened the last screw"). Whether or not Yadav is correct about the devices' *basic* assembly, the plutonium cores were kept separate from the devices and were only inserted in the devices at Pokhran just before the tests.

INDIA'S NUCLEAR WEAPONS PROGRAMME

The end of World War II marked a revolution in world affairs - the recasting of nations and relations between nations, and the emergence of a new technology which fundamentally changed the role of warfare. Within the span of two years and two months, from 1945 to 1947, three critical events occurred whose reverberations have brought the threat of nuclear war in South Asia seemingly daily to the front pages of newspapers everywhere. The three events were - in chronological order - the establishment of the United Nations on 26 June 1945; the dramatic demonstration of the destruction of which even crude nuclear weapons are capable in August 1945; and the calamitous partition of British India into the modern states of India and Pakistan at midnight on 14-15 August 1947.

It is clear to everyone that the legacy of partition is a key driving force behind the nuclear standoff that now exists between India and Pakistan. Partition split apart a region that had been united for millenia amid communal massacres on a scale never before seen, leaving in its wake the unresolved issue of contested Kashmir - a Muslim-majority region held by Hindu-majority India. The skirmishing that has continued now for over fifty years, punctuated by outbreaks of full-scale war (in 1947, 1965, and 1971), have given both nations ample motivation to develop potent weapons to gain advantage over — or restore balance with — the other. Another motivation for India's acquisition of nuclear weapons, less often considered in the West, is the potential threat and regional challenge presented by the nuclear-armed state of China, which faces India along much of its northern border. Disputes covering 80,000 square kilometers of this border region exist:

- China currently occupies the Aksai Chin plateau adjacent to Ladakh in Kashmir;

- India occupies the North-East Frontier Agency claimed by China.

These territorial disputes, a legacy of British rule, erupted into the Sino-Indian War on 20 October 1962, when China launched a massive attack on India to which India was powerless to respond. India had relied for years on a warm relationship with the Soviet Union as a counterweight to China, but with the USSR facing down the United States at the same moment in the Cuban Missile Crisis, India was shocked to find the Politburo suddenly switching to support China in an effort to bolster its own position.

PM Nehru was forced to appeal to the U.S. for help. U.S. naval air forces arrived off the coast, but before the USAF could deploy to India, China halted its attack on 21 November and partially withdrew. China continues to hold the Aksai Chin region captured in the initial advance. The legacy of this incident was the discovery that the Soviet Union was an unreliable ally, and the deep resolve not to be at a similar disadvantage with respect to China in the future.

Finally, an even less well known factor is a deep-seated drive to achieve international influence commensurate with India's size, and its importance throughout history as one of the world's principle civilizations. At the founding of the United Nations in 1945 the composition of the UN Security Council, the world's most influential and powerful international body, was fixed and has never changed from that time.

By an accident of history India was not an independent state at that moment, and its only hope for representation at the conference was the Churchill administration, then in its closing days, which vehemently opposed India's national aspirations. As a result China - with a similar geographic size, population, and state of economic development - was given a seat on Security Council, but India was not.

Nuclear weapons did not exist at the time the Security Council composition was debated, but over time the five Council members all acquired nuclear, then thermonuclear, arms. With the signing of the Nuclear Non-Proliferation treaty in 1970, and the replacement on the Council of the non-nuclear Taipei Chinese government with the nuclear armed government in Beijing shortly thereafter, the de facto principle that Security Council permanent members and the "nuclear club" were one and the same was firmly established.

The crucial importance of the desire for recognition of India as a world power in driving forward the nuclear weapons program, even overshadowing considerations of military necessity and deterrence is underscored by remarks by former weapons program leader Raj Ramanna: "There was never a discussion among us over whether we shouldn't make the bomb. How to do it was more important. For us it was a matter of prestige that would justify our ancient past. The question of deterrence came much later. Also, as Indian scientists we were keen to show our Western counterparts, who thought little of us those days, that we too could do it."

Thus it should be no surprise that India, now tied for third place among the world's largest economies (with Germany), and soon to become the most populous nation on Earth, has concluded that to be given its due in world affairs, it must become a member of the nuclear club as well.

What is notable however is how the world's largest democracy developed such capabilities. The decisions were made by a handful of people, with virtually no input or oversight by the public or the legislature. India's nuclear weapons program from its outset has answered only to the Prime Minister's office, and only the Prime Minister and a select few of his or her appointees have ever had any say in its development and acquisition.

Origin of India's Nuclear Weapon Program

India's indigenous efforts in nuclear science and technology were established remarkably early. The first step was taken by Dr. Homi Jehangir Bhabha in March 1944 when he submitted a proposal to the Sir Dorab Tata Trust (established in honor of Bhabha's own uncle, Sir Dorab Tata) to found a nuclear research institute, over three years before independence and a year before the first nuclear weapon test. This led to the creation of the Tata Institute of

Fundamental Research (TIFR) on 19 December 1945 with Bhabha as its first Director. The new government of India passed the Atomic Energy Act, on 15 April 1948, leading to the establishment of the Indian Atomic Energy Commission (IAEC) not quite one year after independence. At that time Prime Minister Pandit Jawaharlal Nehru declared: We must develop this atomic energy quite apart from war - indeed I think we must develop it for the purpose of using it for peaceful purposes.... Of course, if we are compelled as a nation to use it for other purposes, possibly no pious sentiments of any of us will stop the nation from using it that way."

This note of ambivalence in Nehru's speech foreshadowed his policies on nuclear research for the next decade. Nehru took a prominent role in international politics, founding the Non-Aligned Movement, and advocating nuclear disarmament. However, he refused to foreclose India's nuclear option while other nations maintained nuclear arsenals and supported programs designed to bolster India's weapons potential. In 1954 the Indian nuclear program began to move in a direction that would eventually lead to establishment of nuclear weapons capability. On 3 January 1954 the IAEC decided to set up a new facility - the Atomic Energy Establishment, Trombay (AEET), later to become the "Indian Los Alamos". On 3 August 1954 the Department of Atomic Energy (DAE) was created with Dr. Bhabha as Secretary. This department answered directly to the Prime Minister and has continued to do so down to the present day.

The program grew swiftly. The atomic energy budget increased 12-fold from 1954 to 1956. By 1958 the DAE consumed one third of India's research budget. By 1959 AEET employed over one thousand scientists and engineers. In 1955 construction began on India's first reactor, the 1 MW Apsara research reactor, with British assistance. And in September 1955, after more than a year of negotiation, Canada agreed to supply India with a powerful research reactor - the 40 MW Canada-India Reactor (CIR). Under the Eisenhower Administration's "Atoms for Peace" program the US agreed to supply 21 tons of heavy water for this reactor in Februrary 1956, and the reactor was dubbed the Canada-India

Reactor, U.S. or CIRUS (now commonly written as Cirus). The acquisition of Cirus was a watershed event in nuclear proliferation. Although the sale was made with the understanding that the reactor would only be used for peaceful purposes (the heavy water contract at least made this explicit), it occurred before any international policies were in place to regulate such technology transfers and no provision for inspections were made.

And in fact India was careful to ensure that no effective regulation would accompany the reactor. India refusing to accept fuel from Canada for the reactor and set up a program to manufacture the natural uranium fuel for Cirus indigeneously so as to keep complete control of the plutonium produced there.

This program, led by metallurgist Brahm Prakash, succeeded in developing the techniques for producing the precisely manufactured, high purity material demanded by the reactor.

The reactor was a design ideal for producing weapons-grade plutonium, and was also extraordinarily large for research purposes, being capable of manufacturing enough plutonium for one to two bombs a year.

The acquisition of Cirus was specifically intended by India to provide herself with a weapons option and this reactor produced the plutonium used in India's first nuclear test in 1974; provided the design prototype for India's more powerful Dhruva plutonium production "research" reactor; and is directly responsible for producing nearly half of the weapons grade plutonium currently believed to be in India's stockpile. The sale further set a precedent for similar technology transfers which greatly assisted Israel in obtaining its own plutonium production reactor from France shortly thereafter. The Atomic Energy Establishment, Trombay was formally inaugurated by PM Nehru on 20 January 1957. It acquired its present name — Bhabha Atomic Research Centre (BARC) — on 12 January 1967 when PM Indira Gandhi renamed it in memory of Dr. Bhabha who died in an airplane crash on 24 January 1966.

Apsara, fueled by enriched uranium from the UK, went critical on 4 August 1957, becoming the first operating reactor in Asia outside of the Soviet Union (though only days ahead of Japan's first reactor). Cirus achieved criticality at BARC on 10 July 1960.

As a nation India has always placed a premium on self-sufficiency. It is, in fact, the most self-sufficient large economy in the world and does not import any nuclear fuel. [The traditionally closed nature of economy though accounts for the import/export based Chinese economy far outstripping its growth from the late seventies to the early nineties.] Due to its vast domestic resources of thorium (a potential fuel for breeder reactors) but limited supplies of uranium, from the start of its nuclear program India has always placed strong emphasis on the development of breeder reactor fuel cycles. Breeder reactors require highly concentrated fissionable material for reactor fuel: either highly enriched uranium or plutonium. This provided a peaceful rationale for developing a plutonium separation capability, but the principal impetus for the India's first fuel reprocessing plant was to obtain a nuclear option.

In July 1958 PM Nehru authorized project Phoenix to build a plant with a capacity of 20 tonnes of fuel a year - sized to match the production capacity of Cirus. The plant was based on the U.S. developed Purex process and an American firm, Vitro International prepared the plans for it. Construction of the plutonium plant began at Trombay on 27 March 1961 and was commissioned in mid-1964.

India's civilian nuclear program was also established during this period. Discussions with American firms to construct India's first nuclear power plants at Tarapur were held in 1960-61. An interesting incident sheds light on Nehru's amd Bhabha's thinking at that time. In 1960 Kenneth Nichols, a former U.S. Army engineer who played significant roles in the Manhattan Project, represented Westinghouse in discussions on power plant construction. In a meeting with Nehru and Bhabha, Nichols relates that Nehru turned to Bhabha and asked:

"Can you develop an atomic bomb?" Bhabha assured him that he could and in reply to Nehru's next question about time, he estimated that he would need about a year to do it.... He concluded by saying to Bhabha "Well, don't do it until I tell you to."

CHANGING TACK ON CHEMICAL WEAPONS

These new considerations of national security are also evident from India's dilly-dallying with the Chemical Weapons Convention (CWC) earlier this year. After signing the treaty and ratifying it, in the face of uncertainty about the ratification of the CWC by Russia, China, Pakistan, and especially the USA, India suddenly threatened to withdraw from the treaty. To justify this shift, a senior official of the external affairs ministry said "The main problem here is that in the absence of the above countries [that is, the USA, Russia, China and Pakistan] not ratifying it, the CWC is neither universal nor equitable nor non-discriminatory because, as was the case with NPT and CTBT, certain countries will be keeping chemical weapons, while denying the same to others." Thus the CWC which, prior to this switch, India had praised as a model non- discriminatory treaty, and as a "useful model for our future efforts in the field of global disarmament," suddenly became a discriminatory treaty. But, once it became apparent that the U.S. would ratify the CWC after all, India executed another shift and welcomed the "non-discriminatory" CWC. Subsequently, India has revealed that it possessed chemical weapons and is in the process of destroying them in accordance with the CWC. This proved that India lied on several previous occasions when it declared that it did not possess chemical weapons, and in direct violation of the August 1992 joint declaration with Pakistan on the complete prohibition of chemical weapons."

Along with three nuclear weapons states, namely the USA, Russia, and China, India did not sign the land mines treaty in Ottawa in December 1997.

Domestic Trends and Global Disarmament

These recent shifts in India's attitudes towards global disarmament, and its increasingly strident criticisms of any step-by-step measures towards nuclear disarmament, can only be understood by analysing the domestic debate. Ever since the early sixties, hawkish sections of the Indian policy-making community have argued in the domestic media in favour of building a nuclear arsenal. The 1974 nuclear test is, in part, a display of their influence.

Subsequently, they have not been able to alter the status quo in any significant way.

All this may change. The last few governments in India have been relatively weak and unstable, all formed by coalitions of various parties with different agendas. With the rise in strength of the Hindu fundamentalist Bharatiya Janata Party (BJP), whose election manifestos have consistently endorsed overtly exercising India's nuclear option no party in power has been spared being attacked on its nuclear policy. The BJP has consistently opposed any restraints on the Indian nuclear and missile programs. The BJP's policy is not new, but with no political party strong enough to oppose it, global disarmament initiatives take a back seat to preservation of the nuclear option. In this new political climate, the hawks have begun to dominate the nuclear debate. Citing the pressure imposed by the nuclear weapon states, and particularly the USA, on several of the non-nuclear weapon states and the threshold states to achieve this extension, the hawks managed to increase nationalistic feelings among the elite. The hawks also used the extension to argue that nuclear weapons are here to stay and hence India should go about building its own nuclear arsenal. The effectiveness of this line of argument can be seen subsequently in the domestic CTBT debate. Sections of the Indian population who were otherwise opposed to India going overtly nuclear came to accept that the CTBT, originally championed by India, was a "Western" treaty, and a continuation of the discriminatory nuclear regime set up by the nuclear weapon states.

For the hawks, the rationale for the linkage between a time-bound nuclear disarmament process and the Fissban or the CTBT is two-fold. First, this linkage is needed to be used to gain credibility among the majority of people in India, who support India's official position that India should keep its options open only as long as the other states are not willing to give up their arsenals. Indeed, there is substantial support for global nuclear disarmament among the Indian public. A recent poll conducted by the Kroc Institute and the Fourth Freedom Forum, in conjunction with the Marketing and Research Group (MARG), New Delhi, found that 83% of those polled supported an international agreement for the elimination of all nuclear weapons. The second rationale is that it buys time so that the internal debates can be fought out and some consensus for further nuclear weapons development reached. This extra time is also essential for other reasons. With the increasing norm against nuclear weapons, as codified by agreements like the CTBT, or the decision at the World Court against nuclear weapons, the hawks sense this as their last opportunity to propel India into the ranks of the nuclear weapon states.

The economic liberalization program has also contributed in an indirect way to their campaign. Hand in hand with the 5-10% increases in the Indian economy has been the rise of Indian elite who, like the elite elsewhere, is greatly interested in making their country "powerful." And, conveniently for them, the best example of a country that has recently entered the ranks of the world's rich and mighty is China — which in 1962 had a border war with India and defeated it. Completely ignoring the various economic and social factors that go into making China the power it is, the elite focus on its nuclear arsenal, and in it see their short cut to greatness.

Government Response in Internal and External Constraints

Given the internal and external constraints on India, the hawks have not made much headway. International pressures have become especially important with the economic liberalization process which began in the early nineties, and has led to a greater enmeshing of the Indian economy with the world economy. The weakness and instabililty of the last few governments increases this vulnerability to international pressure. Government response may also be subdued due to calculations of the effectiveness of the nuclear option in security terms. It seems as though policy makers realize that while the nuclear option is useful politically to gain the attention of the five nuclear weapon powers, in particular the USA, its exercise would have little military worth.

In addition to the international and domestic positions offered by government officials and the hawks, there is another point of view that is not exposed to the public eye, but expressed behind closed doors in New Delhi, Washington and elsewhere. Over the past few months, while the crescendo about the Fissban has been building up in the Indian media, several Indian policy-makers have been quietly talking, informally, about trying to make a deal with the United States about the nuclear question. According to these policy makers, India would be quite willing to sign the Fissban — for a price. What exactly the price is has never been stated explicitly, but most of the Indian proposals focus around nuclear and space technology. Despite the strong U.S. opposition to transferring these technologies to India, the hawks are insistent on these for two main reasons. The first reason is to strengthen the alliance with the Department of Atomic Energy. A second, more obtuse, reason is that obtaining nuclear or space related dual technology from the U.S. is a visible display of India's importance.

In part, the informal suggestion that India will be willing to cut a deal over the fissban reflects the Indian view that, through its actions at the CTBT negotiations, India has proved that it is capable of playing hard ball with the great powers, and the time has come for the West, especially the United States, to recognize India's nuclear status. Hand in hand with this attempt to obtain recognition of its nuclear status is India's portrayal of itself in international circles as a trustworthy nuclear state. Indian officials often mention the case of a Middle-Eastern country that asked India for reprocessing technology, only to be denied. The message seems to be that India is responsible enough to be let into the club. And, it is suggested in return for this acceptance, India is prepared to abide by some limitations on its nuclear programs — not due to arm-twisting by the P-5, but because it is a responsible player.

As in the case of the P-5 who, after having developed the requisite capabilities, embraced arms control as an extension of their security policies, India, in the view of the hawks, may be beginning to see itself as "arriving," if not as having "arrived," and so may be considering arms control negotiations in this new light.

In this context, the similarity between the ostensible reason put forward by India — that the CTBT is not linked to time-bound nuclear disarmament — and the Soviet position in 1954 is revealing. Like the five nuclear weapon states, India no longer unconditionally supports global arms control and disarmament measures, such as the CTBT and the proposed Fissban, but accords primacy to what it perceives as its national security interests.

In all these debates, the voices of the doves are seldom heard. There are several reasons for this. First and foremost, the policies of the P-5 towards nuclear weapons makes it very difficult for the doves to persuade the Indian public that the nuclear weapons states are indeed serious about disarmament. In order to change this state of affairs rapid reductions in the size of the existing nuclear arsenals along with measures that de-emphasize the role of nuclear weapons, such as a no-first use commitment and de-mating warheads from missiles, are very necessary.

Another reason, mentioned earlier, is that the Indian elite seem desperate to join the great power club. A third reason is the lack of a strong peace movement. Most other concerned citizens and groups have their hands full with other problems, and as such have not had the time, or the resources, to address nuclear matters. The few groups which are interested in nuclear issues chiefly work on the environmental and social costs related to nuclear energy generation — and even their numbers have been falling. The number of people subscribing to *Anumukti,* the only Indian anti-nuclear journal, has been coming down steadily.

NUCLEAR WEAPONS AND NON-PROLIFERATION TREATY

The Treaty on the Non-Proliferation of Nuclear Weapons, commonly known as the Non-Proliferation Treaty or NPT, is a landmark international treaty whose objective is to prevent the spread of nuclear weapons and weapons technology, to promote cooperation in the peaceful uses of nuclear energy and to further the goal of achieving nuclear disarmament and general and complete disarmament. Opened for signature in 1968, the Treaty entered into force in 1970. On 11 May 1995, the Treaty was extended indefinitely. A total of 190 parties have joined the Treaty, including the five nuclear-weapon States: the United States, Russia, the United Kingdom, France, and China (also the five permanent members of the United Nations Security Council). More countries have ratified the NPT than any other arms limitation and disarmament agreement, a testament to the Treaty's significance. Four non-parties to the treaty are known or believed to possess nuclear weapons: India, Pakistan and North Korea have openly tested and declared that they possess nuclear weapons, while Israel has had a policy of opacity regarding its own nuclear weapons program. North Korea acceded to the treaty in 1985, but never came into compliance, and announced its withdrawal in 2003.

The NPT consists of a preamble and eleven articles. Although the concept of "pillars" is not expressed anywhere in the NPT, the treaty is nevertheless sometimes interpreted as a *three-pillar* system, with an implicit balance among them:

1. *non-proliferation,*
2. *disarmament,* and
3. *the right to peacefully use nuclear technology.*

The NPT is often seen to be based on a central bargain: "the NPT non-nuclear-weapon states agree never to acquire nuclear weapons and the NPT nuclear-weapon states in exchange agree to share the benefits of peaceful nuclear technology and to pursue nuclear disarmament aimed at the ultimate elimination of their nuclear arsenals". The treaty is reviewed every five years in meetings called Review Conferences of the Parties to the Treaty of Non-Proliferation of Nuclear Weapons. Even though the treaty was originally conceived with a limited duration of 25 years, the signing parties decided, by consensus, to extend the treaty indefinitely and without conditions during the Review Conference in New York City on May 11, 1995.

At the time the NPT was proposed, there were predictions of 25-30 nuclear weapon states within 20 years. Instead, over forty years later, only four states are not parties to the NPT, and they are the only additional states believed to possess nuclear weapons. Several additional measures have been adopted to strengthen the NPT and the broader nuclear nonproliferation regime and make it difficult for states to acquire the capability to produce nuclear weapons, including the export controls of the Nuclear Suppliers Group and the enhanced verification measures of the IAEA Additional Protocol. However, critics argue that the NPT cannot stop the proliferation of nuclear weapons or the motivation to acquire them. They express disappointment with the limited progress on nuclear disarmament, where the five authorized nuclear weapons states still have 22,000 warheads in their combined stockpile and have shown a reluctance to disarm further. Several high-ranking officials within the United Nations have said that they can do little to stop states using nuclear reactors to produce nuclear weapons.

Treaty "pillars"

The NPT is commonly described as having three main "pillars": non-proliferation, disarmament, and peaceful use. This "pillars" concept has been questioned by some who believe that the NPT is, as its name suggests, principally about nonproliferation, and who worry that "three pillars" language misleadingly implies that the three elements have equivalent importance.

First Pillar: Non-proliferation

Five states are recognized by the Non-Proliferation Treaty as nuclear weapon states (NWS): China (signed 1992), France (1992), the Soviet Union (1968; obligations and rights now assumed by the Russian Federation), the United Kingdom (1968), and the United States (1968) (The United States, UK, and the Soviet Union were the only states openly possessing such weapons among the original ratifiers of the treaty, which entered into force in 1970). These five nations are also the five permanent members of the United Nations Security Council. These five NWS agree not to transfer "nuclear weapons or other nuclear explosive devices" and "not in any way to assist, encourage, or induce" a non-nuclear weapon state (NNWS) to acquire nuclear weapons (Article I). NNWS parties to the NPT agree not to "receive," "manufacture" or "acquire" nuclear weapons or to "seek or receive any assistance in the manufacture of nuclear weapons" (Article II). NNWS parties also agree to accept safeguards by the International Atomic Energy Agency (IAEA) to verify that they are not diverting nuclear energy from peaceful uses to nuclear weapons or other nuclear explosive devices (Article III).

The five NWS parties have made undertakings not to use their nuclear weapons against a non-NWS party except in response to a nuclear attack, or a conventional attack in alliance with a Nuclear Weapons State. However, these undertakings have not been incorporated formally into the treaty, and the exact details have varied over time. The U.S. also had nuclear warheads targeted at North Korea, a non-NWS, from 1959 until 1991. The previous United Kingdom Secretary of State for Defence, Geoff Hoon, has also explicitly invoked the possibility of the use of the country's nuclear weapons in response to a non-conventional attack by "rogue states". In January 2006, President Jacques Chirac of France indicated that an incident of state-sponsored terrorism on France could trigger a small-scale nuclear retaliation aimed at destroying the "rogue state's" power centers.

Second Pillar: Disarmament

Article VI of the NPT represents the only binding commitment in a multilateral treaty to the goal of disarmament by the nuclear-weapon States. The NPT's preamble contains language affirming the desire of treaty signatories to ease international tension and strengthen international trust so as to create someday the conditions for a halt to the production of nuclear weapons, and treaty on general and complete disarmament that liquidates, in particular, nuclear weapons and their delivery vehicles from national arsenals.

The wording of the NPT's Article VI arguably imposes only a vague obligation on all NPT signatories to move in the general direction of nuclear and total disarmament, saying, "Each of the Parties to the Treaty undertakes to pursue negotiations in good faith on effective measures relating to cessation of the nuclear arms race at an early date and to nuclear disarmament, and on a treaty on general and complete disarmament." Under this interpretation, Article VI does not strictly require all signatories to actually conclude a disarmament treaty. Rather, it only requires them "to negotiate in good faith."

On the other hand, some governments, especially non-nuclear-weapon states belonging to the Non-Aligned Movement, have interpreted Article VI's language as being anything but vague. In their view, Article VI constitutes a formal and specific obligation on the NPT-recognized nuclear-weapon states to disarm themselves of nuclear weapons, and argue that these states have failed to meet their obligation. The International Court of Justice (ICJ), in its advisory opinion on the Legality of the Threat or Use of Nuclear Weapons, issued 8 July 1996, unanimously interprets the text of Article VI as implying that

"There exists an obligation to pursue in good faith and bring to a conclusion negotiations leading to nuclear disarmament in all its aspects under strict and effective international control." The ICJ opinion notes that this obligation involves all NPT parties (not just the nuclear weapon states) and does not suggest a specific time frame for nuclear disarmament.

Critics of the NPT-recognized nuclear-weapon states sometimes argue that what they view as the failure of the NPT-recognized nuclear weapon states to disarm themselves of nuclear weapons, especially in the post–Cold War era, has angered some non-nuclear-weapon NPT signatories of the NPT. Such failure, these critics add, provides justification for the non-nuclear-weapon signatories to quit the NPT and develop their own nuclear arsenals.

Other observers have suggested that the linkage between proliferation and disarmament may also work the other way, i.e., that the failure to resolve proliferation threats in Iran and North Korea, for instance, will cripple the prospects for disarmament. No current nuclear weapons state, the argument goes, would seriously consider eliminating its last nuclear weapons without high confidence that other countries would not acquire them. Some observers have even suggested that the very progress of disarmament by the superpowers—which has led to the elimination of thousands of weapons and delivery systems —could eventually make the possession of nuclear weapons more attractive by increasing the perceived strategic value of a small arsenal. As one U.S. official and NPT expert warned in 2007, "logic suggests that as the number of nuclear weapons decreases, the 'marginal utility' of a nuclear weapon as an instrument of military power increases. At the extreme, which it is precisely disarmament's hope to create, the strategic utility of even one or two nuclear weapons would be huge."

Third Pillar: Peaceful use of Nuclear Energy

The third pillar allows for and agrees upon the transfer of nuclear technology and materials to NPT signatory countries for the development of civilian nuclear energy programs in those countries, as long as they can demonstrate that their nuclear programs are not being used for the development of nuclear weapons.

Since very few of the states with nuclear energy programs are willing to abandon the use of nuclear energy, the third pillar of the NPT under Article IV provides other states with the possibility to do the same, but under conditions intended to make it difficult to develop nuclear weapons.

The treaty recognizes the inalienable right of sovereign states to use nuclear energy for peaceful purposes, but restricts this right for NPT parties to be exercised "in conformity with Articles I and II" (the basic nonproliferation obligations that constitute the "first pillar" of the Treaty). As the commercially popular light water reactor nuclear power station uses enriched uranium fuel, it follows that states must be able either to enrich uranium or purchase it on an international market. Mohamed ElBaradei, then Director General of the International Atomic Energy Agency, has called the spread of enrichment and reprocessing capabilities the "Achilles' heel" of the nuclear nonproliferation regime. As of 2007 13 states have an enrichment capability. Because the availability of fissile material has long been considered the principal obstacle to, and "pacing element" for, a country's nuclear weapons development effort, it was declared a major emphasis of U.S. policy in 2004 to prevent the further spread of uranium enrichment and plutonium reprocessing (a.k.a. "ENR") technology. Countries possessing ENR capabilities, it is feared, have what is in effect the option of using this capability to produce fissile material for weapons use on demand, thus giving them what has been termed a "virtual" nuclear weapons program.

Countries that have signed the treaty as Non-Nuclear Weapons States and maintained that status have an unbroken record of not building nuclear weapons. However, Iraq was cited by the IAEA with punitive sanctions enacted against it by the UN Security Council for violating its NPT safeguards obligations; North Korea never came into compliance with its NPT safeguards agreement and was cited repeatedly for these violations, and later withdrew from the NPT and tested multiple nuclear devices; Iran was found in non-compliance with its NPT safeguards obligations in an unusual non-consensus decision because it "failed in a number of instances over an extended period of time" to report aspects of its enrichment program; and Libya pursued a clandestine nuclear weapons program before abandoning it in December 2003.

In 1991 Romania reported previously undeclared nuclear activities by the former regime and the IAEA reported this non-compliance to the Security Council for information only. In some regions, the fact that all neighbors are verifiably free of nuclear weapons reduces any pressure individual states might feel to build those weapons themselves, even if neighbors are known to have peaceful nuclear energy programs that might otherwise be suspicious. In this, the treaty works as designed.

7

Foundation of China's Nuclear Doctrine

There are two basic starting points for China's nuclear doctrine: China's national security and humanitarianism.

Firstly, the maintenance of China's national security is the fundamental motivation behind the development of nuclear weapons.

China has used its nuclear weapons as a means to prevent its enemies from imposing war on Chinese people. China developed its nuclear weapons under a very special security environment during the Cold War, in which China had faced with the nuclear threats from one or even two superpowers.

Secondly, humanitarianism is one of the most important factors for China in developing its nuclear doctrine. From the first day China successfully tested its nuclear weapons, it has held that these weapons must be totally banned and thoroughly destroyed.

China committed itself to never being the first to use nuclear weapons at any time and under any circumstance.

This also means that China has regarded humanitarianism, which places the most attention on the lives of people at its core, as the one of pillars of Chinese nuclear doctrine. Compared with the nuclear strategy of MAD (Mutual Assurance of Destruction) of the Unites States and the Soviet Union during the Cold War, Chinese doctrine has commanded higher morality within the international community.

Structure of China's Nuclear Doctrine

Similar to the nuclear doctrines of other nuclear-weapon states, China's doctrine has composed five policies: policy of declaration, nuclear development, nuclear deployment, nuclear employment, and nuclear disarmament. Because China has a different strategic culture and is in a different situation, its nuclear doctrine has the following characteristics.

Firstly, the declared policy of China's nuclear doctrine is no-first use of nuclear weapons and self-defence. From the start China has made it very clear that it will not use nuclear weapons first at any time and under any circumstance. No-first use of nuclear weapons has had strategic significance, and is based on deep consideration.

China believes that the final results of wars are decided by people instead of advanced weapons and WMD. The most significant foundation for China's national defence is the concept of People's War. Therefore, implementation of a policy of no-first use of nuclear weapons will affect the results of wars in the future.

The Sacred commitment to no-first use of nuclear weapons fully reflects the point that China's holding of nuclear weapons is totally for self-defence. China had been compelled to develop nuclear weapons, which contain wars.

This no-first use policy allows China to command high morality in the international community. Those countries and people that use nuclear weapons during invading wars will be pinups on the pillar of humanization of the history of humanity.

China's final purpose in developing nuclear weapons is to destroy nuclear weapons. The policy of no-first use is beneficial because it encourages the international community to go forward towards this purpose.

Secondly, China's policy of nuclear development is the building of a lean And effective strategic nuclear force.

Chinese national security has mainly depended on a foreign policy of peace and the integrated power of People's War. Nuclear force is one of the most important pillars and parts of China's armed forces. However, it is not the foundation stone and the core of China's national defence forces. In order to reach the goal of deterring other countries from launching nuclear attacks against China, China must develop a strategic nuclear force with the capability of basic means of retaliation.

China has persisted in the principle of limited development of nuclear weapons, attaching a lot of importance to building a lean and effective strategic nuclear missile force. China does not seek the superiority of numbers in its nuclear force and would not want to have nuclear competition with other countries. China has taken a very self-restrained attitude towards the development of nuclear weapons, so Chinese nuclear arsenal has been kept at a minimal level of self-defence.

Thirdly, China's policy of nuclear weapons deployment is to maintain a second strike capability. China has focused on maintaining this capability in its nuclear weapons deployment—That is the capability of nuclear retaliation. China has never deployed nuclear weapons outside of it. In 1979, the Central Committee of Chinese Communist Party made the decision to build the "Great Wall" Project, the purpose of which was to make China's land-based strategic nuclear force have the capability to survival and retaliate after suffering from a first nuclear strike by other countries.

In the summer of 1995, the "Great Wall" Project—under the Second Artillery— was completed, Therefore, the Chinese land-based strategic nuclear force has had underground positions for fighting, defending, being deposited, commanding and living. Even if struck by nuclear warheads launched from other countries, China's land-based strategic nuclear force can retaliate ten minutes, or after a few days, or even one month living in the underground bunkers.

Some Western experts said that the Second Artillery deploys land-based strategic nuclear missiles in "underground homes" hundreds of meters below ground, which allows them to endure hits from some nuclear bombs, equivalent to hundreds of thousands of TNT.

Strategic nuclear submarines are also an important capability of second strike; they are beneficial for improving strategic stability between China and other nuclear powers. As Deng Xiaoping said, "our strategy has always been defence and will continue its strategic defence in the next twenty years, in which nuclear submarines are also weapons of strategic defence."

Fourthly, China's policy of nuclear employment is self-defence and retaliation. China has persisted in the principle of self-defence and retaliation. The Central Military Commission(CMC) has directly controlled and commanded the nuclear force of China. "The Second Artillery Force sticks to China's policy of no first use of nuclear weapons, implements a self-defensive nuclear strategy, strictly follows the orders of the CMC, and takes it as its fundamental mission the protection of China from any nuclear attack. In peacetime the nuclear missile weapons of the Second Artillery Force are not aimed at any country. But if China comes under a nuclear threat, the nuclear missile force of the Second Artillery Force will go into a state of alert, and get ready for a nuclear counterattack to deter the enemy from using nuclear weapons against China. If China comes under a nuclear attack, the nuclear missile force of the Second Artillery Force will use nuclear missiles to launch a resolute counterattack against the enemy either independently or together with the nuclear forces of other services."

After the armed conflicts between China and the Soviet Union at treasure Islands along China-Soviet border in 1969, the Soviet's attempted to launch surgical nuclear attacks against important military and political targets. Therefore, the Second Artillery Force made final preparations for battle, which showed the firm resolution of China to retaliate and made Soviet leaders give up their attempt to launch nuclear attacks against China. This was the first and only time that China's nuclear missile force of China entered the position of final preparation for battle.

In 1988, Deng Xiaoping put forward the concept of using strategic nuclear missiles as a form of guerrilla warfare, which meant that Deng Xiao asked for an increased mobilization of strategic missiles, so as to improve the capability of nuclear retaliation. Mao Zedong talked about the concept of putting-off nuclear counter-attacks. This would be one of ways of nuclear counter-attacks, which China may choose according to the strategic situation and within the principle of self-defence and retaliation in the future.

Because the possibility of the U.S. being militarily involved an armed conflict between the two sides of Taiwan Strait exists—which could lead to further armed conflict, even Sino-U.S. nuclear conflict, China has to develop the capability to deter the U.S. from interfering militarily in an armed conflict in the Taiwan Strait. China is not a superpower and has a small number of nuclear weapons, so the model of MAD is not suitable for Sino-U.S. nuclear relations. China has some capability for nuclear retaliation. So long as China has the capability for one nuclear warhead to penetrate U.S. missile defence systems and hit American territory after a U.S. launched nuclear attacks against China, or so long as the U.S. cannot assure it could destroy all China's strategic nuclear force after an American first strike against China, it will be very difficult for the U.S. to make the decision to launch nuclear attacks against China.

Fifthly, China's policy of nuclear disarmament regards the complete prohibition and thorough destruction of nuclear weapons as the final goal in nuclear issues. Impacts of China's nuclear Doctrine on the International Nuclear Arms Control China has been the first among the nuclear weapon state, which put forward the concept of the nuclear weapon-free world as the final objective of its nuclear doctrine. Since 1963 China has consistently called for the "complete prohibition and thorough destruction" of nuclear weapons. Thus, China was the first country to regard a nuclear weapon-free world as China's final goal within the international community. China's no-first use policy has greatly reduced the danger of nuclear armed conflicts and has very positive impacts on international nuclear disarmament.

China's minimum deterrence strategy has made China's nuclear arsenal small. China has put forward a set of position on international nuclear disarmament. In 1994, in an effort to step by step, realize the objective of building a world free from nuclear weapons, China put forward a complete, interrelated proposal for the nuclear disarmament process at the 49th session of UN General Assembly.

All nuclear-weapon states should unconditionally declare that they will not be the first to use nuclear weapons and immediately begin negotiations towards a treaty to this effect; efforts to establish nuclear-weapon-free zones should be supported and guarantees given not to use or threaten to use nuclear weapons against non-nuclear-weapon states; a comprehensive nuclear test ban treaty should be negotiated and concluded no late than 1996; the major nuclear powers should implement existing nuclear disarmament treaties as scheduled and further substantially reduce their nuclear weapon stockpiles; a convention banning production of fissile materials for nuclear weapons be negotiated and concluded; a convention prohibiting all nuclear weapons be signed, whereby all nuclear-weapon states undertake to completely destroy existing stocks of nuclear weapons under effective international supervision; the proliferation of nuclear weapons should be prevented while the promoting of nuclear disarmament process and international cooperation in peaceful uses of nuclear energy should be pursued.

Since then, China has also put forward some more views about nuclear disarmament. Up till now, China's stance on nuclear disarmament can be catalogued as follows:

- Nuclear major powers should give up their nuclear first-use policy;
- Nuclear-weapon states with big nuclear arsenals should further reduce their nuclear weapons;
- All nuclear-weapon states should commit themselves not be the first to use nuclear weapons, and should conclude international legally binding documents on this issue as soon as possible;
- All nuclear-weapon states should commit themselves not to use or threaten to use nuclear weapons against non-nuclear-weapon states or nuclear weapon-free zones, and should conclude international legally binding documents on this issue as soon as possible;

- All states deploying nuclear weapons abroad should commit themselves to supporting the appeal of establishing nuclear-weapon-free zones, respecting their positions, and bearing their relevant responsibilities;
- All states deploying nuclear weapons abroad should withdraw their nuclear weapons home; 8
- All states should not develop and deploy weapon systems in outer space and missile defence system, which will disturb strategic security and stability;
- All states should negotiate and conclude international legally binding documents on complete prohibition and thorough destruction of nuclear weapons.

China has repeatedly called for an international convention to ban nuclear weapons, similar to the chemical and biological weapons conventions. China has been officially opposed to the policy of nuclear deterrence, based on the implicit or explicit threat to use nuclear weapons first, and to the deployment of nuclear weapons outside of national territories. China advocates the prevention of proliferation of nuclear weapons as part of the process of eliminating such weapons. Chinese holds that in the process of reaching the objective of complete prohibition and thorough destruction of nuclear weapons, nuclear proliferation should be prevented.

China advocates the total prohibition of nuclear weapon explosion tests during the process of advancing towards the objective of complete prohibition and thorough destruction of nuclear weapons, and nuclear-free world.

On 29 July 1996, Chinese government declared that China suspended its nuclear explosion tests. China actively participated in the negotiations of the Comprehensive Test Ban Treaty (CTBT), showing a constructive spirit and flexible attitude during the negotiations. On 24 September 1996, China signed the CTBT treaty. The treaty is the first international legally binding document, prohibiting any nuclear weapon explosion test or other nuclear explosion test in any environment, in any spot in the world, this is conducive to the process of nuclear disarmament and the prevention of nuclear proliferation, it improves international peace and security.

China endorses the verification measures to be taken in accordance with the regulation of the CTBT treaty. At the same time, China opposes any country who abuses the rights to interfere in China's internal affaire and to harm China's proper security interests. China holds that a prohibition of nuclear test itself is not the objectives, but just one of the steps to realizing the final goal of complete prohibition and thorough destruction of nuclear weapons. However, on 13 October, 1999, U.S. Senate failed in ratifying the CTBT. This failure has exerted great negative influence over the process of international arms control and may lead to new nuclear proliferation. Because of the failure, both India and Pakistan have still refused to sign the CTBT. Concerned with the intention of the United States, some other countries have slowed down the process of their ratification to the Treaty. The Russian State Duma ratified the CTBT on 21 April 2000. If U.S. Senate ratifies the CTBT Treaty in the future, the Chinese National People's Congress will ratify it the next day.

ROLE OF THE NUCLEAR WEAPONS IN CHINA'S MILITARY STRATEGY

Nuclear weapons have been playing an important role in China's national and military strategy. However, they have not played a key role. China's nuclear doctrine has gradually experienced the process change from a counter-nuclear blackmail strategy to a minimum deterrence strategy. Now the most important task of the People's Liberation Army (PLA) is to win partial wars under the situation of high technology. Conventional forces are still the major implements used to win these kinds of wars. Nuclear weapons' major task of China is to deter the enemy from launching an initial nuclear attack against China.

From the first test of a nuclear weapon by China on October 16, 1964, to the mid-1980s, China's nuclear doctrine had been the counter-nuclear blackmail strategy. During the period, China's nuclear weapons had been few and had not reached the standard of the minimum deterrence strategy. This strategy would inflict an unaffordable loss by nuclear retaliation on any superpower that first launched a nuclear attack against China,. Furthermore, during this period, both Chinese Government and the PLA had not accepted the concept of nuclear deterrence. Some of Chinese experts even regarded the nuclear deterrence as a means for the superpowers to impose nuclear blackmail on other countries.

Since China's acquisition of nuclear weapons, it has not only broken the superpowers' nuclear monopolization, but also generated the capability to deny the nuclear blackmail from the superpowers. Identified below are some of the major features of the counter-nuclear blackmail strategy:

Firstly, the counter-nuclear blackmail strategy was established on the foundation of the concept of people determining the results of wars instead of the theory of nuclear taboo. The basic reasons for China developing the counter-nuclear blackmail strategy were:

Nuclear weapons have two distinct characteristics. On one hand, they are weapons of massive destruction that can kill thousands of people. On the other hand, nuclear weapons cannot determine the results of wars.

Territorially, China is very big expansive with a vast of people, so there is deep potential and wide leeway for people's war in China.

Secondly, the counter-nuclear blackmail doctrine was a comprehensive strategy. From October 1964 to 1985, China had prepared to fight a war at short notice, on a large scale, and in which nuclear weapons were used. According to the guideline of China's military strategy of active defence, it sped up the development of missiles with nuclear warheads. At the same time, China actively prepared for defending nuclear wars.

In October 1966, China had its first flight test of a medium-range missile with a nuclear warhead. On May 18, China tested its inter-continental ballistic missile, which flew successfully from West China to the South Pacific. From that time on, China has had the capability to attack a target on another continent.

From 1964, China began to build the areas of the big and small Third Defence Line. After the Armed Conflict between China and the Soviet Union in 1969, the Nine National Congress of Chinese Communist Party declared that China must prepare to fight a war at short notice, on a big scale, and involving nuclear weapons from both the Soviet Union and the United States. From the point on, China began to establish air-raid shelters, some of which withstand nuclear attack, on a big scale throughout the country. In 1972, Chairman Mao Zedong put forward the concept of "Digging deep shelters, Accumulating food in big stockpile, and Not seeking hegemony", which became the national strategy for China guiding the process of China and guided the process to fight a war at shout short notice, on a blarge scale and in which nuclear weapons were used.

Thirdly, China's counter-nuclear blackmail doctrine was of the view that finally winning a war will require conventional weapons. Preparation to fight nuclear wars meant China not only prepared to defence against surprise nuclear attacks from a superpower, but also sought to defeat invading enemy with conventional weapons.

Since 1985, China has gradually transformed its nuclear doctrine from a counter-nuclear blackmail strategy to a minimum deterrence one. The major reasons for this transformation have been the following:

- With the great efforts of many years, China has made great progress in developing its strategic nuclear forces. In September 1989, China finished establishing an integrated nuclear war-fighting system, which can effectively carry out strategic retaliation.
- Since 1986, China has accepted the concept of nuclear deterrence and has regarded the nuclear deterrence as one part of its nuclear doctrine.
- After the PLA's large conventional force reduction, the importance of nuclear weapons in China has been increased. Since 1984, the PLA's Second Artillery has entered the list of day-day combat readiness on duty. So carrying out the minimum deterrence strategy has been beneficial for preventing nuclear war against China.

CHINA'S MISSILE EXPORTS AND ASSISTANCE TO PAKISTAN

China's missile exports and assistance to Pakistan have been a serious proliferation concern for the United States over the years and remain a contentious issue in Sino-US relations. US intelligence reports have revealed that China has transferred complete M-11 missiles, missile related technology, and manufacturing assistance to Pakistan. The US is concerned that Chinese missile transfers could lead to instability in South Asia as India and Pakistan continue to engage in a regional arms race, heightening the risk of military confrontation between the two countries. In this context, proliferation of ballistic missiles into this region is particularly destabilizing, more so in the aftermath of the nuclear tests of May 1998. Chinese missiles and/or technology might also be re-transferred to third parties, further undercutting international nonproliferation efforts.

The United States has made and continues to make serious efforts to dissuade China from transferring missiles, components, and missile related technology to Pakistan. Washington has engaged Beijing in a series of negotiation seeking to obtain Chinese pledges to abide by the Missile Technology Control Regime (MTCR) guidelines and eventually to become a member of the regime. For these purposes, the US has both applied consistent diplomatic pressures, offered economic incentives, and imposed economic sanctions on China. While China made pledges in 1991 and 1994 to the US promising to comply with the main provisions of the MTCR and halt all sales of complete MTCR-class missile systems, it has tended to interpret these pledges narrowly and has continued missile technology transfers and manufacturing assistance to Pakistan, including a second missile factory. More recently, China has also implicitly linked its MTCR commitments to issues of increasing salience to its own security concerns, namely, theater missile defence (TMD), US arms sales to Taiwan, and US intention to deploy national missile defence (NMD) and amend the ABM Treaty. Given the deterioration of Sino-US relations in the aftermath of the NATO bombing of the Chinese embassy, the release of the Cox Report and allegations of Chinese nuclear espionage, the growing tension over the Taiwan issue in the aftermath of Chen Shuibian's election to Taiwan's presidency; and the passage in the House of the Taiwan Security Enhancement Act and the proposed China Nonproliferation Law, bilateral cooperation in arms control and nonproliferation may continue to stagnate. Sino-Pak missile cooperation could remain an irritant to US-PRC relations for some time to come. In this context, recent US intelligence reports alleging continued Chinese transfers of missile technology and technical expertise to Pakistan could impede efforts to mend US-China bilateral relations in the aftermath of the bombing of the Chinese embassy in Yugoslavia.

There are various strategic, commercial, and foreign policy rationales behind Chinese missile exports and assistance to Pakistan. China and Pakistan have enjoyed a solid strategic relationship since the 1960s. Over the years China has provided Pakistan with a wide range of major conventional weapons systems and the two countries have also developed a close partnership in various defence cooperation programs. While this strategic relationship initially grew out of the mutual needs of China and Pakistan in countering the Soviet and Indian security threats, respectively, it continues to serve the two countries' national security interests in the post-Cold War era. Pakistan relies on China as a trusted ally in dealing with India from a position of military weakness; Beijing values its close ties with Islamabad both to extend its influence to South Asia and to balance against India. Commercially, as China began its economic reform and opening up in the early 1980s, defence industries and arms exporting companies were under tremendous pressure to tap into the lucrative international arms market. Pakistan became a valued customer for Chinese arms. Finally, given US concern about and emphasis on missile proliferation issues, Beijing has also found it useful to exploit them as bargaining leverage in dealing with Washington on issues important to China: US arms sales to Taiwan, TMD deployment in East Asia, among others.

China reportedly began discussing possible sales to Pakistan of M-11 missiles and related technology in the late 1980s. The contract for the M-11 sale was reportedly signed in 1988. In April

1991, the United States announced that it had discovered the transfer of an M-11 missile even though China insisted it had never shipped the system to Pakistan. In May 1991, the US imposed sanctions against China. In November 1991, Secretary of State James Baker reached an agreement with then Chinese Foreign Minister Qian Qichen in which Beijing verbally agreed to abide by "the guidelines and parameters of the MTCR" in exchange for the lifting of the sanctions imposed earlier that year. (However, China's pledge said nothing about adhering to the MTCR's annex.) After China sent Washington a letter in February 1992 affirming its earlier MTCR assurance in writing, the sanctions were lifted in March 1992.

However, this commitment did not end the controversy. The September 1992 US decision to sell 150 F-16 fighters to Taiwan led China to withdraw from P-5 talks on conventional arms transfers. In December 1992 reports surfaced that China had transferred 34 complete M-11 systems to Pakistan, in apparent violation of its earlier [1991] pledge. China and Pakistan both denied that the transfer had taken place. In August 1993, the Clinton Administration imposed MTCR related sanctions on China after determining that China had again engaged in missile trade with Pakistan. China denounced the sanctions, calling the US decision "a wrong judgment based on inaccurate intelligence" and threatened to scrap its promise to abide by the MTCR.

The impasse was finally in October 1994 when the two countries issued a joint statement on missile proliferation. In the joint statement, the United States agreed to lift sanctions and in return China promised *to ban all exports* of ground-to-ground missiles exceeding the primary parameters of the MTCR. (The MTCR only calls for a "strong presumption of denial" for such exports.) China also agreed to accept the concept of "inherent capability" which binds China from exporting any missile that is inherently capable of delivering a 500 kg payload over 300 km. This standard would prohibit future exports of the M-11 missile. The US waived the sanctions in November 1994.

Persistent US diplomatic efforts since 1994 have also led China to clarify its MTCR commitment. Beijing has both reaffirmed its obligations to permanently curtail its missile cooperation with Pakistan and indicated that it is actively studying joining the MTCR as a full member. However, serious questions about China's missile export controls remain. Although China promulgated regulations on conventional arms transfers in 1997, it is not clear if they cover missiles and missile-related technology transfers. While an internal control list restricting missile exports exists, Beijing has not revealed its scope, contents, and the extent to which it approximates that contained in the MTCR annex. Developments of the last few months have again derailed the meager progress that had been made between the two Sino-US summits.

The release of the Cox Report, the US bombing of the Chinese embassy in Belgrade, and US intentions with regard to national missile defence (NMD) and theater missile defence (TMD) have effectively put any prospect of China's joining the MTCR on hold. Increasingly, Beijing is demanding a linkage between its MTCR membership and broader issues of US arms sales to Taiwan, and the development, and future deployment of TMD in Northeast Asia. China's continuing transfers of missile technology to Pakistan and Iran may be a means of gaining leverage over the US. However, if China concludes that its fundamental security interests are threatened, it might step up these activities.

Sino-US disagreements over Chinese missile-related activities and missile nonproliferation continue. China has not accepted the MTCR annex and US efforts to get China to adopt legally binding export controls on MTCR items have yet to lead to the publication of regulations on missile exports (although Chinese officials insist they have an internal control list). In addition, suspicion of continued Chinese assistance to the Pakistani missile production facility at Rawalpindi persists and this raises serious questions of Beijing's sincerity in abiding by its pledges.

During and immediately after the Sino-US summit of June 1998, Beijing indicated that it was "actively studying" MTCR membership and renewed once more its missile nonproliferation pledge on curbing its missile technology transfers and assistance to South Asia in the Jiang-Clinton Joint Statement. However, given the recent negative developments in bilateral relations (e.g., the Cox Report, the embassy bombing, TMD), it is not clear that these disagreements will get resolved any time soon. Policy Issues

Chinese missile transfers to Pakistan raise a number of issues for US nonproliferation policy and Sino-US relations. First, China's missile exports and assistance can undermine international missile nonproliferation efforts, in particular the objectives of the MTCR. China's most serious confrontations with the United States over ballistic missile proliferation have involved Chinese transfers of complete M-11 missiles and missile-related technology to Pakistan. The M-11 is a single stage, solid fuelled missile with a reported range of 290 km and a payload of 800 kg. While technically the M-11 missiles do not fall within the MTCR parameter, they have the inherent capability of being able to deliver a 500 kg payload over 300 km. The fact that China has resisted joining the MTCR as a formal member, coupled with its ambiguous interpretation and implementation of its bilateral commitments, raises questions as to the seriousness of Chinese commitment to arms control and nonproliferation.

US concerns over Chinese missile exports to Pakistan focus mainly on regional stability and the potential of further proliferation to other regions where the US has important strategic interests, including the Middle East and the Persian Gulf. The introduction and improvement of ballistic missiles into South Asia could result in a fierce arms race between India and Pakistan, which in turn could be highly destabilizing given the perennial animosity between the two countries; the recent conflicts in Kargil only heightens such concerns. Given the short distances between major population centres of the two countries, poor intelligence, and short warning time, there would be great temptation to launch preemptive strikes in crisis situations. A more serious concern is the mating of nuclear warheads and other WMD with missiles. The further proliferation of ballistic (and cruise) missiles to countries such as Iran, Syria, and Libya could enable these countries to seriously threaten US interests in the Middle East and the Persian Gulf.

Furthermore, China's missile exports and assistance to Pakistan represent a major bone of contention in Sino-US bilateral relations and has the potential to limit and undermine bilateral cooperation in other areas. Over the last decade, Chinese proliferation behaviour, bilateral trade issues, Taiwan and human rights controversies have been the four key obstacles to better US-China relations. US efforts to change Chinese behaviour through both economic incentives and sanctions have achieved noticeable but limited results. While the US has made strong efforts to persuade China to join the MTCR, China continues to resist and remains critical of the regime, in particular its charge that the regime is discriminatory in nature and its exclusion of high-performance aircraft. Continued controversy over Chinese missile-related transfers and assistance to Pakistan points to serious differences between Washington and Beijing with regard to regional security. While the US tends to compartmentalize nonproliferation issues on their own merits, the Chinese have insisted that proliferation issues cannot be separated from underlying security causes.

Finally, differences in interests exist and this may account for the difficulty for a final resolution of the issue. Washington seeks to stem proliferation of WMDs and their delivery systems to the Middle East, the Persian Gulf, and South Asia out of its interests for secure supplies of oil, the security of Israel, and stability on the subcontinent. Beijing, on the other hand, regards its nuclear and missile exports as an important source of foreign exchange as well as a means of gaining influence in these regions. China's refusal to adopt IAEA full-scope safeguards (FSS) may be due to concerns that such measures would deprive it of potential nuclear markets. Regarding continued missile technology transfers and assistance to Pakistan, Beijing's motive may be more strategic than commercial. Islamabad has remained an important factor in Beijing's strategic calculations regarding South Asia and a useful counterweight to India.

Three issues confront the Clinton administration: the credibility of Chinese commitments to missile nonproliferation; whether the US should impose sanctions on China as required by domestic laws; and balancing the management of bilateral relations and the enforcement of nonproliferation legislation. The charges about renewed Chinese missile technology cooperation with Pakistan occurred at a particularly sensitive moment as Beijing and Washington are resuming both the security and arms control dialogues; as the Senate is to begin debates on PNTR on China, with some senators proposing the "China Nonproliferation Law" bill and seeking to amend the bill with provisions requesting annual review of Chinese missile proliferation activities; and as the deadline of a task force investigation of the 1992 Chinese sale of 34 M-11 missiles is approaching or may have already been passed. While both China and the Clinton administration have the incentives to reach a compromise to avoid sanctions, the room for such an outcome remains limited.

New Developments

Suspicions persist regarding China's continued missile cooperation with Pakistan. It has been speculated that the Shaheen-1 IRBM, which Pakistan tested in April 1999, is actually modeled on Chinese M-9 missiles. A February 1999 CIA report stated that "Chinese and North Korean entities continued to provide assistance to Pakistan's ballistic missile program during the first half of 1998. Such assistance is critical for Islamabad's efforts to produce ballistic missiles...China's involvement with Pakistan will continue to be monitored closely." A September 1999 National Intelligence Council (NIC) report stated that "Pakistan has Chinese supplied M-11 short-range ballistic missiles..." This is the first time that the US government has publicly verified that China actually supplied Pakistan with these missiles. The NIC report referred to the transfer of 34 M-11 missiles delivered in November 1992, but there is no evidence that China has resumed the transfer of complete missile systems to Pakistan. However, an unclassified CIA report to Congress released in February 2000 suggests that "some [Chinese] ballistic missile assistance [to Pakistan] continues." Following the September 1999 NIC Report Republican Senator Jesse Helms, chairman of the Senate Foreign Relations Committee, threatened to block the appointment of Acting Assistant Secretary of State for Nonproliferation Affairs Robert Einhorn to a permanent position unless the Clinton administration formed a task force to impose sanctions on China. A task force was formed and given a six month deadline to make a determination, which is expected to be in late

May or June 2000. US and Chinese reportedly have been meeting to reach a compromise to avoid sanctions. China is unlikely to become a full member of the MTCR, but a compromise on strengthening China's nuclear export controls may be possible.

The recent US intelligence reports suggest that despite Chinese pledges to the contrary, it has continued to provide Pakistan with specialty steels, guidance systems and technical expertise in the latter's effort to develop long-range ballistic missiles. These and other allegations have apparently led to the proposal by Republican Senator Fred Thompson and Democratic Senator Robert G. Torricelli of legislation aimed at monitoring Chinese missile proliferation activities and mandating automatic sanctions should "credible evidence" indicates that specific Chinese exports and transfers have taken place. US Assistant Secretary of State for Nonproliferation Robert Einhorn travelled to Beijing in early June to seek commitment from China not to export missiles and missile technology to Iran and Pakistan. The July meetings in Beijing between Chinese officials and John Holum, Undersecretary of State for Security and Arms Control, and Secretary of Defence William Cohen are expected to focus heavily on China's alleged missile assistance to Pakistan.

On 21 November 2000, the State Department announced that it was waiving sanctions on Chinese entities for the past sales of missile technologies to entities in Iran and Pakistan. These exports, which date back to 1992, violated the 1990 Missile Control Act which calls for sanctions on entities engaged in export of MTCR-controlled items. The sanctions were for the export of both MTCR category I and category II items. The US also pledged to resume discussions with China as soon as possible on extending the 1995 US-China Agreement on International Trade in Commercial Launch Services. Under this accord, US companies can export satellites to China for launch on Chinese rocket boosters.

In response to these actions, the Chinese Foreign Ministry issued its most stringent and specific policy statement on missile nonproliferation to date. China stated "China is opposed to the proliferation of weapons of mass destruction...China has no intention of assisting, in any way, any country in the development of ballistic missiles that can be used to deliver nuclear weapons (i.e., missiles capable of delivering a payload of at least 500 kg to a distance of at least 300 km.)"

This statement appears to build on China's past commitment in the 1998 US-China Joint Statement on South Asia not to provide missile technologies to Pakistan or India. As part of the recent commitment, the Chinese government importantly promised, for the first time, to issue export control laws covering missile technologies. In the past, Chinese officials have stated that its controls on missile exports were governed by internal documents and not public laws. The Chinese pledged that the new laws would include such regulations as license application and review, end-user certifications, and a "catch-all" clause. The Chinese statement did not, however, specifically reference the MTCR or its control list and the statement did not mention when China would issue the new export control law. Some experts argue that these latter elements represent a loop-hole in the accord. The Chinese government also denies that it engaged in illegitimate trade with either Iran or Pakistan. The *China Daily* reports Chinese Foreign Ministry spokesman, Sun Yuxi refuting US allegations that China supplied Iran and Pakistan with missiles. Sun denounced the allegations as "rumors with ulterior motives." Sun said the PRC has exercised strict control on the export of missile technologies..

According to CIA Director General Tenet, whatever the current policy of Beijing on missile assistance to Pakistan, previous aid has enabled Islamabad to move rapidly toward serial production of solid propellant engines. Future assistance cannot be ruled out. The concern is that continued development of the Shaheen-II will require additional Chinese assistance.

In August 2001, concerns about China's continued missile technology assistance to Pakistan reemerged. According to a report in the *Washington Times*, a Chinese company has sent a shipments of missile components to Pakistan. The leaked intelligence information noted that the China National Machinery & Equipment Import & Export Corp., known as CMEC, reportedly supplied the missile components for Pakistan's Shaheen-1 and Shaheen-2 missile programs. A U.S. spy satellite reportedly detected the latest shipment as it arrived by truck at the mountainous Chinese-Pakistani border May 1. It was one of 12 missile component transfers sent by ship and truck detected by U.S. intelligence agencies since the beginning of the year. After bilateral consulations failed to resolve this dispute, in September 2001 the US government imposed economic sanctions on a Chinese company for shipping missile technology to Pakistan in violation of a bilateral agreement in November 2000 and US law. The US government said that the China Metallurgical Equipment Corporation in late 2000 and early 2001 shipped missile technology to Pakistan that would assist its Shaheen 1 and Shaheen 2 programs. The sanctions, under the 1990 Missile Control Act, ban US companies from doing business with the Chinese entity for two years. The Bush administration has also invoked a ban on new licenses for U.S. companies to put their satellites on Chinese rockets or transfer satellite technology. These transfers were subsequently confirmed in September CIA report on global proliferation developments.

The Chinese government vociferously denied a Chinese company had shipped proscribed missile technology to Pakistan. The Foreign Ministry spokesman said: Over a period of time, the US has repeatedly alleged that MECC was engaged in missile proliferation activities according to its so-called "intelligence information". In-depth investigations by the Chinese side indicate that MECC has never engaged in any activities as alleged by the United States and the US allegation is groundless. However, the US side is bent on making the erroneous decision based on its wrong intelligence information, in disregard of the constructive position and the investigation results of the Chinese side. Such a US move is totally groundless and irresponsible, which the Chinese side can never accept.

The Foreign Ministry called for the US to immediately lift the sanctions. China threatened repercussions of the sanctions were not lifted. "China strongly urges the US side to immediately withdraw its wrong decision, so as to avoid any damage to Sino-US cooperation in non-proliferation. Otherwise, the US side should bear all the responsibilities for the consequences arising therefrom."

THE ROLE OF NUCLEAR WEAPONS IN CHINESE DEFENCE POSTURE

China has long maintained that its nuclear weapons development is largely driven by the need to respond to nuclear coercion and blackmail. The role of nuclear weapons, in this context, is purely defensive and retaliatory, rather than war-fighting, as some western analysts suggest. Indeed, in the early years, China even rejected the concept of deterrence, regarding it as an attempt by the superpowers to compel others with the threat of nuclear weapons. This probably explains the glacial pace with which China introduced, modified, and modernized its small-size nuclear arsenals over the past four decades. Mainly guided by the principle that nuclear weapons will only be used (but used in a rather indiscriminate way) if China is attacked with nuclear weapons by others, nuclear weapons in China's defence strategy serve political rather than military purposes.

PLA analysts emphasize that the terms "nuclear strategy" and "nuclear doctrine" are rarely used in Chinese strategic discourse; instead, a more commonly used term refers to "nuclear policy," which in turn is governed by the country's national strategy. Hence, the deployment and use of nuclear weapons are strictly under the "supreme command" of the Communist Party and its Central Military Commission. Nuclear weapons are for strategic deterrence only; no tactical or operational utility is entertained. If and when China is under a nuclear strike, regardless of the size and the yield, it warrants strategic responses and retaliation. Chinese leaders and military strategists consider the role for nuclear weapons as one of defensive nuclear deterrence (*ziwei fangyu de heweishe*). Specifically, the country's nuclear doctrine and force modernization have been informed and guided by three general principles: effectiveness (*youxiaoxing*), sufficiency (*zugou*), and counter-deterrence (*fanweishe*). China's 2006 Defence White Paper emphasizes the importance of developing land-based strategic capabilities, both nuclear and conventional, but provides no specifics on the existing arsenal, the structure of the Second Artillery Corps (China's strategic nuclear force) order of battle, or the projected size of the nuclear force. It indicates only that China will continue to maintain and build a lean and effective nuclear force. While Chinese analysts acknowledge that deterrence underpins China's nuclear doctrine, it is more in the sense of preventing nuclear coercion by the superpower(s) without being coercive itself, and hence it is counter-coercion or counter-deterrence. Rather than build a large nuclear arsenal as resources and relevant technologies have become available, a path pursued by the superpowers during the Cold War, China has kept the size of its nuclear weapons modest, compatible with a nuclear doctrine of minimum deterrence. According to Chinese analysts, nuclear weapons' role in China's defence doctrine and posture is limited and is reinforced by the NFU position, a limited nuclear arsenal, and support of nuclear disarmament.

China's 2006 Defence White Paper for the first time describes at length the country's nuclear doctrine. Reaffirming its long-held NFU principle and calling for the comprehensive prohibition and complete elimination of nuclear weapons, the white paper emphasizes the defensive nature of its nuclear strategy, stating that

> Its fundamental goal is to deter other countries from using or threatening to use nuclear weapons against China. ... China upholds the principles of counterattack in self-defence and limited development of nuclear weapons, and aims at building a lean and effective nuclear force capable of meeting national security needs. It endeavours to ensure the security and reliability of its nuclear weapons and maintains a credible nuclear deterrent force. ... China exercises great restraint in developing its nuclear force. It has never entered into and will never enter into a nuclear arms race with any other country.

This position is reinforced in China's latest white paper on defence, released in January 2009. Specifically, the paper lays out the circumstances in which Beijing may contemplate the use of nuclear weapons in retaliation against nuclear attacks against it:

> In peacetime the nuclear missile weapons of the Second Artillery Force are not aimed at any country. But if China comes under a nuclear threat, the nuclear missile force of the Second Artillery Force will go into a state of alert, and get ready for a

nuclear counterattack to deter the enemy from using nuclear weapons against China. If China comes under a nuclear attack, the nuclear missile force of the Second Artillery Force will use nuclear missiles to launch a resolute counterattack against the enemy either independently or together with the nuclear forces of other services.

While NFU remains China's official policy regarding nuclear weapons use, it is clear that Beijing also emphasizes the importance of maintaining an effective and reliable strategic force composed of both nuclear and conventional weapons capabilities. Nuclear weapons would be used for strategic retaliation and counterstrikes, while conventional weapons would be used for precision attacks, presumably in an offensive posture. In essence, China's nuclear doctrine, the size of its nuclear arsenal, and scope and speed of its modernization will depend on a host of politico-strategic considerations, Sino-U.S. relations, and developments in the revolution in military affairs (RMA).

China continues to modernize its nuclear arsenal, not so much in quantitative terms, but focusing more on the survivability and effectiveness of a credible second-strike capability. To that goal, efforts are under way to develop and deploy new-generation land-and submarine-based ballistic and cruise missiles. Among the five nuclear weapon states, China claims to maintain the smallest number of operational nuclear weapons. The most recent publicly available sources estimate that China's current nuclear forces consist of approximately 176 deployed warheads and an unknown number of additional warheads in the stockpile. China's strategic arsenal is deployed on a triad that includes 121 land-based missiles, 55 strategic bombers, and an unspecified number of submarine-launched ballistic missiles on board the newly deployed *Jin*-class nuclear-powered submarine. Of this relatively small arsenal, only a limited number of missiles (about two dozen) are capable of striking targets throughout the continental United States (compared to the hundreds of U.S. missiles that could strike Chinese targets). In addition, China's medium-range ballistic missiles, such as the DF-4 and DF-21, could effectively reach U.S. bases in Guam and Japan.

CHINA'S STRATEGIC FORCES TODAY

China does not publish information about the size of its nuclear weapons arsenal. The United States intelligence community, however, has released considerable amounts of information. Although some of this information is contradictory—the intelligence community is certainly not a monolith—some assessments can be made by comparing quantitative assessments from the intelligence community with qualitative descriptions provided by authoritative Chinese sources.

China appears to maintain the smallest operationally deployed nuclear force (and perhaps the smallest stockpile) of any of the five nuclear weapon states party to the Treaty on the Non-Proliferation of Nuclear Weapons. According to unclassified U.S. intelligence assessments, China "has over 100 warheads deployed operationally on ballistic missiles. Additional warheads are in storage." Declassified documents from the 1990s place classified estimates of the total stockpile, including a small stockpile of aircraft-delivered gravity bombs, between 200 and 250 warheads.

The majority of these missiles were developed in the 1960s and 1970s, beginning with the 1965 *banian sidan* plan ("eight years, four missiles") to develop medium-, intermediate-, and intercontinental-range ballistic missiles by 1972. As it turns out, China did not complete deployment of its first-generation large liquid-fuelled ballistic missiles until the deployment of the first DF-5 intercontinental ballistic missiles (ICBMs) in silos beginning in 1981.

In the 1980s, China focused on developing solid-fuelled, mobile ballistic missiles to replace its first generation of ballistic missiles. Although China deployed the first of these new missiles, the DF-21, beginning in the early 1990s, flight-testing of the DF-21 continued through the 1990s, and China did not begin large-scale deployments in earnest until around 2000. China is just now beginning deployments of the DF-31 and DF-31A, which will replace China's DF-4 and DF-5 missiles.

China is also developing a submarine-launched variant of the DF-31, called the JL-2. China has built at least two new ballistic missile submarines since 2007. The Office of Naval Intelligence believes China may build as many as five of the new submarines to replace China's lone Xia-class nuclear-powered ballistic missile submarine, which is not believed to be operational. Although the JL-2 may become operational as soon as 2010, China appears to have rather limited capabilities for communicating with submarines at sea and probably has not established operational practices for conducting deterrent patrols.

The growth in China's ballistic missile arsenal is not confined to China's nuclear forces. China has also developed new conventionally armed solid-fuel short-range ballistic missiles, the DF-11 and DF-15, which it deploys in very large numbers near Taiwan. China has also deployed a conventional variant of the DF-21, the DF-21C, and is further developing a fourth modification to serve as an anti-ship ballistic missile. Finally, China has deployed a new land-attack cruise missile—the ground-launched DH-10—as part of a broad effort to acquire ground-, air-, and sea-launched cruise missiles.

This process of replacing liquid-fuelled ballistic missiles with solid-fuelled ballistic and cruise missiles underpins China's ongoing strategic modernization. Although many observers have linked the deployment of the DF-31 and DF-31A to recent U.S. missile defence deployments, it is important to keep in mind that these programs date to the mid-1980s and were supposed to have been completed many years ago.

China is not developing new warheads for its new ballistic missiles. The warheads for the new nuclear delivery systems—the DF-31, DF-31A and JL-2—were tested during the 1990s, before China signed the CTBT in August 1996. Since that time, China has observed a moratorium on nuclear tests. Without resuming yield testing, China would have significant difficulty in designing and certifying a new design, such as those incorporating insensitive high explosives. China does appear to have a significant stockpile stewardship program that may make use of hydro-dynamic experiments at the Lop Nor Test Site.

China may also have a small stockpile of gravity bombs for delivery by aircraft, but no aircraft appear to have the primary mission of nuclear warhead delivery, and nuclear warheads do not appear to be deployed at Chinese airbases. Before permanently moving its nuclear testing underground in the 1980s, China tested numerous nuclear weapons by dropping them from aircraft; however, Chinese officials have stated that the purpose of "airdrop" tests was to reduce test debris that would assist foreign intelligence agencies in analysing the test results.

China probably does not deploy tactical nuclear weapons, although it has the capability to do so and successfully tested an enhanced radiation weapon or "neutron bomb" in 1988.

If China's modernization seems unusual, perhaps it is because China is only now completing the deployment capabilities that other countries have possessed for decades.

This is not to suggest that missile defence and other aspects of U.S. strategic modernization have no effect on Chinese decisions. China has developed and flight-tested a sophisticated suite of penetration aids for the DF-21 and DF-31 family of ballistic missiles. Some Chinese specialists have argued that China may increase the number of nuclear warheads capable of reaching the United States, rather than simply replacing the DF-4 and DF-5 on a one-to-one basis.

It remains to be seen whether China will increase its number of nuclear warheads as much as current U.S. intelligence community predictions, which anticipate very large increases in Chinese nuclear forces to respond to U.S. missile defence efforts. In 2001, the U.S. intelligence community asserted that the number of Chinese warheads capable of reaching the United States could grow to 75–100 by 2015. In 2006, the National Air and Space Intelligence Centre warned that the number of Chinese nuclear warheads that could reach the United States "could expand to well over 100 in the next 15 years."

Although such increases are within China's economic and industrial capabilities, especially if China were to deploy as many as five new ballistic missile submarines, it is also possible that China's modernization will occur within the general parameters of its overall force posture, characterized by keeping warheads in storage and a restrictive nuclear no-first-use declaratory policy.

China's nuclear arsenal also stands out from the other nuclear powers not merely due to its small size, but also because China keeps its nuclear forces off alert and under the strictures of a no-first use pledge.

By all indications, Chinese nuclear warheads are not normally mated to their missiles. Robert Walpole, then national intelligence officer for strategic and nuclear programs at the CIA, stated in 1998 that "China keeps its missiles unfueled and without warheads mated." The warheads are stored at nearby, but separate, bases. Press reports of Chinese mobile ballistic missile exercises published by the state-run Xinhua News Agency indicate that nuclear warheads would be mated in the field to mobile ballistic missiles before launch, similar to the procedure used by Soviet Mobile Technical Rocket Bases (PRTB, in Russian) stationed in East Germany and elsewhere during the Cold War.

Anecdotal evidence from public descriptions of Chinese exercises and doctrinal materials suggest that Chinese forces expend considerable effort training to conduct retaliatory missions in the harsh environment after a nuclear strike. One Chinese textbook that is used to train cadres is forthright about the difficulty of maintaining a survivable retaliatory capability under a no-first-use doctrine. "According to our principle of no first-use of nuclear weapons," the text *Zhanyi Xue* (Operational Studies) warns future commanders, "the nuclear retaliation campaign of the Second Artillery will be conducted under the circumstances when [the] enemy has launched a nuclear attack on us. ... The personnel, position equipment, weapons equipment, command telecommunication system and the roads and bridges in the battlefield will be seriously hurt and damaged."

Whether Chinese leaders will change these features of their nuclear posture is difficult to predict. Western analysts have long predicted, for example, that China would eventually move away from a no-first-use posture—yet China's political leaders continue to appear committed to the policy. In part, the judgment that China would dump no-first-use has been based on voluminous criticisms of no-first-use in Chinese military writings. The considerable ink spilled in Chinese military publications complaining about "no-first-use" is probably the best evidence that the policy remains in place. Dissatisfaction among some Second Artillery commanders with no-first-use might also explain the growing deployments of conventionally armed ballistic missiles, which are presumably subject to less doctrinal interference from senior leaders and Chinese nuclear weapons scientists.

Fundamental changes are more likely to result from ongoing changes in China's domestic politics, rather than as a mechanistic response to changes in U.S. strategic capabilities such as missile defence or conventional strike. China's small cadre of scientists and engineers continue to play a significant role in matters relating to nuclear policy—but today, unlike in Nie's era, they are no longer the only voices on nuclear policy. As part of an effort to ensure that military priorities are better reflected in defence science and technology investment, the General Armaments Department replaced the Commission on Science and Technology for National Defence, which was run by Nie's son-in-law as late as the mid-1990s. Although the GAD itself may be a distinct interest group, relative to the Second Artillery or the Navy, it is presumably much less independent than in Nie's day.

Moreover, the Second Artillery and the Navy are vastly more professional today than even ten years ago. In the past it would have been difficult to imagine the parochial service interests overriding a desire for central control over China's nuclear forces—as embodied in aphorisms such as "the party must control the gun, the gun must never control the party." But today China is very different: the PLA is far more professional than ever before, and China's leaders were children when the United States subjected China to nuclear threats.

STRATEGY FOR WEAPONS AND EQUIPMENT DEVELOPMENT

Weapons are tools used to carry out armed conflicts. It is an important component of the military's combat power. It is the major element that determines the success and failure of a war. The development of modern weaponry, contained and controlled by national defence science and technology and national defence economic realities, have affected a succession of military scientific theories.

The Development of Modern Weaponry and National Defence Science and Technology

On June 7, 1981, the Israeli Air Force sent out 14 aircraft and bombed a nuclear reactor 20 km southeast of the Iraqi capital of Baghdad. "The bombs landed precisely on the main building where the nuclear reactor was located." On May 2, 1982, during the Falklands War between England and Argentina, England's SSN Conqueror fired two wire-guided TIGERFISH torpedoes and sank the only 13,000-ton large cruiser, General Belgrano, in the Argentina Navy. Two days later, the Argentina air force flying the French manufactured SUPER ETENDARD fighters needed only one EXOCET AM39 air-to-ship missile to sink the large, superbly equipped and costly ($200 million) SHEPHERD class destroyer from a distance more than 45 km away. On May 25, Argentina sank the British Navy's 18,000-ton troop transport, an ATLANTIC SEA TRANSPORT [Daxiyang Yunsongze] class ship. In June 1982, in the air battle above Syria's Bekka Valley, the Israeli Air Force won an important battle by using all types of jamming methods and precision-guided weapons like air-to-surface missiles and television and in 2 days completely destroyed all the surface-to-air missile sites in the Bekka Valley.

In the surprise attack on Grenada on October 25, 1983, the United States used many surveillance methods and sent out an E-2C high-altitude, early-warning aircraft with antijamming capability, and hi-tech F-15s and F-16s, which had been remodeled and equipped with infrared sighting equipment, laser-guided bombs, and radar-guided self-seeking air-to-surface missiles, to achieve its predetermined military objectives with very little cost. During the military conflict over the Gulf of Sidra between the United States and Libya between March 24-25, 1986, and in the air attack on Libya by the United States on April 15, the United States used hi-tech weapons such as laser-guided bombs, "Rockeye" cluster bombs, TRIDENT radar-guided, self-seeking air-to-surface missiles and for the first time, used its high speed antiradiation missile "HARM" as well as other hi-tech equipment such as new infrared sighting equipment.

The United States lost only one F-111 fighter-bomber and in turn sank and seriously damaged two Libyan cruisers, destroyed one missile launching site, destroyed about 5 to 12 Soviet made MIG-23s and 3 to 5 IL-76 transports, and achieved combat successes on 5 predetermined targets. Since the 1980s, several local area conflicts have vividly shown, and people have clearly understood even before the smoke cleared, that modern weapons have assumed some new characteristics under the impetus given them by the advances made in national defence science and technology.

One is electronics. With the development of microelectronics, computers, satellite communications, lasers, and other technologies and greater improvements seen in communications, navigation, radar, telemetering, remote control, remote sensing, and modern electronic command, control, and communications systems because of electronics and the radio, various kinds of weapons systems are extensively using electronic equipment and technology. From the perspective of the cost accounting of weapons systems, the percentage of the costs of the electronic equipment within each of these weapons systems is relatively sizable. In aircraft, it is 33 percent; in missiles, 45 percent; in space vehicles, 66 percent; in military vessels, 22 percent; and in combat vehicles, 24 percent. Electronic equipment has already become an indispensable component of modern weapons systems. It has also become the nerve centre of modern weapons systems. With the development of the fifth generation of computers, artificial intelligence, and robotic technology, it is possible that troops could be equipped with simple artificial intelligence weapons systems in the future.

Second is the change in guidance systems. Since the 1950s, along with the development and discovery of new technologies like wireless, television, infrared, laser, microwave, inertia guidance, photoelectricity, acousto-electronics, sensors, and precision measuring and automation, precision-guided weapons systems (cruise missile, surface-to-air missile, air-to-surface missiles, air-to-air missiles, surface-to-surface missiles, ship-borne missiles and antitank missiles) have appeared along with terminal precision-guided weapons warheads for guided artillery shells, guided bombs, and guided torpedoes. The guidance system changes in these weapon systems have greatly increased their capabilities for automatic searches and identification and attack, and have increased tenfold the precision of these weapons systems, to the point of near perfect accuracy.

Third is covertness. Weapons are tools for the destruction of the enemy but at the same time, they are also the major target of offensives by the enemy. The new technological revolution has searched for and provided advanced equipment, ways, and methods for the modern battlefield, and together with troops, weapons have now become a serious threat. In the history of combat, to increase battlefield survivability of weapons, man has thought of many kinds of decoys and camouflage. With the development of invisible light technology (like infrared, ultraviolet, laser, microwave, and others), surveillance technology and various anticamouflage technology, original camouflage mechanisms have lost a great deal of their effectiveness. To increase their battlefield survivability, weapons systems have begun moving toward the direction of concealment. "Concealment" is the use of various types of scientific technology to decrease detection by radar, infrared, photoelectricity, and weapons sighting systems. It is the adoption of a specialized technology through systems research and design. Major "concealment" methods include:

- Having the weapons system's structural distribution and design be scientifically rational and still be able to decrease the effective reflecting surfaces of radar, electromagnetic spectrum, and laser.
- Decreasing infrared radiation and the noise level of engines within the propulsion system in the weaponry.
- Selecting coatings that will absorb and shield radar waves and infrared radiation as well as effectively reduce radar reflecting surfaces. For coating on surfaces of the weaponry, new wave-absorbing structured materials made of composite materials and electromagnetic spectrum "absorbing material" are now being selected. There is also the use of different kinds of concealment technology and

use of different methods for different weapons systems, such as missiles, aircraft, ships, tanks, vehicles, and artillery. The U.S.'s B-1B bomber is a weapons system that uses rather advanced stealth technology. Structurally, it uses swing-wing. The outer shape of the body and wings are designed for radar reflecting surfaces. It uses a turbofan engine and a bypass culvert that dispenses the mixed hot and cold air to decrease the heat radiation strength of the jet. It uses the radioactive isotope polonium 210 and curium 242 as well as ferrite as its surface coating. Cover coating the aircraft surface with these substances decreases the radar reflecting surfaces and will furthermore absorb and shield radar, electromagnetic spectrum, and laser radiation. From what we have seen in localized wars during recent years, covert technology has raised the survivability of weapons systems in close concealed contact with the enemy and in surprise attacks. It has also played a role in decreasing wastefulness in terms of consumption.

Fourth, focused energy, is different from radiation mass destruction weapons like chemical, atomic, and nuclear weapons. A focused-energy weapon directs energy into beam power that kills the enemy or destroys a target directly. (It is also called a directed energy or directed beam energy weapon.) The rapid rise of laser technology, particle beam technology, microwave technology, and plasma technology has provided the foundation for the creation of focused-energy technology. In recent years, there has been rapid development in focused-energy weapons, and at present, the phase of theoretical experimentation has largely been completed and has entered the prototype stage of research. According to reports, the Soviet Union is in the process of researching three kinds of high energy laser weapons for its anti-air defence. It could complete the research work for a practical model against a star wars weapon in the 1990s and deploy a small quantity of them. There is intense research going on for various kinds of tactical laser artillery and guns and the coming of directed-energy weapons in theatres of war are not far away. The combined use of these and conventional weapons systems will result in greater casualties and destruction.

War and the need for the development of weapons power are the motivations for weapons development. As long as war, an abnormal development of mankind, persists, the military will strive to find more sophisticated weaponry and suggest the need for development of weapons. With this "demand as an incentive," opposing sides, all wanting victory, will initiate national defence construction "monitors" for "military expenditures" for large investments in national defence science and technology and support for research work in the leading edge of technology and advanced weapons systems. The greatest "investment returns" in weapons development for national security and arms superiority would be a pioneering spirit in new ideas, exploitation, and creation of new technologies. In other words, national defence science and technology could apply all kinds of new technologies to both the research of weapons and their production, thus acting as "technology boosters." In this way, the research disciplines within national defence science and technology could become the "breeding grounds" for high technology development; furthermore, the new achievements of science and technology would most appropriately find their first applications within the military.

IDEOLOGICAL AND BUREAUCRATIC ROOTS OF CHINA'S NUCLEAR POSTURE

Why does China's nuclear posture look so different from those of the other nuclear weapon states? The most compelling explanation is that Chinese policy makers have tended to make decisions about China's strategic forces that suggest a widespread belief that deterrence is achieved early and with a small number of forces. This view contrasts with the norm among Western security experts, who tend to believe that deterrence can be achieved only through difficult choices, sustained with intelligent effort, and will heavily depend on the technical details. This is the view expressed in Albert Wohlstetter's 1958 Rand monograph (and later an article in *Foreign Affairs*), *The Delicate Balance of Terror,* which helped to shape the dominant Cold War attitudes in the United States about deterrence.

A different view is that, beyond a certain point, the technical details matter very little, if at all. The balance of terror is anything but delicate. An enemy who *can* be deterred, *will* be deterred by the prospect of a counterattack, even if it consists of only a few nuclear weapons. Drawing on his experience during the Cuban Missile Crisis, McGeorge Bundy later argued that decision makers are unlikely to "double-check the detailed consequences of an exchange, or to review how such a war might be fought." National leaders are likely to have "a healthy disrespect for such exercises," recognizing that the avoidance of a nuclear war is imperative.

Mao's famous remark that "The atomic bomb is a paper tiger" is often treated as evidence of a dangerous irrationality in Chinese attitudes toward nuclear weapons. But, as Mark Ryan found in his study of the formation of Chinese attitudes about nuclear weapons during the Korean War, the first generation of Chinese Communist leaders formed highly accurate assessments about the physical limitations of nuclear weapons and the political constraints on the U.S. use of nuclear weapons. Having successfully endured nuclear threats from the United States, Chinese leaders saw nuclear weapons as tools of political coercion that could be met with resolve and, eventually, possession of similar capabilities.

Some context may be helpful. Chinese Communist leaders first used the term "paper tiger" to refer to reactionaries, not nuclear weapons, in 1946. The reference is a metaphorical allusion to "an older Maoist revolutionary maxim which holds that men and politics, rather than weapons and economic power, are the determining factors in war." In context, referring to nuclear weapons as paper tigers merely indicates that the balance of nuclear weapons is not likely to be decisive in conflict—a statement that the technical details matter very little. Calling nuclear weapons paper tigers is simply the "healthy disrespect" that Bundy predicted any world leader would have for plans to fight a nuclear war. It is perhaps no more colourful than similar remarks by U.S. and Soviet leaders.

Of course, even if world leaders talk about nuclear weapons as though the details don't matter very much, the United States and the Soviet Union still expended enormous efforts tending to those details during the Cold War, deploying very large, diverse, and highly alert forces. The bureaucratic realities of China's nuclear weapons development, however, were different and seem to have reinforced the tendency toward minimalism suggested by the ideological description of nuclear weapons as paper tigers.

Although most histories of China's nuclear weapons program begin with a decision made by Mao in 1955, another date is perhaps more consequential. The leadership consensus behind pursuing nuclear weapons in the mid-1950s was not difficult to understand: Chinese leaders expected substantial Soviet assistance. But that consensus eventually cracked under the budgetary and technical constraints imposed by the suspension of Soviet technical assistance and the chaos of the Great Leap Forward.

In particular, many military leaders wanted to cut strategic programs—nuclear weapons and ballistic missiles— to free up money for ships, tanks, and aircraft that would be needed to defend China from the United States or the Soviet Union. In the summer of 1961, the Central Committee resolved the controversy during a meeting at the seaside resort of Beidaihe, selecting strategic programs for modernization at the expense of conventional forces. Marshal Nie Rongzhen, the head of China's defence science and technology complex after 1958, carried the day, arguing that strategic programs would serve as an organizing endeavour for national science and technology, a rationale that linked the development of "sophisticated weapons" to the broader theme of China's national economic development and emphasized the possession of advanced capabilities, rather than their battlefield uses.

This bureaucratic history may explain why China chose to invest very little in strategic bombers: advocates for the aircraft industry had aligned themselves with opponents of the strategic weapons programs. It may also explain the small number of ballistic missiles that China acquired: Since the advocates were largely scientists and engineers responsible for designing new missiles and warheads, the natural bureaucratic emphasis was on continuing research and development, rather than procurement. Finally, Nie and his political allies tended to be less alarmist than their political opponents about the international security situation. It is not a coincidence, for instance, that Nie was one of the four marshals who argued in 1969 that China ought to be open to U.S. overtures to improve relations.

All of these factors led advocates for the nuclear and ballistic missile programs to argue for a relatively small nuclear force that represented China's possession of the most advanced strategic capabilities.

The emphasis on possession, rather than use, of nuclear weapons is evident in how the Chinese describe their arsenal, both in terms of vocabulary and the content of declaratory policy. Chinese leaders tend to eschew using the word "deterrence" to describe the purpose of China's nuclear forces. The Chinese word for "deter" (*weishe*) echoes the Latin root shared with "terrorism"—*terreo*, to frighten. As a result, *weishe* carries a much stronger sense of *terror* or blackmail than the oddly clinical "deterrence" and "compellence." Chinese-speakers seldom use "deterrence" to describe China's posture, although the word sometimes appears in English-language translations and Western-oriented scholarship. The National Defence White Papers, for instance, tend to use "counterattack" rather than "deterrence"—with the exception of the 2004 paper, which used both.

China's rejection of the credibility of nuclear threats—what Thomas Schelling eloquently called "the threat of damage, or of more damage yet to come, that can make someone yield or comply," helps explain why many Chinese avoid using the word "deterrence" to describe China's arsenal. Chinese leaders rejected the credibility of such threats to make one either yield or comply; either "counterattack" or "reprisal" seem a better choice for the purpose they had in mind. One can see echoes of this difference in contemporary debates. The National Academies' recently released *English–Chinese, Chinese–English Nuclear Security Glossary* was delayed for many months by a dispute over whether to include the term "limited nuclear deterrence."

It is in this context—the ability to counter coercion—that we should understand China's no-first-use pledge. Where Western writers have tended to see such a pledge as a self-imposed constraint placed upon the state making the pledge, Chinese policy makers seem to view the pledge as a statement about the nature of nuclear weapons—an outright rejection of the value of nuclear threats—and, as a result, an observation on the reason that China's own small, vulnerable force still enjoys a kind of parity with the United States.

New Challenges in Sino-U.S. Crisis Stability

In the United States, we tend to think about two implications that will arise from China's deployment of new mobile ballistic missiles. Some argue that a more survivable Chinese deterrent will increase the threat to the United States, discouraging Washington from coming to the aid of Taiwan in a crisis. Others have suggested that the deployment of more survivable Chinese strategic forces will prove stabilizing because a U.S. president would be less likely to initiate a nuclear strike against Chinese targets.

Both of these views emphasize the role of nuclear weapons in deterring a *deliberate* attack. Yet the prospect that either a Chinese or U.S. political leader would initiate nuclear hostilities seems extremely remote. A very different concern is the possibility of an accident or miscalculation arising from the interaction of alert U.S. and Chinese forces.

China's strategic forces have been placed on alert only once, in 1969 during the Sino-Soviet crisis. This event remains confusing—Lin Biao, Mao's heir apparent who would later die attempting to flee China, allegedly aft er a failed coup attempt against Mao, appears to have placed the Second Artillery on alert without going through established procedures.

The event may have reinforced concerns within the Chinese leadership about the need to maintain control over the country's nuclear forces. Today, however, China is changing rapidly. Chinese leaders will have an arsenal comprising new solid-fuelled missile systems that maximize survivability by standing alert—either by placing mobile missiles in the field or patrolling submarines at sea—and a vastly more professional military. Even if Chinese leaders do not keep forces on alert as a peacetime routine, in a severe crisis they may be tempted to raise the alert level of Second Artillery forces to demonstrate their resolve. *Zhanyi Xue* suggested such a course of action, calling it "anti-nuclear deterrence combat"—"the military operation that shows our nuclear power and will."

Based on press reports of exercises, in a crisis China would disperse mobile ballistic missiles and fuel missiles in fixed sites. How would American policy makers react, especially if U.S. forces were placed on alert? The history of U.S. alert operations suggests that they have an inherent escalatory potential. In studies of the four U.S. DEFCON-3 or higher alerts, Scott Sagan found that orders were frequently misunderstood or ambiguous events misinterpreted to confirm the sense of crisis, and he concluded that "keeping the alert at the desired level will be extremely difficult, and the degree of further grave escalation uncertain." The inherent risk is captured by President John F. Kennedy's sardonic remark, upon learning that a U.S. U-2 plane had strayed into Soviet airspace during the Cuban Missile Crisis, that "There's always some son-of-a-bitch who doesn't get the message."

One can imagine, for instance, the potential for escalation if Chinese missile submarines put out to sea during a crisis. U.S. attack submarines would surely attempt to tail them. What would happen if two submarines collided? Or if the Chinese submarine suffered a crippling accident, like the torpedo explosion that sank the Russian submarine *Kursk*? Would Chinese policy makers, in a crisis atmosphere, be able to distinguish the loss of contact with submarines from early efforts to eliminate their deterrent? How would U.S. policy makers react if China appeared to prepare mobile ballistic missiles that could perform antisatellite missions? Or anti-ship DF-21D missiles that, externally, are identical to China's nuclear-armed DF-21 and DF-21As?

8

South Asia Security Challenges: Terror Campaign and Nuclear Proliferation

CHALLENGES IN DEFENCE PLANNING

Defence planning is essentially a subset of overall national level planning in the political, economic and social spheres and has to be evolved in the context of global and proximate factors affecting the nation.. It has also to take into account the philosophy and ethos animating the national psyche; in other words the historical and cultural forces which have shaped the collective memory and outlook of the people over the centuries.

The Cold War, was a classic example of the factors stated above. There were fundamental philosophical differences between the adversaries – the western bloc, advocating the virtues of free enterprise and its own interpretations of democracy, and the Soviet bloc, equally strongly asserting the merits of the socialist system as the only one genuinely meeting democratic aspirations and assuring social equality and economic well-being of the people as a whole, rather than for a few. Fifty years of the Cold War could not conclude the capitalism-socialism debate, though, in the end, it did push the socialist forces into, perhaps temporary, retreat. This was because the struggle was really for power and domination. "The evil empire" of Ronald Reagan's description may have withered away, but the necessity for the US to target the so called "rogue states" has not disappeared. Many examples can be found of philosophical differences leading to stand-offs, usually with the USA as one of the parties.

The USA-Cuba divide is a long-standing one. USA-Venezuela stand-off is just developing and resonating in other Latin American countries. Sometimes the differences are couched in the language of anticipated threats, such as in US-North Korea, or US-Iran relations. The true reasons and underlying causes are buried in verbiage and obfuscation. A more serious rift has developed over the selective and poorly conceptualised US war on terrorism, launched for spurious reasons in Iraq, when the real source of terror was elsewhere and far more complex. Differing religious beliefs and rigidities are often cited as causes but do not sufficiently explain conflicts within the same religion, as between Protestants and Catholics in Northern Ireland or the Shias and Sunnis in Iraq and elsewhere.

Planning for the security and defence of a vast country like India with its particular geographic location, historical experiences and associations, social, ethnic, religious and cultural diversity, political and economic structure and a large, relatively poor, democratically governed population, is a complex and challenging task. It is rendered more so in the context of the national and international situation in the last sixty years or so, embracing post-World War II de-colonisation, partition, the creation of Pakistan and later Bangladesh, conflicts with Pakistan and China, the Cold War and its aftermath, the disintegration of the Soviet Union, the re-definition of NATO's role, and of most recent and decisive significance, the September 11, 2001 terror attack on the United States mainland. This last factor is significant because it resulted in a major re-orientation in US foreign policy.

Strategic Overview

Planning for defence pre-supposes identification of threats and contingencies. Until about five years ago, the strategic situation for India was difficult but relatively clear. Pakistan was a definite threat, conventional, clandestine and nuclear. China was a strategically reducing threat, though its international power, influence and economy were growing. Uncertainties in Bangladesh and Nepal required us to be vigilant for fall-out effects. There were problems in the north-east of insurgent groups exploiting the ethnic ties and jungles in Myanmar, and the destabilising spill-over effects of the activities of the Liberation Tigers for Tamil Eelam(LTTE) in Sri Lanka. The presence in our proximate waters, of non-littoral naval forces in substantial numbers, such as those of the US, which has been traditionally supportive of Pakistan, had to be taken cognisance of. Also the fact that warfare at sea, because of its distinctive characteristics of rapidity of concentration and dispersal of forces, mobility, flexibility and speed of execution, requires a different, longer term approach to threat assessment. Strategically the global situation is now evolving in a manner less inimical to India's interests than in the preceding fifty years. Yet the end of the Cold War did not see any easing of pressures on India. On the contrary, economic sanctions and technology denials were increased so as to coerce India to conform to norms of international behaviour prescribed by dominant world powers, led by the US and the European Union on the one hand and China on the other. The reason was the desire of the P-5, the five permanent members of the UN Security Council, who are also the N-5, the self-certified nuclear powers, to preserve their monopoly power status in the face of India's challenge through the nuclear tests of 1998.

Yet, the re-evaluation of foreign policies by leading powers set off by the September 11, 2001 terrorist attack on the USA, has initiated processes that are, by and large, beneficial to India. An indication of this is the US declaration of seeing India as a strategic partner for the 21st century, and its efforts to legislate exceptions to its domestic laws to allow supply of nuclear materials for peaceful civilian use to India by the cartel operated by the Nuclear Suppliers Group (NSG).

Nearer home, the pathological hostility of the Pakistanis establishment towards India is rooted in its quest for a national identity, which no novel interpretations, distortions or reinventions of sub-continental history seem able to provide. It will be a long time before there can be normal relations with Pakistan because they are influenced more by the internal contradictions and dynamics of the Pakistani state rather than considerations of mutual benefits through good relations. Since the Pakistan army is the self-appointed guardian of the undefined "ideology of Pakistan", normalcy will come when the Army decides it should be so; or the cost-benefit equation alters.

With China, there is perceptible progress on resolving disputes and fostering economic and cultural relations. As for Nepal, Bangladesh, Myanmar and Sri Lanka, there is no significant positive change, and because of shared borders, internal problems in those countries will continue to spill over into India. Instability in Afghanistan remains a cause of concern, especially because of Pakistan's dubious role, and this will have its impact on the pursuit of India's energy and strategic interests in Central Asia.

Non-littoral naval forces in significant numbers are still present in the Indian Ocean, but there is no coercive or inimical intent as in the past. Indeed, the Indian Navy holds regular friendly exercises with them on a routine basis. China's long term plans for a naval presence in the region have to be taken note of. There are ample signs of Chinese maritime interest, starting from building and operating communications facilities in Myanmar to financing and building Pakistan's Gwadar Port on the Makran coast, collaboration in building warships for the Pakistan navy at Karachi shipyard, as well as port building in Sri Lanka. On the western rim of the Indian Ocean, China is vigorously pursuing options in Africa, underlined by the meeting of 49 heads of state/government in Beijing in early November this year.

National Objectives in the Long Term

Planning for defence has to be in the framework of national objectives over a period of decades ahead, even if these are not publicly articulated. USA does not hesitate to state its intention to remain the dominant global technological, space and military power for the foreseeable future and tailors strategic policies accordingly. China has, by its actions, investments and developments over the years, demonstrated that it intends to be at least the equal of the USA, though with "Chinese characteristics".

Pakistan makes no secret of its intention to be "different" from India, and to compete with and undermine India at every opportunity.

India too has shown in various ways that it intends to be in the forefront of nations in every sphere: economic, technological, industrial and human development. What about military capability? Does it wish to have only a capacity to ward off aggression by land and sea? Or does it aspire to play a larger role in the region? If it emerges as the world's third or fourth largest economy in a few years, would a commensurate military role follow? Or are national objectives to be largely achieved by a combination of diplomacy and economic policies? If it aspires for a permanent seat in the UN Security Council, is it prepared for the increased diplomatic and military responsibilities attached? Many of these seemingly philosophical issues require to be debated to facilitate meaningful defence planning for the future.

DIMENSION IN THE SECURITY SECTOR

It is difficult if not impossible to measure outcomes in much of the security sector, the importance of security as an enabling factor in development becomes very clear in its absence. Moreover, it is also difficult to identify performance indicators that do not inadvertently generate inappropriate incentives for security agencies. Nevertheless, and notwithstanding data limitations, as in the case of other public services it is necessary to monitor performance as best possible and in the process generate useful information for feedback and decision making. Appropriate performance indicators inevitably will vary across sectors, and as important as the information itself is ensuring that it feeds into subsequent decisions including through the budget process. While detailed consideration of performance indicators and monitoring in the security sector would get into technical aspects beyond the scope of this volume, some initial ideas for different sectors are put forward below, for illustrative purposes and further consideration. The Government, in defining its MDGs, has established targets, indicators, and baselines for the security sector (mainly for Defence), and moving toward a performance-based budgeting system for the security sector will keep efforts focused on outcomes.

In the container of *defence,* PFM specialists generally consider that indicators of preparedness (although they are more akin to output indicators than to outcome indicators) are the most appropriate performance indicator in peacetime. Another set of indicators which may be useful are the number, types, and results of training exercises conducted. It should be noted in this context that the Government has put forward the level of defence expenditures as a ratio to GDP as a (negative) performance indicator for its MDG target of enhancing security. While other things equal, a lower level of defence expenditure allows a greater proportion of Government budgetary resources to be spent on other development priorities, the relationship between the level of defence expenditure and actual security is complex and unlikely to be linear in either the positive or the negative direction.

Intended for *the police,* and for the *internal security* system more generally, the ultimate outcome of local security and rule of law is very difficult to measure but can be roughly proxied by some indicators. Official crime statistics are a partial and not very accurate (negative) indicator of security and rule of law, since they are affected by various factors such as the extent to which crimes are reported and recorded. Hence these are hard to use in monitoring performance over time or especially across countries. Household surveys generating information on the number and types of crime encountered by households can provide a useful check on the validity of official statistics, and they can also shed light on people's perceptions of the local security situation and their degree of trust in police. The effectiveness of the police and prosecutorial services can be measured by the percentage of different categories of cases resulting in convictions, based on which type of evidence (confessions, physical evidence etc.). The availability of female police officers and separate detention facilities for women are also indicative of mitigating the risks women face during detention.

In adding, the performance of the *justice system* can be measured by various indicators like numbers of cases handled, timeliness of processing court cases, and households' perceptions of the justice system and their indications of willingness (or otherwise) to use formal justice channels when seeking redress. The existence of Family Courts and Juvenile Courts and their functioning is also indicative of how sensitively and even-handedly the justice system deals with women and children. Furthermore, Afghanistan has signed a number of international conventions related to gender, including the Convention on the Political Rights of Women and on Elimination of all forms of Discrimination Against Women, which like the other international conventions ratified will require legislative and administrative measures to give legal backing to the nation's commitment to fair treatment and advancement of its women. In the container of *mine action,* outcomes of mine clearance activities (land and areas free of landmines - with clear linkage to ultimate development benefits) can be specified and measured reasonably well, and compared with the costs of mine clearance. On the other hand, the performance and effectiveness of mine awareness-raising activities are difficult to measure.

For *counter-narcotics,* the outcome indicator at the national level can be specified relatively clearly: progressive and sustained reduction over time and eventual elimination of the opium economy on a sustainable basis (i.e. pressures to resume cultivation are manageable), accompanied by a corresponding reduction in trade in opiates (the latter may occur with a lag due to remaining inventories). However, measuring the performance of various actors and activities involved in counter-narcotics activities is not easy, and linking such performance to progress toward achieving this strategic objective is even more difficult. Given the variety of activities encompassed under the counter-narcotics rubric - ranging from eradication and interdiction to judiciary and penal development, demand reduction, and rural development programs - performance indicators for the different components will need to be appropriate to their varying characteristics.

More generally, in all parts of the security sector *basic indicators of inputs* can be useful in measuring performance. Examples include number and ratio of staff on the job (confirmed by spot-inspections), percentage of staff in security services properly equipped, proportion of staff who have received designated training, percentage of budget resources spent (covering both Core and External Budget to the extent possible), etc. A related option is *expenditure tracking surveys,* which are rarely used in the security sector as compared with social sectors, but which are feasible and provide information on actual flows of funds to, for example, police stations.

Unit costs, although not an outcome indicator, nevertheless can be useful performance indicators of the efficiency with which inputs for service delivery are being provided. All this leads to a rather formidable agenda for generating and effectively utilizing monitoring information. While there will be a need to focus attention and resources on this aspect, developing performance indicators and monitoring progress can start with small steps and make progress incrementally over time.

One promising option is to generate and regularly monitor basic financial information on security sector expenditures in the Core Budget, and encourage donor partners to provide similar information on as consistent a basis as possible for External Budget expenditures in the security sector. This will provide useful information on expenditure of funds (a critical input) that can be monitored. To illustrate how straightforward monitoring of basic financial data can provide meaningful insights and feedback for resource allocation and other budgetary decision-making, compares estimated actual expenditures with budget targets for various categories of security sector expenditures in 2003/04 and 2004/05. Key points that emerge from these simple comparisons include the following:

There are sizable deviations between budgeted and estimated actual spending for most categories of security expenditures and also major fluctuations over time, suggesting that there is still a way to go before the budget targets become reasonably good predictors of actual expenditures. Within the security sector, External Budget expenditures are substantially higher in relation to budget targets than are Core Budget expenditures. Defence expenditures tended to perform better in relation to budget targets than other parts of the security sector, especially in 2004/05.

Finally, comparing the security sector with the budget as a whole, it is clear that the security sector achieves considerably higher expenditures in relation to budget targets than does the overall budget.

Another important area for basic input monitoring is employment levels. Staffing data, which have suffered from inconsistencies, need to be improved and regularly monitored throughout the security sector, including staff in security services paid through the External Budget. Such data can be augmented with indicators of numbers or proportions of staff on duty and available to carry out their duties.

Building on monitoring of basic data on inputs, simple indicators of output/performance could be compiled and used in monitoring. It is more important to collect and effectively utilize simple information than to devise highly sophisticated data and monitoring systems which are difficult to implement and become a burden on scarce Government capacity.

Finally, the institutions concerned need to take on the role of monitoring and evaluation and treat it as a serious part of their work. Most important they need to make meaningful use of performance indicators in decision making.

Intensification funds Execution

The budget can be a useful policy tool only if it is properly executed. The Government has made significant progress in developing institutions and systems to raise fiduciary standards, including implementation of the AFMIS in the Treasury, establishment of the Central Procurement Facility, and promulgation of procurement, public finance and expenditure management, and audit laws. However, because most of the expenditures in the security sector are in the External Budget, these systems are bypassed. Ongoing reforms to strengthen accountability mechanisms will develop institutions and systems that give civil servants the incentives and tools to use public resources effectively, but this will take some time. Many of these reforms will also reduce corruption, which may be considerable in certain parts of the security sector.

Currently, execution of the ordinary budget proceeds largely in accordance with the usual process of meeting day-to-day recurrent costs for both the security services and associated civilian staff. Based on the approved annual budget, quarterly advances are provided to security sector entities, against which recurrent costs (O&M) and food allowances are paid. In nearly all cases, execution of the development budget is via donor funded projects in the External Budget. The only notable exception is DDR.

The ANA payment system has been a parallel budget execution system, although OMC-A is strengthening the budget department of MoD, and future salaries are expected to be paid through the new payroll system. The US Army/OMC-A maintain full expenditure authority over US Government funding. Salaries for AMF were provided through the national budget, but the AMF has now been phased out through DDR. Food allowances for the ANA had been provided in-kind directly by the US Army but are now paid through the Core Budget. Investment expenditures are procured directly by the US Army. Core Budget funding is accounted for through the Government / Treasury accounting system. In the case of reimbursement through ARTF, expenditures are verified through AFMIS by the ARTF Monitoring Agent. The Auditor General's Office currently conducts an audit of Government accounts, although the audit methodology (sampling frame and extrapolation technique) needs to be upgraded. In reporting all operating expenditures, the standard economic object classification is used, allowing comparative analysis between sectors.

Implementation of the External Development Budget differs substantially from the recurrent or operating budget in that, with the exception of some Core Budget funding for law enforcement (US$16.8 million in 2004/05), mine action (US$3.9 million), and Justice (US$3.1 million), all other development budget spending is drawn from the External Budget. The External Budget is fully projectized, under funding from bilateral donors. As a consequence, donors procure works, supplies, and services directly through their own procurement services. For the External Budget, accounting and auditing procedures are determined by the policies of each bilateral donor. As financial information is internal to bilateral agencies, actual recurrent spending in the External Budget remains unknown. However, given the requirement to move toward an integrated security budget, greater disclosure will be required to enable the longer-term fiscal implications of External Budget spending to be calculated.

Procurement. An external Procurement Advisor (Agent) has been retained by the Government, reporting to the Afghanistan Reconstruction and Development Services (ARDS) and supervised by the Ministers of Planning and Reconstruction. However, in spite of being the procurement agent for over 17 national Ministries, it has not so far handled procurement for any part of the security sector. A new Procurement Law has recently been passed. Hitherto, procurement of supplies, services, and works in the security ministries has not been unified around a single procurement system due to the different sources of finance and the multiplicity of actors. Instead, all core operating budget expenditures appear to follow the various procurement laws established by the budget entities directly. What is more, none of the 110-150 procurement staff from line ministries who have received training in basic and specific procurement rules have come from security-related ministries. With the approval of the new Procurement Law, this situation will need to change. Indeed, OMC-A has embarked on adapting procurement processes for MoD to the new law. Currently, Government security sector funding is limited to payroll and non payroll recurrent costs, so no large procurements have taken place to date.

LOTFA has its own set of procurement procedures and policies, covering both payroll and purchase of supplies such as vehicles and radio sets as well as works contracts for construction of police offices. Procurement is based on open international competitive bidding overseen by the management support unit, which is formally responsible for "procurement of goods, services and works on a transparent and competitive basis."

Procurement of defence items by bilateral agencies is determined by the bilateral procurement policies of the different contracting authorities (US DoD, UK Government, and so on).

Clearly, if procurement policies are to be unified within the framework of the national budget, bilateral commitments in support of national security will need to be progressively drawn within the national budget framework. In essence, this would require that defence and non-defence procurement be harmonized to enhance (i) transparency, (ii) cost-efficiency, (iii) and cost-effectiveness. However, given bilateral donors' procedures and interests, this is unlikely to be possible any time soon. In the case of counter-narcotics, large contracts are being tendered, with few market operators able to deliver in such a complicated political and security environment, and contract costs probably reflecting this situation.

In the case of mine clearance, there are some issues related to procurement (i.e. contracting) for this activity. While very specific to de-mining, these issues and the options for addressing them do provide an illustration of how constraints elsewhere in the security sector might be addressed. The general message is that while the specific features may vary, it is extremely important to ensure that sound procurement principles are followed.

Another area of procurement related to the security sector - very important in the current situation in Afghanistan - is procurement by international security forces for various goods and services that they require, ranging from certain security services to water, fuel, other goods, construction, construction materials, etc. Although difficult to ascertain with any precision, these activities are sizable and comprise a significant source of demand in the Afghan economy. Such contracts in many cases comprise an opportunity for development of the Afghan private sector which should be exploited. As argued with respect to other security-related procurement, these also should follow good-practice principles for procurement, particularly with respect to transparency and competition. However, it appears that such principles often are not followed in contracting for services by international military forces.

Accounting and reporting. As indicated earlier, accounting standards and reporting requirements should be uniform as between the security sector and non-security sectors. Within the Core Budget this condition is basically met, although there is room for further improvement in the case of security as well as other sectors. Major improvements in terms of timeliness, quality, and harmonized information standards for expenditures in the External Budget are needed. It is also very important that information on staffing and payrolls be improved in both Core and External Budgets.

External scrutiny and audit. It is essential that security expenditures be properly audited by a suitable external auditor, and that findings of audit reviews are made available to the Government and public. Core Budget expenditures (including those on security) are audited through regular Government procedures, whose quality needs to be improved. But it is very important that External Budget expenditures have proper external scrutiny and audit, and that findings are shared with the Government. LOTFA's accounts also need to be regularly audited by an external auditor on a timely basis. With the formation of Parliament, review of audit reports by the legislature should become a regular practice.

In sum, security expenditures within the Core Budget are essentially subject to similar control mechanisms, accounting and reporting requirements, and procurement arrangements as in the rest of the Core Budget. The main difference is the absence of a strong internal audit function - a role that in the case of the civilian budget is to a large extent played by the Monitoring Agent of the ARTF. The absence of such a mechanism - albeit extraordinary (and temporary) - in the security sector means a weaker control framework despite the beneficial application of other elements of the budget execution process for the Core Budget.

Security spending in the External Budget occurs outside these Government processes. Although this spending is subject to financial controls exercised by donors, associated disadvantages are potentially very important with respect to the quality and consistency of information flows, and procurement. Another major problem is the wide variety of salary levels, payment channels, and top-up arrangements in the security sector, which risk fragmenting the accountability and loyalties of security sector staff.

SECURITY, DEVELOPMENT AND PERSPECTIVE

Security, an essential public good, is widely seen as a central issue for Afghanistan's reconstruction and development. Security impacts on the whole range of development issues faced by Afghanistan, ranging from state building and capacity development to revenue collection, service delivery, and encouraging private sector-led growth. For the purpose of Afghanistan's National Development Strategy (ANDS), currently under preparation, the Government has added a Millennium Development Goal (MDG) on enhancing security to the internationally agreed list of MDGs. This demonstrates the importance assigned by the Government to security and rule of law as a critical development issue. Afghanistan's external partners (including the World Bank) have consistently highlighted the importance of security as a key enabling factor for Afghanistan's reconstruction and development And most important, the Afghan people themselves emphasize the importance of security and the protection of property rights in their daily lives and for building their livelihoods and communities.

More specifically:

- Security and rule of law as public goods have been grossly underprovided in Afghanistan during the past quarter-century, with state functions in this regard usurped by factions, regional and local powerbrokers, and external actors. Remedying this situation is an urgent, high-priority task.
- Improving security is also a core component of the state-building agenda, seen by most Afghans as an essential function of an effective, accountable government.
- Moreover, an adequate level of security is a critical prerequisite for effective delivery of other public services.
- Politically, security improvements have been and will continue to be essential for the success of Afghanistan's transition toward political normalcy.
- Economically, security and law and order, along with the protection of property rights, are required for robust private

sector development, which will be the only way to achieve sustained rapid economic growth over the medium term.

- Insecurity and narcotics are closely linked-insecurity is the environment in which Afghanistan's opium economy thrives, and the drug industry is a major source of instability and insecurity.
- And finally, from the individual, household, and community standpoints, security and rule of law are extremely important components and enabling factors in the quality of life, as is almost universally recognized by Afghans.

In addition to its importance as a central development issue for Afghanistan, the security sector accounts for a very high proportion of the country's total public expenditures as well as external assistance and raises major public expenditure management issues including risks to fiscal sustainability and possible crowding out of spending on other basic services. Therefore the security sector is also very important from a public finance management perspective. In view of these considerations, the Government of Afghanistan requested that the security sector be included in the World Bank's Public Finance Management (PFM) Review, and this volume is the result. There are in addition a number of specific rationales for the World Bank's engagement in analytical work on Afghanistan's security sector as part of the PFM Review and from a development perspective. First, as indicated above, security is of central importance for Afghanistan's development prospects, including in particular the state-building agenda. This means it has to be incorporated in the country's development strategy and planning (which the Government is doing), and that development partners need to be engaged in areas of their competence.

Second, given the great importance of security spending in the national budget (accounting for around 40% of total Core and External Budget expenditures), the security sector must be incorporated in the analysis of expenditure composition, budget prioritization and trade-offs, downstream expenditure implications of decisions and investments, fiscal sustainability, etc. These issues lie at the heart of the PFM Review. Third, a weak PFM system in the security sector (and particularly if the security sector gets left behind while improvements in the PFM system are occurring elsewhere) would adversely affect the overall progress of PFM reform and institutional strengthening, distort choices made by the Government, reduce the effectiveness and efficiency of public spending, and increase vulnerability to corruption. All of these areas are of concern to the Bank.

And fourth, security sector expenditures are largely donor-financed, raising important issues of aid management, aid harmonization, and aid effectiveness, as well as capacity development and effectiveness of technical assistance. These issues comprise an important part of the overall PFM agenda and hence need in the context of the security sector to be included in the PFM Review.

The main objectives of this review of security sector expenditures in the context of the PFM Review and taking a development perspective are as follows:

- To gain as complete an understanding as possible of the current level and structure of security related expenditures, recent trends, and likely future expenditure requirements based on current plans.
- To assess the extent to which coherent strategies, for the security sector and the major parts of the security sector, guide public expenditure allocations.
- To review the processes for determining funding levels, expenditure allocations, budget execution, and post-execution functions, with a view to assessing the extent to which they follow sound PFM principles.
- To describe the institutional framework for the security sector and ascertain the extent to which it embeds or is conducive to sound public financial management.
- To assess the strategic coherence and consistency and the fiscal sustainability of security sector expenditures.

This chapter sets forth the conceptual framework for analysis of security sector expenditures from a development and public finance management perspective. It first provides a working definition of the security sector. The chapter goes on to outline key linkages between security and development (based on recent international thinking on this subject). It then discusses key public finance management principles and their application to the security sector.

Some background on the historical legacy from the long period of conflict in Afghanistan, and summarizes the progress made in building the security sector since 2001. It then overviews Afghanistan's security sector at present-its legal basis, size, institutions, salient characteristics, and coordination-and at the end outlines the key security issues faced by Afghanistan from a development perspective. PFM principles and their application to the security sector, the implications for Afghanistan including gaps and constraints, and the Afghan budget process for the security sector.

The crucial issue of the fiscal sustainability of security sector decisions and investments, which is an important driver of the fiscal sustainability of Afghanistan's public finances as a whole. Building on the analysis of fiscal sustainability, At strategic prioritization and sequencing issues in the security sector and how these can be managed in particular through the national budget process. The budget execution for effective and efficient use of funds provided to the security sector.

Meaning of the Security Sector

The security "system" is defined broadly in OECD (2005b) as including the following main components: core security actors, security management and oversight bodies, justice and law enforcement institutions, and non-statutory security bodies. A broad definition of the security sector along these lines makes the most sense from a development and PFM perspective, as all different parts of the security sector have significant development implications as well as varying budgetary implications (for both expenditures and revenues). However, some components clearly do not apply to Afghanistan (e.g. coast guards), while other institutions like Parliaments have not been functioning and hence are not relevant for analysis of recent developments and the current situation (although the role of the legislature will be important starting in the very near future). Moreover, non-statutory security bodies, although they have been major actors in Afghanistan (and mirror the breakdown of the formal security system during the protracted conflict), for the most part do not have direct budgetary implications and would require a very different mode of analysis. Therefore they are not looked at closely in this volume except in terms of their immediate budgetary implications-notably the Disarmament, Demobilization, and Reintegration (DDR) program-although their development implications and impact on the formal security sector will be kept in mind.

In sum, consistent with the overall objectives and approach of the PFM Review and in line with the increasingly recognized development implications of the security sector, this volume uses a broad definition of the security sector but focuses on those components which are of major importance from a PFM perspective.

In terms of budget categories and programs, those that form part of the security sector and which are analyzed in the PFM Review include: defence, police and other internal security services, intelligence, counter-narcotics, the judiciary and penal system, mine clearance, and the DDR program.

The main security institutions in Afghanistan which will be looked at in the PFM Review include the following: (i) *government security management and oversight bodies:* National Security Council and National Security Advisor, Ministry of Defence, Ministry of Interior, Ministry of Counter Narcotics, Ministry of Border and Tribal Affairs, Ministry of Justice, Ministry of Finance, and the Auditor General's Office; (ii) *security services:* Afghan National Army (ANA), Afghan National Police (ANP), National Border Guards, Counter-Narcotics forces, National Directorate of Security (NDS-responsible for intelligence), Customs General Directorate under MoF, remnants of earlier military and police forces (the former subjected to DDR); and (iii) *justice and legal institutions:* Supreme Court, Judiciary, Attorney General's Office and prosecutorial offices *(saranwal).*

Excluded from detailed analysis in this volume are the non-statutory security bodies, including remaining unofficial militias and armed factional groups, private body-guards, and security companies. Foreign and international armed forces operating in Afghanistan also will not be analyzed in detail, except to some extent the Provincial Reconstruction Team (PRTs) which are intended to help strengthen governance and carry out reconstruction activities. However, the overall size and cost of these forces will be considered and their impact on the fiscal and PFM aspects of the formal security system will be taken into account. The absence of a Parliament means that its oversight role with respect to security can be incorporated in terms of future options and recommendations, but not in relation to the analysis of recent developments and the current situation. Independent and civil society institutions which play a monitoring and advocacy role with respect to security, such as the Afghanistan Independent Human Rights Commission (AIHRC) are extremely important but are not analysed in detail in this volume.

NATIONAL SECURITY POLICY AND STRATEGY

The concept of national security rests mainly on the proposition that many foreign and domestic political, economic and military issues are inter-related, each with implications on the other. In India's case, this has been highlighted by insurgencies and other political events, particularly in border-states, and other outside pressures, which are brought to bear on the country's economy and technological progress from time to time. A response to this type of environment calls for a highly focussed national security policy and strategy. Effective guidance on national security and defence policy objectives is fundamental to the defence planning process. National security is a relative matter without a firm criteria but unless firm national security objectives are set and a defence policy evolved, there can be no military doctrine or balancing of defence effort with other national objectives and priorities such as maintaining a viable economy and supporting development of society.

The lack of a cohesive national security strategy and defence policy has many implications. First, it results in the absence of clear political direction regarding politico-military objectives, which is the very basis of sound defence planning. Secondly, there is inadequate coordination of defence plans and economic development. Finally, science and technology policies for defence, general industrialisation and other development programmes are not coordinated properly to achieve security goals and objectives.

Perspective Planning

A Defence Plan has to be prepared on the basis of a 15-year long perspective planning system, such that the first five years of the plan are very firm (Definitive Plan), the second five years less firm (Indicative Plan) and the third five-year term tentative (Vision Plan). There has to be a reasonably firm allocation of financial resources for the first five years and an indicative allocation for the subsequent period. Perspective planning needs to be done in the Integrated Defence Headquarters, where military, technical and R&D experts take an integrated view of future threats and challenges. This has to be based on future battlefield scenarios, and array of forecasts, evaluation of strategic options and force mixes, and analysis of potential technical and industrial capabilities. Based on this, the respective Service should work on their perspective plans and the R&D and Defence Production/Supplies experts should spell out their requirements in terms of effort, technology and indigenous production.

Integrated Planning

As stated earlier, the CDS, who would be the cornerstone of integrated operational planning for defence, has not been appointed. India's defence planning, therefore, continues to be Service based. Often, the threat perception of one Service is at variance with that of another Service. What emerges is essentially a sum of total of Service or department wise programmes. The focus is not on overall goals or priorities but on what is required by a particular Service. In its endeavour to lay the groundwork for an increased share of the budget, each Service tends to exercise its own priorities, favouring its own plans to the detriment of joint plans.

Subjects like surveillance, air defence, electronic warfare, and amphibious operations, which relate to more than one Service, do not get adequate attention. Integrated planning for defence is essential for creating balanced force structures and for the successful execution of all military missions. In fact, it is the most effective manner of ensuring effective defence. According to Charles Hitch, "the revolution in military technology has not only changed the character of our military programmes, it has also to a significant degree blurred the lines of demarcation among various Services". Most major military missions today require the participation of more than one military service. Therefore, the principal concern now must be centred on what is required by the defence establishment as a whole to perform a particular mission—not what is required by a particular Service to perform its individual part of that 'mission'. The areas of commonality in modern weapon systems are immense and growing rapidly. Communications, guidance systems, missiles, radars, lasers—even traditional equipment such as guns, fuses, ammunition and vehicles are common. Integrated defence planning is necessary in view of escalating costs of these weapons and equipment.

Self-reliance in Defence Technology

The DRDO has a network of 51 laboratories and establishments. The Scientific Advisor (SA) to the Raksha Mantri (RM) is the Secretary of this Department. The DRDO has a staff of 30,000, including 6,800 scientists and engineers. It receives approximately four to six per cent of the defence budget annually.

The DRDO is engaged in the pursuit of self-reliance in critical technologies relevant to defence. It formulates and executes a programme of scientific research, design and development for the induction into the Armed Forces of state-of-the-art weapons and other equipments. In April 1984, the DRDO envisaged a programme "to transform the Department into a leader of international class with the mission to capture and retain commanding heights in critical technologies". A 'mission mode' organisational structure and approach was approved by the Government with a view to increasing the element of self-reliance from the current 30 per cent to 70 per cent by 2005. This goal, however, is nowhere in sight.

The Department has developed more than 1,100 items of weapon systems and equipment with a production value of over Rs 6,000 crore. But it has not been able to make any major contribution to the state-of-art weapons and equipment. Most of its programmes, like Prithvi (sea borne version), Trishul (short-range surface to air missile), Akash (medium-range surface to air missile), Nag (anti-tank missile), Light Combat Aircraft with Kaveri engine, Pinaka (multiple-barrel rocket system), MBT Arjun, Electronic Warfare equipment, new radio sets for the Army, Sonar system for Navy, and many other items, are way behind schedule.

Despite the media hype, the costs have been heavy. MBT Arjun, when it goes into production mode, will have more than 60 per cent imported components, including several crucial components like the engine and gun control system. It will cost over Rs 25 crore a piece whereas the cost of a T-90 tank, which is as superior (if not more), is less than Rs 10 crore along with technology transfer. Matters have come to such a pass that the Armed Forces have stopped believing media reports about the so-called 'successful trials' of weapons and equipment.

Because of the failure to deliver the required weapons and equipment, defence planning and Force structuring by the Services has suffered continuously. The DRDO's inability to deliver in time has caused a crisis of confidence and constant dissatisfaction in the Services. In order to ensure smooth progress towards self-reliance in defence technology, the Government must undertake a periodic performance audit of DRDO projects to reinforce efforts in areas of success and weed out projects that are unproductive.

NUCLEAR SECURITY AND TERRORIST ATTACKS

Nuclear power plants, civilian research reactors, certain naval fuel facilities, uranium enrichment plants, and fuel fabrication plants, are vulnerable to attacks which could lead to widespread radioactive contamination. The attack threat is of several general types: commando-like ground-based attacks on equipment which if disabled could lead to a reactor core meltdown or widespread dispersal of radioactivity; and external attacks such as an aircraft crash into a reactor complex, or cyber attacks. The United States

9/11 Commission has said that nuclear power plants were potential targets originally considered for theSeptember 11, 2001 attacks. If terrorist groups could sufficiently damage safety systems to cause a core meltdown at a nuclear power plant, and/or sufficiently damage spent fuel pools, such an attack could lead to widespread radioactive contamination. The Federation of American Scientists have said that if nuclear power use is to expand significantly, nuclear facilities will have to be made extremely safe from attacks that could release massive quantities of radioactivity into the community. New reactor designs have features of passive safety, which may help. In the United States, the NRC carries out "Force on Force" (FOF) exercises at all Nuclear Power Plant (NPP) sites at least once every three years.

Nuclear reactors become preferred targets during military conflict and, over the past three decades, have been repeatedly attacked during military air strikes, occupations, invasions and campaigns. Various acts of civil disobedience since 1980 by the peace group Plowshares have shown how nuclear weapons facilities can be penetrated, and the groups actions represent extraordinary breaches of security at nuclear weapons plants in the United States. The National Nuclear Security Administration has acknowledged the seriousness of the 2012 Plowshares action. Non-proliferation policy experts have questioned "the use of private contractors to provide security at facilities that manufacture and store the government's most dangerous military material". Nuclear weapons materials on the black market are a global concern, and there is concern about the possible detonation of a small, crude nuclear weapon by a militant group in a major city, with significant loss of life and property. *Stuxnet* is a computer worm discovered in June 2010 that is believed to have been created by the United States and Israel to attack Iran's nuclear facilities.

Fusion Power

Fusion power is a developing technology still under research. It relies on fusing rather than fissioning (splitting) atomic nuclei, using very different processes compared to current nuclear power plants. Commercial plants and prototype generators are not anticipated before 2030-2050. Nuclear fusion uses only tiny amounts of fuel at any time, and requires precisely controlled conditions to generate any net energy. Fusion reaction processes are so delicate that this level of safety is inherent; no elaborate failsafe mechanism is required.

The fuel itself is extremely safe at any temperature outside that of a working fusion reactor and only tiny amounts are used. If the reactor were damaged or control impaired, or the fuel supply stops, reactions and heat generation would cease almost immediately. For the same reason, there is also no risk of a thermal runaway or nuclear meltdown, since any significant change will render the reactions unable to produce excess heat. In comparison, a fission reactor is typically loaded with enough fuel for one or several years, enough fuel in a sufficiently small space will always produce thermal runaway or "meltdown", and no additional fuel is necessary to keep the reaction going. In the event of fire, calculations suggest that the total amount of radioactive gases from a typical fusion plant would be so small, about 1 kg, that they would have diluted to legally acceptable limits by the time they blew as far as the plant's perimeter fence.

In general terms, fusion reactors also create less radioactive material than a fission reactor, the material it would create is less damaging biologically, and the radioactivity "falls off" within a time period that is within existing engineering capabilities. The main byproduct is a small amount of helium, which is harmless to life. Of more concern is tritium, which, like other isotopes of hydrogen, is a very light gas, and difficult to retain completely. Although volatile and biologically active, the health risk is lower than most other radioactive contaminants, due to tritium's short half-life (12 years), very low decay energy (~14.95 keV), and the fact that it does not bioaccumulate (instead being cycled out of the body as water, with a biological half-life of 7 to 14 days). However the effect of widespread fusion power may require attention in this area.

Unlike fission reactors, whose used fuel rods and other waste remains highly radioactive for thousands of years, most of the radioactive material in a fusion reactor would be the reactor core itself, which would be dangerous for about 50 years, and low-level waste another 100. Fusion reactors can more easily be designed using "low activation" materials that do not easily become radioactive, such as vanadium or carbon fiber. Although the core of a decommissioned reactor will be considerably more radioactive during those 50 years than fission waste, the relatively short time period makes waste management fairly straightforward. By 300 years it would have the same radioactivity as coal ash.

More Stringent Safety Standards

Matthew Bunn, the former US Office of Science and Technology Policy adviser, and Heinonen, the former Deputy Director General of the IAEA, have said that there is a need for more stringent nuclear safety standards, and propose six major areas for improvement:

- operators must plan for events beyond design bases;
- more stringent standards for protecting nuclear facilities against terrorist sabotage;
- a stronger international emergency response;
- international reviews of security and safety;
- binding international standards on safety and security; and
- international co-operation to ensure regulatory effectiveness.

Coastal nuclear sites must also be further protected against rising sea levels, storm surges, flooding, and possible eventual "nuclear site islanding".

ALLEGED NUCLEAR TERRORISM ATTEMPTS AND PLANS

In June 2002, U.S. citizen Jose Padilla was arrested for allegedly planning a radiological attack on the city of Chicago; however, he was never charged with such conduct. He was instead convicted of charges that he conspired to "murder, kidnap and maim" people overseas. In November 2006, MI5 warned that al-Qaida were planning on using nuclear weapons against cities in the United Kingdom by obtaining the bombs via clandestine means.

In June 2007, the FBI released to the press the name of Adnan Gulshair el Shukrijumah, allegedly the operations leader for developing tactical plans for detonating nuclear bombs in several American cities simultaneously. The Alexander Litvinenko poisoning with radioactive polonium "represents an ominous landmark: the beginning of an era of nuclear terrorism," according to Andrew J. Patterson. Security specialist Shaun Gregory argued in an chapter that terrorists have attacked Pakistani nuclear facilities three times in the recent past; twice in 2007 and once in 2008.

Obama Administration

Nuclear weapons materials on the black market are a global concern, and there is concern about the possible detonation of a small, crude nuclear weapon by a terrorist group, in a major U.S. city, with significant loss of life and property. The Obama administration says they will focus on reducing the risk of such nuclear threats and aims to strengthen homeland nuclear security.".

Pakistan

After several incidents in Pakistan in which terrorists attacked three of its military nuclear facilities it became clear that there emerged a serious danger that they would gain access to the country's nuclear arsenal, according to a journal published by the US Military Academy at West Point. In January 2010 it was revealed that the US army was training a specialised unit *"to seal off and snatch back"* Pakistani nuclear weapons in the event that militants would obtain a nuclear device or materials that could make one. Pakistan supposedly possesses about 80 nuclear warheads. US officials refused to speak on the record about the American safety plans.

Recovering Lost Weapons & Material

In August 2002, the United States launched a program to track and secure enriched uranium from 24 Soviet-style reactors in 16 countries, in order to reduce the risk of the materials falling into the hands of terrorists or "rogue states". The first such operation was *Project Vinca,* "a multinational, public-private effort to remove nuclear material from a poorly secured Yugoslav research institute."

The project has been hailed as "a nonproliferation success story" with the "potential to inform broader 'global cleanout' efforts to address one of the weakest links in the nuclear nonproliferation chain: insufficiently secured civilian nuclear research facilities."

In order to reduce the danger of attacks using nuclear waste material, European Union Commissioner Loyola de Palacio suggested in November 2002 the creation of common standards in the European Union, especially in the new member states operating Soviet-era reactors, for subterranean nuclear waste disposal. In November 2007, burglars with unknown intentions infiltrated the Pelindaba nuclear research facility near Pretoria, South Africa. The burglars escaped without acquiring any of the uranium held at the facility.

Nuclear Proliferation and the Potential Threat of Nuclear Terrorism

For many centuries, security strategies have been based on boundaries: the strategic placement of cities and borders to take advantage of natural barriers; defences that relied on walls, trenches and armadas; and the use of ethnic and religious groupings or other categories to distinguish friend from foe. In the 20th Century, the advent of airplanes, submarines, ballistic missiles and weapons of mass destruction began to undermine this approach to security — by making borders increasingly porous, and by enabling the remote delivery of destruction on a scale previously not envisioned.

But the forcing factor — the change that has altered the international security landscape so drastically that it has compelled a fundamental reevaluation of security strategies — is, in fact, globalization. The global community has become interdependent, with the constant movement of people, ideas and goods. Many aspects of modern life — global warming, Internet communication, the global marketplace, and yes, the rise in international terrorism — point to the fact that the human race has walked through a door that cannot be re-entered. Our approaches to national and international security must be in keeping with this reality.

Today, our focus is on nuclear proliferation and the potential threat of nuclear terrorism in Asia and the Pacific — and I am pleased at the opportunity to share with you my perspectives on the challenges we face, and how the IAEA is working to strengthen nuclear security and the nuclear non-proliferation regime. But I would emphasize at the outset that, while much of our work must begin locally and regionally, we must not forget to think globally, because ultimately the existence of a nuclear threat anywhere is a threat everywhere, and as a global community, we will win or lose this battle together.

Nuclear Proliferation and Nuclear Verification

Turning first to the threat of nuclear weapons proliferation: the *Treaty on the Non-Proliferation of Nuclear Weapons (NPT)*remains the global anchor for nuclear non-proliferation and nuclear disarmament. Despite flaws in the system, implementation of the NPT continues to provide important security benefits — by providing assurance that, in the great majority of non-nuclear-weapon States, nuclear energy is not being misused for weapon purposes. Although the NPT is sometimes perceived as a project of the industrialized world, its benefits extend across any geopolitical divide.

Still, it is clear that the events of the past few years have placed the NPT and the regime supporting it under unprecedented stress, exposing some of its limitations and pointing to areas that need to be adjusted. A number of conspicuous lessons and insights can be gained from the recent experience of the IAEA in verifying undeclared nuclear programmes in Iraq, Iran, Libya and North Korea.

Perhaps the most important lesson is that verification and diplomacy, used in conjunction, can be effective. The Iraq experience demonstrated that the nuclear inspection process — while requiring time and patience — can be effective even when the country under inspection is providing less than active cooperation. When international inspectors are provided adequate authority, aided by all available information, backed by a credible compliance mechanism, and supported by international consensus, the verification system works. The report recently issued by the Iraq Survey Group confirmed the conclusions the IAEA was providing to the United Nations Security Council before the war, when we said we had found no evidence to suggest that Iraq had reconstituted any element of its former nuclear weapon programme — a conclusion that clearly came as a relief to all concerned.

Looking more broadly at recent IAEA experience in other countries, it is clear that, for nuclear verification to be successful, IAEA inspectors must have adequate authority. The "any time, any place" authority granted by the Security Council in the case of Iraq was extraordinary, and it is not likely that countries would voluntarily grant the IAEA such blanket rights of inspection.

Nonetheless, within the NPT framework, adequate authority can be achieved in those countries that accept the so-called "additional protocol" as a supplement to their NPT safeguards agreement. The additional protocol provides the Agency with significant additional authority with regard to both information and physical access. As illustrated by the IAEA's experience in Iraq before the first Gulf War, without the authority provided by the protocol, our ability to verify nuclear activities is mostly limited to the nuclear material already declared — with little authority to verify the absence of undeclared, or clandestine, nuclear material or activities. By contrast, our recent efforts in Iran and elsewhere have made clear how much can be uncovered when the protocol is applied.

Perhaps the most disturbing lesson to emerge from our work in Iran and Libya is the existence of an extensive illicit market for the supply of nuclear items, which clearly thrived on demand. The relative ease with which a multinational illicit network could be set up and operated demonstrates clearly the inadequacy of the present export control system. The fact that so many companies and individuals could be involved (more than two dozen, by last count) — and that, in most cases, this could occur apparently without the knowledge of their own governments — points to the shortcomings of national systems for oversight of sensitive equipment and technology. It also points to the limitations of existing international cooperation on export controls, which relies on informal arrangements, does not include many countries with growing industrial capacity, and does not include sufficient sharing of export information with the IAEA. Clearly, it is time to change our assumptions regarding the inaccessibility of nuclear technology. In a modern society characterized by electronic information exchange, interlinked financial systems, and global trade, the control of access to nuclear weapons technology has grown increasingly difficult. The technical barriers to mastering the essential steps of uranium enrichment — and to designing weapons — have eroded over time. Much of the hardware in question is 'dual use', and the sheer diversity of technology has made it much more difficult to control or even track procurement and sales.

The only reasonable conclusion is that the control of technology is not, in itself, a sufficient barrier against further proliferation. For an increasing number of countries with a highly developed industrial infrastructure — and in some cases access to high enriched uranium or plutonium — the international community must rely primarily on a continuing sense of security as the basis for the adherence of these countries to their non-proliferation commitments. And security perceptions can rapidly change. This leads to the important conclusion that ways and means should be found to better control the sensitive parts of the fuel cycle — namely, the production of enriched uranium and the reprocessing of plutonium.

The concept of multilateral control or oversight over proliferation sensitive parts of the nuclear fuel cycle has been the subject of many studies and initiatives over the years. Recent non-proliferation and security challenges make it important and appropriate that we revisit this subject. Several months ago, I appointed a group of senior experts to look into various options for multilateral control. I also asked the group to look into how to guarantee the supply of reactor technology and fuel, and the possibility of setting up an international scheme for the management and disposal of spent nuclear fuel. The group plans to submit a report next March, before the NPT Review Conference, on the results of its study.

The evolution of the North Korean situation over the past 18 months also carries an important lesson — that is, that the international community cannot afford not to act in a timely manner in cases of non-compliance, and before available options are narrowed. Beginning in the mid-1980s, the Democratic People's Republic of Korea (DPRK) took seven years to fulfill its obligations under the NPT to conclude a safeguards agreement with the Agency. In 1992, shortly after this agreement was concluded and the IAEA began inspections, we sounded the alarm that the DPRK had not reported its total production of plutonium. From that time forward, the DPRK has been in continuous non-compliance with its NPT obligations, and has not allowed the IAEA to fully verify its nuclear programme. At the end of 2002, the DPRK capped that non-compliance by ordering IAEA inspectors out of the country, dismantling the monitoring cameras, breaking IAEA seals and, a few weeks later, declaring its withdrawal from the NPT.

Naturally, all of these actions were promptly reported by the Agency to the Security Council — but with little to no response. This lack of timely action may have complicated finding a solution, and may have conveyed the message that breaking the non-proliferation norms with impunity is a doable proposition — or, worse, that acquiring a nuclear deterrent will bring with it a special treatment. The final lesson, an insight that has been demonstrated repeatedly, is that insecurity breeds proliferation. It is instructive that nearly all nuclear proliferation concerns arise in regions of longstanding tension. In other words, nuclear proliferation is a symptom, and the patient cannot ultimately be cured as long as we leave unaddressed the underlying causes of insecurity and instability — such as chronic disputes, the persistent lack of good governance and basic freedoms, the growing divide between rich and poor, and newly perceived schisms based on ethnic or religious differences.

It is in this context that I have begun to stress not only the value but also the limitations of the IAEA's role. While the Agency can use verification effectively to bring to closure questions of compliance with legal and technical requirements, the long term value of these efforts can only be realized to the extent that they are reinforced by all other components of the non-proliferation regime, and followed by the necessary political dialogue among concerned States to address underlying issues of insecurity, and to build confidence and trust. I should note that verification, supported by diplomacy, has been an important part of the efforts so far in Iran and Libya, and in that sense I can only hope that the continuation of the six-party talks on the DPRK nuclear programme will yield results that will include, inter alia, full IAEA verification.

THE TROUBLE WITH TERRORISM

Charles Townshend writes in "Terrorism": "Terrorism upsets people. It does so deliberately. That is its point, and that is why it has engrossed so mush of our attention in the early years of the 21st century. Insecurity can take many forms, but nothing else pays quite so sharply on our sense of vulnerability. After September 11 we found ourselves in an apparently open-ended and permanent state of emergency, a "war against terrorism", whose ramifications are as inscrutable as terrorism itself. Terrorism is never easy to understand, and least of all in the aftermath of a terrorist attack. When society feels under threat, attempts at rational analysis are often openly resisted as giving aid and comfort to, or even sympathizing with, the enemy. Yet without such analysis, combating Terrorism seems a baffling contest against an indefinite threat. Although Terrorism can sometimes took rational, more often it seems to go straight off the chart of common sense – to be not only unjustifiable, but atrocious, mad or mindless."

The Problem of Definition

"Both political and academic efforts to get to grips with terrorism have repeatedly been hung up on the issue of definition, of distinguishing terrorism from criminal violence or military action. In a word it is labelling because terrorist is a description that has almost never been voluntarily adopted by any individual group. It is applied to them by others, first and foremost by the governments of the states they attack. States have not been slow to brand violent opponents with this title, with its clear implications of inhumanity, criminality, and – perhaps most crucially – lack of real political support. Equally, states find it quite easy to produce definitions of Terrorism. The USA, for instance, defines it as ' the calculated use or threat of violence to inculcate fear, intended to coerce or intimidate governments or societies'; the UK as 'the use or threat, for the purpose of advancing a political, religious, or ideological course of action, of serious violence against any person or property'."

"In the states view, only the state has the right to use force – it has, as academics tend to say, a monopoly on the legitimate use of violence. But outsiders may wonder whether all use of violence by non-state actors is equally unjustifiable, even it is formally illegal. The very first revolutionary terrorists in the modern sense believed themselves justified in opposing with violence a repressive regime in which no freedom of political expression or organization was permitted."

"Thus arose a notorious adage that one person's terrorist is another's freedom fighter. This relativism is central to the impossibly of finding an uncontentious definition of Terrorism." "Terrorism is a distinctive form of modern political agency, intended to threaten the ability of a state to ensure the security of its members' – and thus its claim to legitimacy. To get closer to a definition of Terrorism we need to unpick its political logic. For the core of nearly all definitions of Terrorism – the use of violence for the political ends – is too similar to the definition of war to be much of use."

Terrorism & War

"Clearly war and terrorism are intimately related. It is hard to imagine a war that did not generate extreme fear amongst many people, and sometimes this is more than a by-product of violence – it is a primary objective." "The essence of Terrorism, by contrast, is surely the negation of combat. Its targets are attacked in a way that inhibits self-defence. But, of course, what marks Terrorism out in the public mind is its readiness to attack not just selected but also random targets; in the indiscriminate bombings of a street market, a store, or a bar, we see a deliberate flouting of the international law of war, and a refusal to accept as binding the prevailing moral distinctions – b/w belligerents and illegitimate targets. So the vital part of the US definition is the non-combatant targets against whom violence is perpetrated."

The Terror Process

I. Seizing attention: shock, horror, fear, or revulsion: this is certainly the most straightforward stage. The thirst for order and security impels societies to establish conventions and boundaries to regulate violent coercion: when these are transgressed, shock is generated.

II. Getting the message: what do terrorists want: by no means all-terrorist groups rush to claim responsibility for their actions, or if they do so, deliver a comprehensible rationale or demand. When terrorist acts are left unsigned-like 9/11 attacks – it is up to the onlookers to fill in the blanks. The results can be varied. George W. Bush assured his citizens that the 9/11 attacks were 'intended to frighten our nation into chaos and retreat'. But retreat from what, or where? American commentators, both official and unofficial, showed a marked reluctance to accept a surely well-established view that Usama bin Laden's primary motive against the US was the defilement of Saudi Arabia by the presence of US troops. Instead they preferred more abstract explanations of the attacks rooted in envy or hostility towards American prosperity and democracy.

III. Fight or flight? – The response: partly because the assessment of motives can be quirky, responses can be unpredictable or contradictory. If the demands are comprehensible and fulfillable, fear may drive people to comply. It is easy enough for people to fulfil minimal demands – to keep quiet and defuse to help the police, for instance; but bigger political demands can't usually be delivered directly. The people who are most likely to be intimidated or alarmed are the people who in most political structures are outside the decision-making sphere.

Strategies of Terror

T. P. Thornton proposed two basic varieties: enforcement and agitational terror. The function of the enforcement terror is likely to be limited, aimed at preserving the security of the rebel organization by deterring the public from giving information to the security forces. To succeed in this, the organization needs a sufficiently extensive surveillance system to persuade people that assisting the authorities will be detected: most terrorist groups are simply too small for this. Agitational terror is likely to grasp at mush extensive, longer-term goals: revolution of some kind, or 'national liberation'. Some of these goals are more feasible than others.

"Terrorist action may be auxiliary-one element of a larger military or guerilla strategy; it may be confined to limited goals; or it may be absolute – the pursuit of political goals through the systematic use of terror alone. It is this absolute, independent terror strategy, rather than terrorist action per se, that should properly be labelled terrorism. "Thus Terrorism properly so-called is not just the use of violence for political ends; not just outrageous violence; not just violence by the armed against the unarmed; it is conceived as a free-standing, sufficient, and decisive political strategy."

Terror & Politics

"Thinking about the terror process leads to the conclusion that the essential distinction b/w war and terrorism lies in their operational logic: war is ultimately coercive, terrorism is impressive. War is physical, terrorism is mental. Terrorism operates, therefore, through subjective psychological pressure.

Women & Terrorism

From Vera Zasulish, who carried out the first Narodnik armed attack when she shot the governor of St. Petersburg in 1878, to Waffa al-Edress, the first female Arab suicide bomber in Israel in January 2002, women have been frontline actors and, consequently, pioneer recasters of gender roles.

SECURITY-ENHANCING EFFECTS OF GLOBALIZATION

The threat-eroding impact of globalization in the region has been generated mainly, though not exclusively, through economic means that exposed the attractiveness of the market economy to ASEAN states and integrated them into the world economy. Despite various security concerns in the domestic and regional contexts, regional states have generally responded positively to the process of globalization. There has been a common view, at least among core members of ASEAN, that globalization served to promote and accelerate economic development. ASEAN countries realized that an open economy would best serve their respective pragmatic national economic strategy of promoting growth through attracting foreign investment and expanding their export share in the world market. They also realized that resistance to the increasing power of global capitalism would be futile. It was also acknowledged that the core of this global capitalist system – the West – served as an important source of capital, technology, goods and services.

The result of three decades of such outward-looking development strategy is evident on two fronts. On the regional front, it elevated the level of economic interdependence among ASEAN countries to an unprecedented scale. Even though intra-ASEAN economic exchanges and co-operation had been slow at the beginning of the Association's life, changes attendant from the end of the Cold War forced ASEAN leaders to realize that their economies were rapidly involved in market-driven processes towards regional and international economic integration. Rather than each country going its own way, they thought that by joining forces they could enhance their collective position and increase the gains from integration in the world economy. In addition, they believed that governments could facilitate this market-driven integration. As demonstrated by the agreement to form an ASEAN Free Trade Area (AFTA), ASEAN governments realized that improving and strengthening intra-ASEAN economic co-operation have become imperative for the viability and relevance of ASEAN for its members. This reflects ASEAN's judgement, though rarely stated, that the only way to survive in the world economy was to promote greater economic co-operation and integration in ASEAN. Growing interdependence among ASEAN countries then became a logical consequence of the deepening of regional economic co-operation.

The implication of such interdependence for regional security has been well noted. Hadi Soesastro, for example, maintains that economic interdependence and integration "contribute to economic growth and development of the region as a whole. As people's well-being in the region increases the region becomes more stable; this in turn improves regional security." Steven Chan writes that "the deepening and widening networks of interests that characterize increasing interdependence should moderate international tension."

Scalapino argues that "given... the growth of economic interdependence, the destructiveness of a major war to all parties, victor and vanquished alike, would be enormous." In a similar vein, Harris points out that the pattern of behaviour for most of the Asia-Pacific powers seems to follow the proposition that "the growing economic interdependence of nations... provides strong incentive for countries, even the major powers, to adopt trading (and investment) strategies for the development and maintenance of relationship in international society." All in all, there was a widely held belief that economic interdependence has been conducive to regional co-operation and stability.

Indeed, the primary contribution of economic interdependence to security in Southeast Asia has been to contain or prevent actual and potential conflict from arising to the extent that could damage intra-ASEAN relations. Growing interdependence does increase the cost of the use of force as a means to solve differences. The acknowledgement of this logic, primarily due to the imperative of a stable external environment for national development, has been central in the policy of ASEAN member states towards each other. Consequently, ASEAN no longer sees the outbreak of war or a military confrontation among member states as an immediate security concern. Seen in this context, growing interdependence can be regarded as a factor that explains why Southeast Asia has enjoyed a relatively long period of stability. To that effect, it can be argued that globalization has increased interdependence among Southeast Asian countries, and therefore reduced the likelihood of war among them.

However, economic interdependence alone, while necessary, is not a sufficient condition for peace. Keohane and Nye, for example, warn that "we are not suggesting that international conflict disappears when interdependence prevails. On the contrary, conflict will take new forms and may even increase..."Indeed, there has been no convincing evidence that growing economic interdependence in ASEAN has successfully removed the sources or potential of conflict among its members. This is also partly due to the nature of Southeast Asian security being characterized by the more salient dimensions of internal security. Nor does interdependence remove any possibility for new conflicts to arise. In fact, globalization has brought with it more than just integrating forces that drive economic interdependence among states. Globalization has also brought threat-intensifying effects, which blend old and new threats to national and regional security.

the Blending of Old and New Threats

There are three dimensions of security-eroding effects of globalization in Southeast Asia. First, globalization has perpetuated some old security concerns. Second, it has forced states to respond to new non-traditional threats. Third, it has increased the security burdens of regional states. While this latest dimension of security-eroding effects of globalization does not necessarily represent a threat as such, it could nevertheless contribute to the erosion of security in the region.

As for the old security concerns, globalization has served the function of reinforcing the internal security concerns of Southeast Asian states. It has been mentioned earlier that the primary threat to national security for Southeast Asian states has been internal in nature. They were worried about anything that would erode state sovereignty, challenge regime legitimacy and the central role of the state, and undermine domestic stability. The forces of globalization did just that, and will continue to do so.

First, the source of challenges to state sovereignty brought about by globalization can be found in the process of opening up a national economy and integrating it into the global economy. Indeed, one of the crucial aspects of globalization has been its implication for the central role of the state as the dominant actor, not only in international relations but also in domestic politics. This, in turn, puts the state in a rather problematic situation. On the one hand, it has been argued that globalization poses a challenge to the sovereignty of state and limits state power. The state no longer serves primarily as a buffer, or shield, against the world economy. The scope for state autonomy is then reduced in the context of economic globalization. On the other hand, the state may attempt to preserve its central role by seeking material gains from globalization. The state may increasingly facilitate globalization, acting as an agent in the process.

Within the Southeast Asian context, the attempt to seek material gains from globalization during the 1990s may have helped the state to retain its role as a principal agent of development. This role is indeed crucial for the state since it serves as a primary factor that sustains the security of the regime. It is also imperative for the government to welcome the positive impact of globalization on economic development since it encourages growth and brings about new economic opportunities. Both of these serve as important sources of regime legitimacy. On the other hand, economic growth driven by states' integration into the economic globalization process may also bring about political consequences, primarily through the free flow of information, made possible by the revolution in information technology that carries with it new ideas and cultural values. Such political consequences have manifested themselves, among other things, in the rise of new groups in society that demand greater participation in policy process and politics, and the absorption of new ideas and demands (such as democracy, human rights, and social justice). Under such circumstances, the governments of Southeast Asia undoubtedly feel the autonomy-eroding impact of globalization. Indeed, there has been a rise in challenges to regime legitimacy and changing state–society relations as two attendant effects of globalization, in countries like Indonesia, Thailand, the Philippines, and (to a lesser degree) Malaysia.

The second security concern has been the effect of globalization on the permeability of the state to foreign penetration. A state's participation in the globalization process, which requires greater and deeper integration into the global economy, makes it more exposed to external influences. States with such outward-looking development strategy are confronted with growing economic interdependence as an inevitable consequence of globalization. In such circumstances, globalization then erodes the autonomy of governments in formulating and implementing national economy strategies and policies. For most developing countries in Southeast Asia, which view independency and autonomy as two significant political values, the autonomy-eroding effect of globalization clearly serves as one source of insecurity feeling.

The suspicion that there will always be foreign forces trying to exploit the vulnerability and weakness of developing countries for their own benefits has been prevalent among regional countries. The growing permeability of states due to the revolution in information and communication technology (ICT), which intensifies the internationalization and globalization process of values, strengthens the sensitivity of regional states to a growing threat posed by the penetration of foreign values into their domestic domain. There are worries among Southeast Asian leaders that the globalization process may threaten social and cultural values in the society.

The third security concern is the impact of globalization on social structure and relations. Again, concerns over this issue are closely linked to the paramount importance of internal order for Southeast Asian countries. For example, it has been argued that a special challenge for Southeast Asia in assuring "domestic tranquillity is that of ethnic and religious relations." Indonesia's government, owing to the fragile nature of ethnic and religious relations in the country, has been the most sensitive on this issue.

On more than one occasion, government officials have warned that "globalization can strengthen the influence of liberalism which foster individualism, and deteriorate our nationalism, which, in turn, can encourage ethnic separatism to the effect of undermining the authority of the government." The problems of ethnic divisions are also present in Thailand, the Philippines, and (to a lesser extent) Malaysia and Singapore. Ethnic tension in the region has been exacerbated not only by uneven distribution of the positive results of the economic globalization process, but also by the gap existing among different ethnic groups in tapping those advantages.

The fourth security concern is the impact of globalization on national unity and territorial integrity. The globalization process has not produced the same positive effects on every group in the society. Since globalization fosters competition, there will be winners and losers. Those who feel that they are left behind in the process might harbour separatist tendencies, such as the case in Indonesia, Thailand, the Philippines and Myanmar. As Southeast Asian states see territorial integrity as the basis for their existence and identity as an independent and sovereign nation-state, separatist tendencies are seen as a grave danger to the maintenance of that core value. Given the growing permeability of states, concerns over the spillover of domestic problems into the regional stage have been heightened. Indeed, given the surge of insurgencies in the region, Southeast Asian states are once again faced with the twin challenges of preventing internal conflicts from undermining regional security, on the one hand, and avoiding external factors from complicating domestic problems, on the other.

While globalization has perpetuated the existing internal security concerns, the nature of threats to the national security of Southeast Asian states has also become more complex due to the emergence of new threats. Security problems such as piracy, disputes over fishing ground, drug trafficking, arms smuggling, environmental degradation, terrorism, ethnic and communal violence, and transnational organized crimes have become a cause of common concern. There has also been a growing concern among Southeast Asian states over threats to human security such as poverty, hunger, human rights abuses, and infectious diseases. Even though these problems have been common in Southeast Asia for many decades, the growing frequency of their occurrences and the magnitude of the threat to the security of both the state and the people can be attributed to globalization. The growing threat of terrorism since 11 September 2001, the health crisis triggered by the problem of Severe Acute Respiratory Syndrome (SARS) in 2003, and now Avian flu, clearly demonstrate how security threats in Southeast Asia have become increasingly transnational, and therefore blurred the distinction between internal and external security. These problems serve as the latest reminder to all regional states that security interdependence has become an undeniable reality in Southeast Asia. What happens in one country certainly has an impact on others.

The transnational nature of security threat in Southeast Asia has been exemplified by the problem of terrorism. The current threat posed by terrorist network such as the *Jamaah Islamiyah* has been far too lethal compared to the previous terrorist acts perpetrated by communist insurgencies in the 1950s–1960s (Malaysia, Singapore, Thailand, the Philippines, and Indonesia) and religious extremists in the early 1980s (Indonesia).

Previous terrorist attacks in some ASEAN states were motivated purely by domestic grievances and perpetrated by disgruntled domestic groups.

The *Jamaah Islamiyah* constitutes a completely different form of terrorist threat. It is, first and foremost, a network whose activities encompass almost all Southeast Asian states.

It also has global links with global terrorist networks elsewhere, even though the exact nature and extent of those links are still not well defined. Globalization has facilitated the creation of such networking through the skilful use of internet and other forms of modern communication technology by the terrorists. The network has also been forged by ease of travel in the era of globalization.

In between the internal and transnational security concerns, Southeast Asian states are also concerned with traditional security issues. Regional security concerns as a consequence of globalization have not been confined to non-conventional security issues alone.

In a traditional sense, globalization facilitates changes in international and regional power structure. It provides opportunity for aspiring powers to acquire new status and exercise greater influence within an existing regional and international political structure.

In Southeast Asia, the rise of China constitutes the most salient aspect of traditional security concerns. China has demonstrated well how a state's participation in the process of globalization has led to a dramatic improvement in national strength and capability. Over the last ten years or so, China has consistently demonstrated its ability to sustain economic growth at an impressive rate higher than that of its Southeast Asian neighbours. Along with its economic development, China's military capability has also improved significantly vis-à-vis Southeast Asian countries.

In other words, China's participation, taking advantage of the process of economic globalization, has increased significantly the stature and standing of this country in the region.

The concern with China relates, first and foremost, to the question of how China is going to use its new stature and influence in achieving its national interests and objectives in the region. Moreover, in economic terms, it is not yet clear whether China would become a competitor or a partner to ASEAN states.

However, it is important to note that China has repeatedly assured regional states that its rise would be peaceful and China would continue to play a positive role in the stability and security of the region.

The third aspect of security-eroding effects of globalization in Southeast Asia has been the increase in the security burdens of regional states.

Globalization clearly increases the need for new resources required for sustaining economic development of those states participating in the process of globalization. Here, three interrelated problems could arise.

First, there has been an increase in the demand for gas and oil. Second, for littoral Southeast Asian states, the 200 nautical mile Exclusive Economic Zones (EEZs) serve as the most important sources of gas and oil, and also of marine resources such as rich fish stocks, and therefore "policing these Zones is becoming increasingly important for ASEAN economies."

As a consequence of the first two, the third problem stems from the overlapping territorial claims, especially over areas rich in such natural resources, which have become more difficult to resolve.

In other words, these three problems have increased the security burdens of Southeast Asian states, which calls for not only the need to protect owned resources, but also to reinforce claims over disputed territories.

Indeed, globalization could also exacerbate these traditional security concerns that have already existed in the region even before the economies of regional states became more integrated with the global economy. Southeast Asia remains a region fraught with unresolved territorial disputes and border problems among the regional states. Malaysia, for example, has territorial disputes with Indonesia, Singapore, and the Philippines. Indonesia and Singapore also have an unresolved problem of boundary demarcation.

The problem of borders security is evident in the case of Thailand–Myanmar and Thailand–Cambodia relations. The security-eroding effects of this particular problem have been demonstrated in the case of Malaysia–Indonesia disputes, first over Sipadan–Ligatan Islands, and now over the jurisdiction of Ambalat in the Sulawesi Sea.

In addition to unresolved territorial disputes and maritime boundary issues, the water issue and Singapore's growing need for space through land reclamation have often disrupted Malaysia–Singapore relations.

The above discussion clearly reveals that globalization has presented the governments of Southeast Asia with an array of threats, old and new, to national security.

In this context, however, it is important to note that there are differences among regional states with regard to which threat they perceive as more pressing to national and regional security, depending on the degree of their success in managing globalization. Of all the Southeast Asian countries, Singapore, Malaysia, Thailand, the Philippines and Indonesia have been the ones most exposed to globalization.

However, the ability of these countries to manage the process of globalization differs. Malaysia and Singapore, for example, "have managed to take advantage of most of the globalization components that they consider beneficial, but still avoid those (boundary breakdown/penetration and enlargement) that threaten to overthrow their respective internal orders."Meanwhile, despite also benefiting from globalization, Indonesia, and to a lesser extent Thailand and the Philippines, could not escape some negative effects of globalization that they sought to avoid, especially on the internal order of these countries.

This reality has resulted in two different sets of globalization-induced security concerns between the two groups of states. On the one hand, owing to their success in managing the negative impacts of globalization on internal order, Singapore and Malaysia are more worried about terrorism, piracy and environmental problems.

Indonesia, Thailand and the Philippines, while sharing those same worries with Malaysia and Singapore, are also faced with those challenges that intensify their internal security concerns, such as threats to territorial integrity posed by armed separatist movements, communal violence, and internal instability. While these differences lead to the same response at regional level, regional states differ with regard to responses at national level, especially in defence policy.

SAFETY AND SECURITY PAKISTAN'S NUCLEAR ARSENAL

Determined to retain and expand its nuclear capabilities but shaken by the reaction to A.Q. Khan's global nuclear entrepreneurship, in 2004 Musharraf's government had sharply reversed its earlier policy of keeping all nuclear matters under the wrap.

It hoped thereby to assure the world that Pakistan's nuclear weapons were in safe hands. A stream of highly placed official visitors made a beeline for Washington's think-tanks and military colleges across the United States. A few years earlier this would have been unthinkable. Visits from top officials of the Strategic Plans Division (SPD), which is charged with the possession, maintenance, and safety of Pakistan's nuclear weapons became routine, and still continue.

It is especially significant that the director general of the SPD, Lt. Gen. Khalid Kidwai, is a visitor to the US. He was, for example, invited to a special guest lecture to the faculty, students, and guests of the Naval Postgraduate School in Monterey where he sought to debunk the notion that Pakistani weapons could fall into the hands of religious extremists, were on hair-trigger alert, or be used irresponsibly.

Other Pakistani military officers associated with the nation's nuclear program are paid by US funding sources for writing reports and papers for US think-tanks and research institutes. Still others are in the process of writing books that will reveal the true history of the Pakistani nuclear program xlviii.

To safeguard Pakistan's crown jewels is a relatively recent preoccupation that dates to the September 11, 2001 attack. Although Pakistan's military government insisted that there was no danger of any of its nuclear weapons being taking for a ride, it did not take chances.

Several weapons were reportedly airlifted to various safer, isolated, locations within the country. This nervousness was not unjustified – two strongly Islamist generals of the Pakistan Army (the head of Pakistan's ISI intelligence agency, Lt. General Mehmood Ahmed, and Deputy Chief of Army Staff, General Muzaffar Hussain Usmani), close associates of General Musharraf, had just been removed. The seriousness of betraying the progeny of Pakistan's intelligence services was something that Musharraf feared – and for good reason.

Internationally, there are widespread fears that instability in Pakistan could make its nuclear weapons and stocks of nuclear explosive material dangerously vulnerable to theft. As could be expected, Pakistan's position has been one of emphatic denial: the Foreign Ministry claims that our [nuclear] assets are 100 percent secure, under multiple custody. Soothing words, however, have not taken away a general sense of worry. Pakistan is now in the grip of a full-fledged insurgency by Islamic groups. Some of these view Pakistan's nuclear weapons as belonging to the *Ummah*, rather than Pakistan alonel. This has enhanced the feeling internationally that Pakistan's nuclear weapons, fissile materials, and other nuclear components are unsafe.

The dangers to Pakistan's nuclear weapons are potentially four-fold:

- From India and the US, separately or together. Israel is a distant possibility but not to be ruled out.
- From outside: Islamic militants attacking a nuclear storage site or facility with the purpose of capturing a nuclear weapon.
- From inside: Islamic elements in the army who have responsibility for protecting and operating nuclear sites or facilities.
- From a collaboration between insiders and outsiders.

There is concern in Pakistan of the growing Israeli-Indian strategic alliance, underscored by the supply of four Phalcon AWAC-type systems.

These have the capability of tracking Pakistani aircraft over the entire geographical area. India has already acquired two Israeli Green Pine radars, capable of tracking missiles at a distance of 400 km. These are normally used in conjunction with the Arrow II anti-missile system.

These early-warning systems could be effectively used by Israel to launch a pre-emptive strike at Pakistan's nuclear facilities with India's direct assistance or by using India as a base. Only an extreme crisis would result in India or the US, whether acting together or separately, to attack a nuclear armed state with all the obvious dangers this contains.

Even a massive use of force is unlikely to net all of well-hidden and well-protected Pakistani nuclear weapons. Moreover, the job would be incomplete unless the major nuclear weapon facilities, reactors, and uranium enrichment plants were also destroyed completely. This would involve nothing short of total war.

On the other hand, Islamic extremists may seek a weapon for ultimate use against a US or European city. But, because it would be much easier to arrange, they may seek the destruction of an Indian or Pakistani city, with the hope of provoking total war between Pakistan and India. This would be consistent with the suicide bombing strategy followed by Al-Qaida elsewhere. In the extremist mindset, it is best if infidels are killed. But if Sunni Muslims are killed, they will simply make it to heaven a bit earlier.

Defending against other nations as well as internal enemies poses a difficult security dilemma: Pakistan would like to keep the location and details of its nuclear weapons secret in order to increase their chances of a strike by India, the US, or Israel. On the other hand army insiders are already, by definition, in the know. Perhaps in collusion with an external Islamic group they could be plotting a move unknown to the Nuclear Command Authority (NCA), the SPD, or the Chief of Army Staff. How could such an attempt be foiled?

Only partial safety is possible no matter what the technical fix. One obvious mechanism is to reduce the readiness level. Pakistan is widely believed to store the fissile core and bomb mechanisms separately in safely guarded vaults. As early as December 1999, it had requested senior US officials visiting Islamabad for Permissive Action Links (PALs) that are directly integrated into the firing mechanism and electronics of a nuclear weapon, as well as Environment Sensitive Devices (ESDs), in order to enhance protection against unauthorized use or accidental nuclear detonations.

At that time, the US had declined for obvious reasons: these devices make it possible for the weapons to be maintained at a higher state of alert for the same level of safety, thereby increasing the threat perceived by India. But subsequent to a reversal of Pakistan's relationship with the US after 911, it is possible that the US may have acceded to Pakistan's request without demanding that Pakistan reveal the location or details of its nuclear weapons. According to an ISIS report, US Secretary of State Colin Powell had offered nuclear protection assistance to Pakistan after 911li. Pakistan found the offered technology to be quite rudimentary but nevertheless accepted it under the condition that the end point usage would remain opaque. Other aspects of the assistance included training courses for Pakistani nuclear weapons personnel in US labs where they were instructed on nuclear safety and security issues.

David Albright, a US nuclear security analyst, prescribed the following forms of additional assistance to Pakistan in the aftermath of 911:

"Generic physical protection and material accounting practices; theoretical exercises; unclassified military handbooks on nuclear weapons safety and security; more sophisticated vaults and access doors; portal control equipment; better surveillance equipment; advanced equipment for materials accounting; personnel reliability programs; and programs to reduce the likelihood of leaking sensitive information. In addition, aid could focus on methods that improve the security of nuclear weapons against unauthorized use through devices not intrinsic to the design of the nuclear weapon or through special operational or administrative restrictions. Excluded assistance would include nuclear weapons design information aimed at making more secure, reliable or safer nuclear weapons or devices, PALs, coded launch control devices, and environmental sensing devices."

While technical measures to reduce the chances of nuclear sabotage and accident must undoubtedly be implemented, there is a fundamental tension that cannot be avoided – a perfectly safe nuclear weapon is also one that cannot be used. Hence, by definition, it is useless. In times of crisis and war, when casualties and passions run high, there will be a strong urge to weaken the safety mechanisms in place.

NUCLEAR THREAT REDUCTION IN INDIA AND PAKISTAN

The Carnegie Endowment for International Peace (CEIP) published a draft report, 'Universal Compliance: A Strategy for Nuclear Security', in June 2004. The report proposes a strategic blueprint for US leadership to rethink international nuclear nonproliferation and global nuclear security. In this report, the recommended measures for nuclear risk reduction between India and Pakistan include:

- o Establishment of national risk reduction centres in both countries to administer agreed upon confidence-building measures.
- o Acommitment not to develop, produce, and use 'tactical' nuclear weapons.

- o Agreement not to flight-test missiles in the direction of the other country.
- o Agreement to flight-test missiles only from designated test ranges.
- o Provision of advance notification of the movement of missiles for training purposes.

The Henry L. Stimson Centre's report, 'Reducing Nuclear Dangers in South Asia', argues that: "The stability-instability paradox that was formulated in the West to characterise the dangers of nuclear deterrence is alive and well in South Asia.

This paradox holds that, while offsetting nuclear capabilities might indeed prevent a full-blown conventional or nuclear war, the presence of these fearsome weapons could also encourage the use of violence at lower levels in the expectation that escalation would be contained by a mutual desire to avoid the nuclear threshold."

And that, "Kashmir has been inflamed since the advent of covert nuclear capabilities on the subcontinent, and tensions have grown even more pronounced with the demonstration of overt nuclear capabilities in 1998. The region is now experiencing crises with greater frequency and severity."

The report includes extensive deliberations during two workshops, November 14-18, 2002, and May 20-23, 2003, with participants from the US, India and Pakistan, convened by the Stimson Centre to discuss escalation control and scenarios that could lead to crossing of the nuclear threshold. It provides the following 'doable' steps in the near term:

- o Establishment of national risk reduction centresto serve as focal points for the administration of confidence-building measures.
- o Missile-related measures to formalise and properly implement the agreement concerning prior notification of missile launches; to formalise and extend the time-line for such notifications; to forego missile flight tests in the direction of the other country; to flight test missiles only from designated test ranges; and to provide advance

notification of the movement of missiles for training purposes.

- o Clarifying terminology or developing common terminology on nuclear-related programmes, deployment, and doctrine could reduce misunderstanding and increase crisis stability.
- o Leadership declarations affirming responsible nuclear stewardshipcould help defuse nuclear dangers and facilitate an improvement in bilateral relations.
- o Increased awareness of nuclear dangers, particularly with regard to the possible acquisition of nuclear materials by terrorist groups, would be advisable.

In the Stimson Centre's report, the proposals collected in the workshops on escalation control are grouped in five categories: improving bilateral relations; nuclear risk reduction and strategic restraint; safety and security measures; and, improving intelligence through communication.

Both the reports, by CEIP and the Stimson Centre, have this presumption that 'deterrence' may not work between India and Pakistan as similar to the Cold War experience.

Such assumptions are not completely invalid for the two countries did resort to nuclear rhetoric during the 1999 Kargil conflict and indulged in 'nuclear signalling' during the period of crisis in 2001-2.

In addition, the absence of a doctrine without no-first-use policy and repeated calls from the Pakistani side to lower the threshold could have a certain bearing on the thinking of Western analysts. Already, the strategic debate had reached a slightly higher level than was normally prevalent in the subcontinent when the Indian Army Chief stated that a limited war with Pakistan is possible.

For any future war in the subcontinent, the two most likely scenarios discussed in the Cooperative Monitoring Centre Occasional Paper of Sandia National Laboratories, are: a breakdown along the common border in Kashmir, and failure of nuclear policy. The authors propose an alternative approach through which India and Pakistan can begin to cooperate in managing their common border to prevent a breakdown. The ultimate concern in the report about the existence of nuclear weapons is the possibility of their use in a time of conflict. The following are the enumerations in the Cooperative Monitoring Centre Occasional Paper that focuses on the monitoring of nuclear safety, security, and stability:

- o The ability to assess the current operational and deployment status of nuclear weapons is perhaps the most critical factor in near-term crisis prevention.
- o Developing measures to prevent escalation.
- o National decisions to include both technical and procedural mechanisms to restrict use of weapons and delivery systems will permit more time to attempt diplomatic solutions to conflict before initiating weapons use.
- o Another element of nuclear stability is determining the readiness of launch systems. There may be a number of indicators associated with launcher alert status. These include: Flight parameters loaded, other software updates (if appropriate); Vehicle fuelled (missile or aircraft); Crews readied; Delivery vehicle in launch location (moved to launch point); Transporter system in ready position (e.g., transporter erector launcher [TEL] in raised launch position); Weapon armed. While most of these indicators of launch preparation are difficult to monitor, some, such as missile fuelling and launcher movements, might be monitored through electronic sensors.
- o There is the possibility of use through miscalculation or misinterpretation.
- o Sharing information on any of the concerns for safety, security or accident will require an infrastructure of capabilities and procedures. These include methods for providing timely, reliable, secure, accurate, and authenticated communications.
- o Ensuring safety of nuclear weapons and materials will primarily be a state responsibility because of the highly classified nature of most safety issues. These issues involve

detailed design, as well as material and handling details. An expanded mission for hotlines between the Directors-General of Military Operations and between the Heads of State might be established to address this critical issue.

Acknowledging the fact that only the Indian and Pakistani governments can decide whether and on what basis, to establish new risk reduction measures, the 'Working Group Report of the Centre for Strategic and International Studies (CSIS)' recommends the following steps for nuclear risk reduction:

- o A new communications mechanism-nuclear risk reduction centres (NRRCs) in India and Pakistan-should be established to complement existing bilateral channels.
- o The main functions of the NRRCs would be to provide each party a dedicated, secure means of: (a) notifying the other side about activities or events on its territory that might be wrongly perceived or misinterpreted that could lead to conflict, (b) sharing information that the two countries are obliged to exchange under existing security agreements, and (c) seeking and receiving clarifications about ambiguous events on the other' sterritory. Other functions could include the conduct of joint exercises of certain NRRC notification procedures, technical back-up during crises, and support for consultations on the implementation of existing confidence-building measures (CBMs).
- o Adequate infrastructure already exists in South Asia to support a wide range of secure communication options, including data, voice, video, or a combination of these.

  The approximate cost for a dedicated cable permitting teletype and voice communication would be US$10,000-50,000 annually. For a dedicated satellite channel permitting teletype, voice, and video, the annual cost would be roughly US$560,000.
- o The centres would operate on a continuous, round-the-clock basis. Written messages using agreed formats would be the norm, although voice and video capability would

also be desirable. It would be the prerogative of each government to decide where it would institutionally house its NRRC and to determine how its NRRC would relate to other government organisations. The Indian and Pakistani solutions to these questions need not be symmetrical.

The Working Group Report concluded, that "the circumstances in South Asia today are very different from the circumstances surrounding the current US-Russian relationship and the relationship that existed when the US-Soviet Centres were brought into being. To tailor a new communications mechanism to the needs of South Asia, the mechanism could appropriately take on a wider range of functions than the US and Russian Centres."

Rodney W.Jones assumes that there lies intense political conflict over Kashmir and that the escalation in South Asia has the potential of becoming a nuclear war. In one of the papers presented during the fourth nuclear stability roundtable during March 12-13, 2002, in Washington on 'Military Asymmetry and Instability in Emerging Nuclear States: India and Pakistan,' he suggests the following conditions of nuclear stability in the region:

- o High nuclear threshold (strong conventional defence)
- o Secure second strike capabilities (robust C4I)
- o Rough parity in size and defence space
- o Neither falling behind the other's first strike edge (good early warning?) Supposing that "nuclear deterrence might provide the security that allows a general improvement in security relations" in South Asia, the UNIDR (United Nations Institute for Disarmament Research) research paper depicts various aspects of nuclear confidence-building measures between India and Pakistan. Commenting on the current conflict situation between the two countries, the authors of the paper subscribe to developing CBMs in connection with the 'central issue-Kashmir'. An interim suggestion is made to work on the possibilities of addressing the 'central sore-cross-border terror raids' from Pakistan.

With regard to nuclear CBMs, according to the UNIDR paper, India and Pakistan should share the development of respective nuclear doctrines and security concepts to have clarity over 'red lines'; develop mechanisms on notification of ballistic and cruise missile tests; create nuclear risk reduction centres with robust safety systems to deal with the issues of accidental or unauthorised use; and install a secure and dedicated line of communication including safe command and control systems between the national authorities (the nature or constitution of national authority remains undefined).

The paper categorically puts the 'Kashmir issue' to be discussed as in the final stages of CBMs between the two countries.

The UNIDR study concludes that the two countries should seize the ripe moment (that has begun since the two countries agreed to peace talks during the sidelines of the SAARC summit in January 2004) in the context of possibility of conflict.

"Any future terrorist incident might provoke India into punitive action, which in the worst case might lead to uncontrolled or accidental responses, all the way to a nuclear exchange. This suggests that, although the nuclear aspects will have to be part of the general discussions on security, it might also be worth considering whether they can be made separable, in case the moment passes too quickly."

The aspect of geographical proximity of the two countries is also discussed in one of the reports dealing with nuclear threat reduction measures. Based on some hypothetical South Asian launch point-target combinations, the missile travel time between India and Pakistan is estimated between 8 to 13 minutes.

Taking account of the danger of false alarms and miscalculations, the Pugwash Discussion Paper of 2002 suggests that a posture of De-alert (most basic measures would be to keep the weapons de-mated from delivery systems; use of locking devices), and installation of best available safety measures into the weapons, like use of Insensitive High Explosive (IHE) and fire-resistant pits would significantly reduce the risk of inadvertent or unauthorised use of weapons.

From the above discussed strategic policy recommendations, there emerge two sets of proposals that could draw attention of the diplomats and strategic planners of India and Pakistan.

In the first set, one can identify mechanisms for escalation control and nuclear force management within each state.

The second set includes possible measures of nuclear CBMs by the two countries to work towards long lasting stability in the region.

Control and Nuclear Force Management

- o Leadership declarations affirming responsible nuclear stewardship (avoidance of shrill rhetoric).
- o Developing strategies to avoid escalation of conventional confrontation to nuclear exchange level.
- o Avoiding sensitive targets in the event of a conventional war.
- o Raising the level of nuclear threshold (strong conventional defences).
- o Securing second strike capabilities.
- o Review of decision-making to develop, produce, and use 'tactical' nuclear weapons.
- o Regular assessment of each other's current operational and deployment status of nuclear weapons (missile fuelling and launcher movements might be monitored through electronic sensors).
- o Determining the readiness of launch systems.
- o Improvements in intelligence to avoid miscalculation or misinterpretation.
- o Acquisition of technology to help provide prompt and accurate information concerning missile launches and nuclear detonations.
- o Advancement in respective command and control mechanisms including establishment of effective early warning systems.
- o Refraining from giving pre-delegation of authority to use nuclear weapons.

- o Effective physical safety of nuclear materials and installations.
- o Ensuring safety and security of nuclear weapons and materials.

Steps Required for Nuclear CBMs

- o Improving bilateral relationship.
- o Sharing knowledge of decision-making processes.
- o Agreement on advance notification of missile testing and movements.
- o Flight test missiles only from designated test ranges.
- o Provision of advance notification of the movement of missiles for training purposes.
- o Review of policy decisions related to tactical nuclear weapons (including development, production, or use).
- o Establishment of multi-layered, reliable, secure, accurate, and authenticated communication mechanisms.
- o Establishment of Nuclear Risk Reduction Centres (NRRCs).

Most of the above-mentioned studies on South Asia suggest that problems related to Kashmir may be the spark to trigger a nuclear exchange between India and Pakistan.

Linking of the Kashmir issue with Indo-Pak nuclear strategy is quite complex.

In fact, such an assumption indirectly endorses (and is born out of) Pakistan's nuclear blackmailing. In reality, it is the Pakistani military that has crossed the Line of Control (LoC) in the past to provoke Indian defence.

Pakistan does not adhere to no-first-use (NFU) and keeps making frequent calls to lower the nuclear threshold in the apprehension of India taking reprisal measures to stop Pakistan-sponsored terrorism in Indian territory.

Pakistan insists on Kashmir being the 'core' issue of stability/instability between India and Pakistan. India maintains that the scourge of 'terrorism' in South Asia has adverse implications for both regional and international security. In between the two exclusive views, remains a pertinent question unanswered-who is to guarantee that if the issues related to Kashmir remains resolved, towards which India has already been making significant efforts, Pakistan's military-ISI sponsored terrorist activities in other parts of India would end?

In such a complex security environment, bilateral confidence-building measures alone would keep the escalation under manageable limits.

Bibliography

Ajey Lele: *Strategic Technologies for the Military : Breaking New Frontiers*, Sage, Delhi, 2009.

Allison, Graham, *Nuclear Terrorism: The Ultimate Preventable Catastrophe*, New York: Times Books, 2004.

Anil, K.C.: *Military and Democracy in South Asia : Challenges, Politics and Power*, Sumit Enterprises, Delhi, 2009.

Barber B.R.: *Strong Democracy. Participatory Politics for a New Age*. Berkeley, University of California Press, 1984.

Ben Wisner : *At Risk, Natural Hazards, People's Vulnerability, and Disasters*, London, Routledge, 1994.

Bhat, T.P. : *India and China : Trade Complementarities and Competitiveness*, Bookwell, Delhi, 2008.

Buzan, Barry & Eric Herring: *The Arms Dynamic in World Politics*, London: Lynne Rienner Publishers, 1998.

Chitkara, M.G. : *China-Pak Relations Challenges Before New Millennium*, APH, Delhi, 2001.

Cochran, Thomas B. *Nuclear Weapons Databook*. Cambridge, MA: Ballinger Publishing Company, 1987.

Damrosch, L.F.: *Law and Force in the New International Order*, Boulder, Westview Press, 1991.

Deepak, B R : *India and China : 1904-2004 : A Century of Peace and Conflict*, Manak, Delhi, 2005.

Dixit, A.K. : *Military Wars and Rescue Techniques*, Cyber Tech Pub, Delhi, 2010.

Drewes, Jeanne : *Computers: Planning for Disaster*, Law Library Journal, Winter, 1989.

Dunn, Lewis A., *'India, Pakistan, Iran: A Nuclear Proliferation Chain'*, Colorado: Westview Press, 1977.

Fatima, T. : *Islamic Law and Judiciary*, Deep & Deep Publications, New Delhi, 2001.

Freedman, Lawrence. *The Evolution of Nuclear Strategy*. Studies in International Security, #20. New York: St. Martin's Press, 1981.

Friedman, G.: *The Future of War of Cyber Crimes*, N.Y., Random House, 1996.

George Perkovich: *India's Nuclear Bomb: The Impact on Global Proliferation*, University of California Press: Berkeley, 1991.

Goel, Suresh : *Military, Security and Intelligence Agencies*, MD Publications, Delhi, 2009.

Hasan-Askari Rizvi, *Nuclear Terrorism and South Asia*, Albuquerque, NM: Sandia National Laboratories, February 2003.

Huntington, S.P.: *The China Modernisation Military and the State*, N.Y., Vintage Books, 1964.

Janowitz, M.: *The Professional Soldier: A Social and Political Portrait*, N.Y., The Free Press, 1960.

Kapur, C.K. : *Chinese Military Modernisation*, Manas, Delhi, 2003.

Khan, Saira: *Nuclear Proliferation Dynamics in Protracted Conflict Regions: A Comparative Study of South Asia and the Middle East*, Vermont: Ashgate Publishing Ltd, 2002.

Kunju, N. : *Indo-Pak : Nuclear Cold War*, Reliance, Delhi, 2002.

Leena Parmar: *Military Sociology : Global Perspectives*, Rawat, Delhi, 1999.

McPhee, John. *The Curve of Binding Energy*. New York: The Noonday Press, 1992.

Posen, B.R.: *The Sources of Military Doctrine*, Ithaca, 1984, Cornell Univ. Press.

Radhakrishna: *Military Ethics: Guidelines for Peace and War*, Sumit Enterprises, Delhi, 2009.

Samuel P. Huntington: *The Soldier and the State : The Theory and Politics of Civil-Military Relations*, Natraj Pub, Delhi, 2005.

Schroeer, Dietrich, *Science, Technology, and the Nuclear Arms Race*, Ontario: John Wiley & Sons, 1984.

Sidney Fox: *Klaus Dose, Molecular Evolution and The Origin of Life*, New York: Marcel Dekker, 1977.

Stephen Reyna : *The Political Economy of African Famine*, Philadelphia, Gordon and Breach Science Publishers, 1991

White, J. R.: *Terrorism: An introduction: 2002 update*, Belmont, CA: Wadsworth, 2002.

Winston, Mark L.: *Travels in the Genetically Modified Zone*, Cambridge, Harvard University, 2004.

Index

A

Arms Race, 1, 3, 14, 16, 25, 32, 36, 37, 38, 51, 52, 87, 91, 95, 96, 193, 207, 211, 218.
Arms Trade, 45, 46, 67, 75, 77, 92, 93, 98, 99, 100.
Arms Transfers, 44, 45, 46, 47, 48, 49, 64, 81, 84, 221, 222.

C

Chinese Nuclear Weapons, 40, 43, 44, 224.
Conventional Operations, 106.
Cruise Missiles, 91, 110, 150, 151, 153, 154, 155, 156, 157, 219, 221.

D

Defence Planning, 235, 239, 253, 254, 255, 256.
Domestic Stability, 56, 272.

F

Foundation, 162, 197, 198, 199, 205, 228.

G

Global Threats, 5.

H

Horizontal Proliferation, 116.

I

India and Pakistan, 107, 110.

M

Mass Destruction, 9, 55, 214, 228, 261.
Missile Exports, 207, 208, 210, 211, 212, 215.

N

National Defence Economy, 19, 20, 22, 23.
National Defence Policies, 5.
National Security Policy, 253.
Nuclear Arms Control, 14, 201.
Nuclear Arms Race, 1, 3, 33, 39, 54, 195, 221.
Nuclear Deterrence, 16, 35, 55, 81, 150, 203, 205, 206, 217, 232, 234, 284, 288.
Nuclear Doctrine, 19, 106, 121, 125, 126, 127, 143, 197, 198, 201, 204, 206, 217, 218, 219.
Nuclear Establishment, 176.
Nuclear Neighbourhood, 121.
Nuclear Proliferation, 9, 37, 117, 120, 121, 134, 136, 160, 187, 215, 216, 289, 292.
Nuclear Security, 3, 17, 260, 262, 283.
Nuclear Threshold, 25, 129,

130, 131, 132, 284, 288, 290, 291.

S

Security, 2, 3, 4, 5, 6, 7, 8, 11, 14, 15, 16, 17, 19, 38, 40, 41, 44, 47, 50, 55, 56, 64, 70, 75, 80, 82, 89, 92, 93, 94, 95, 98, 106, 114, 116, 122, 124, 127, 134, 135, 136, 143, 144, 171, 176, 179, 181, 182, 186, 188, 189, 190, 192, 196, 197, 198, 203, 204, 207, 208, 210, 212, 213, 214, 218, 229, 232, 235, 236, 237, 239, 240, 241, 242, 243, 244, 245, 246, 247, 248, 249, 250, 251, 252, 253, 254, 256, 257, 259, 260, 261, 262, 263, 264, 265, 267, 268, 269, 270, 271, 272, 273, 274, 275, 276, 277, 278, 279, 282, 283, 285, 286, 287, 288, 289, 291, 292.

Security Policy, 6, 124, 253.

Small Arms Development, 71.

Small Arms Trade, 74, 75, 77, 94, 99, 100.

T

Terror Campaign, 235.

Terrorist Attacks, 103, 276.

W

Weapons Development, 17, 20, 23, 28, 134, 189, 198, 218, 230, 237, 245.

❑❑❑